PAPERBACK SONGS

THE '60s

MELODY LINE, CHORDS AND LYRICS
FOR KEYBOARD • GUITAR • VOCAL

HAL•LEONARD®

ISBN 0-634-06419-3

Printed In Canada

HAL•LEONARD®
CORPORATION
7777 W. BLUEMOUND RD. P.O. BOX 13819 MILWAUKEE, WI 53213

Visit Hal Leonard Online at
www.halleonard.com

Welcome to the PAPERBACK SONGS SERIES.

Do you play piano, guitar, electronic keyboard, sing or play any instrument for that matter? If so, this handy "pocket tune" book is for you.

The concise, one-line music notation consists of:

MELODY, LYRICS & CHORD SYMBOLS

Whether strumming the chords on guitar, "faking" an arrangement on piano/keyboard or singing the lyrics, these fake book style arrangements can be enjoyed at any experience level – hobbyist to professional.

The musical skills necessary to successfully use this book are minimal. If you play guitar and need some help with chords, a basic chord chart is included at the back of the book.

While playing and singing is the first thing that comes to mind when using this book, it can also serve as a compact, comprehensive reference guide.

However you choose to use this PAPERBACK SONGS SERIES book, by all means have fun!

CONTENTS

(contents continued)

ABRAHAM, MARTIN AND JOHN

Words and Music by
RICHARD HOLLER

Medium Rock beat
F Am Gm7 B♭
Has an - y - bod - y here seen my old friend
F Gm7
A - bra - ham,
John,
Mar - tin,
Bob - by,
can you tell me where he's
C7sus C7 Dm
gone?
1.-3. He freed a lot - ta
4. I thought I saw him
Am Gm7 B♭
peo - ple, but it seems the good die
walk - in' up o - ver the
F Gm7 C Gm7
young. But I just looked a - round and he's
hill with A - bra - ham, Mar - tin and

1, 2
3, 4
B♭ F Fsus F Fine
gone. Has gone.
John.
B♭ Am7 Gm7 B♭
Did - n't you love the things they
F Am7 B♭ Am7
stood for? Did - n't they try to
Gm7 B♭ Gm7 B♭ F
find some good for you and me?
3
Cm7 E♭ B♭
And we'll be free. Some -
Am Gm7 C7sus C7 D.S. al Fine
day soon it's gon - na be one day. Has

ALL YOU NEED IS LOVE

Words and Music by JOHN LENNON
and PAUL McCARTNEY

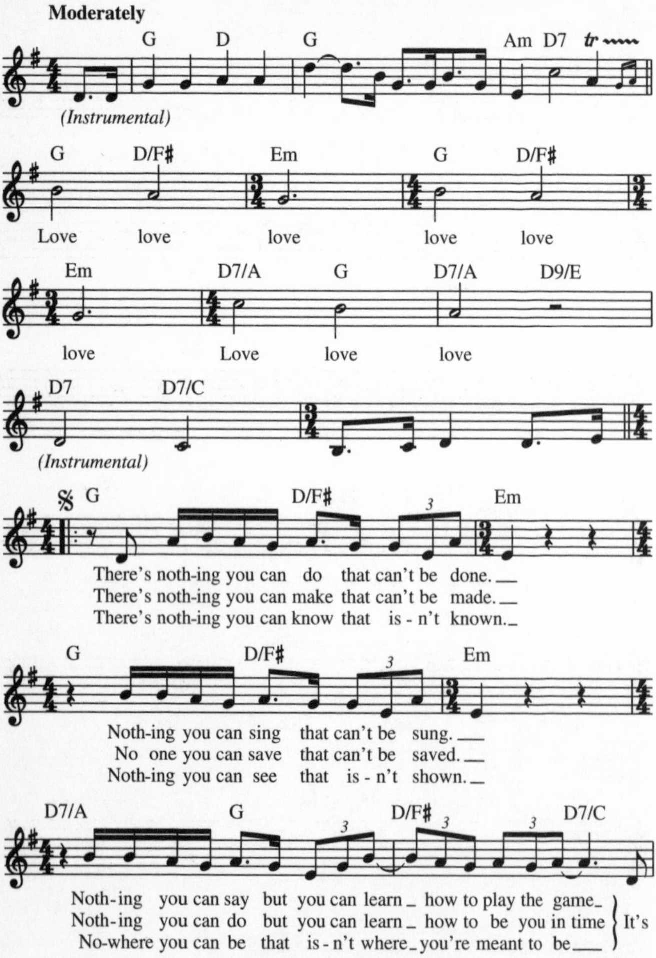
Moderately
G D G Am D7 tr
(Instrumental)
G D/F# Em G D/F#
Love love love love love
Em D7/A G D7/A D9/E
love Love love love
D7 D7/C
(Instrumental)
G D/F# 3 Em
There's noth-ing you can do that can't be done.
There's noth-ing you can make that can't be made.
There's noth-ing you can know that is - n't known.
G D/F# 3 Em
Noth-ing you can sing that can't be sung.
No one you can save that can't be saved.
Noth-ing you can see that is - n't shown.
D7/A G 3 D/F# 3 3 D7/C
Noth-ing you can say but you can learn how to play the game
Noth-ing you can do but you can learn how to be you in time
No-where you can be that is-n't where you're meant to be
It's

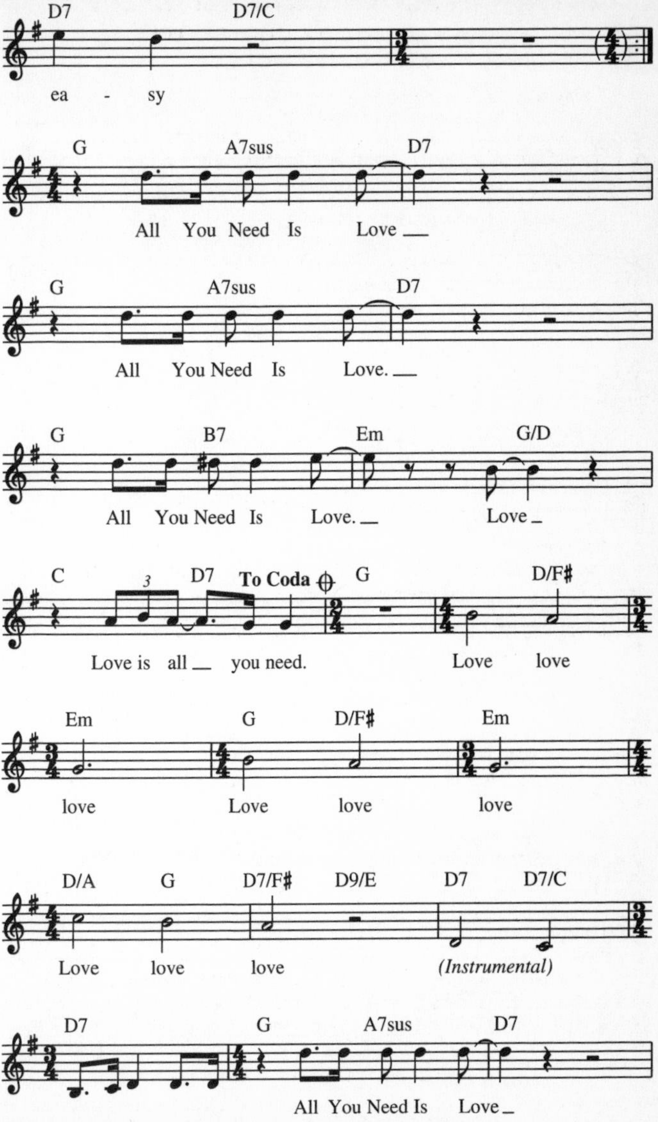
D7 D7/C
ea - sy
G A7sus D7
All You Need Is Love
G A7sus D7
All You Need Is Love.
G B7 Em G/D
All You Need Is Love. Love
C D7 To Coda G D/F#
3
Love is all you need. Love love
Em G D/F# Em
love Love love love
D/A G D7/F# D9/E D7 D7/C
Love love love
(Instrumental)
D7 G A7sus D7
All You Need Is Love

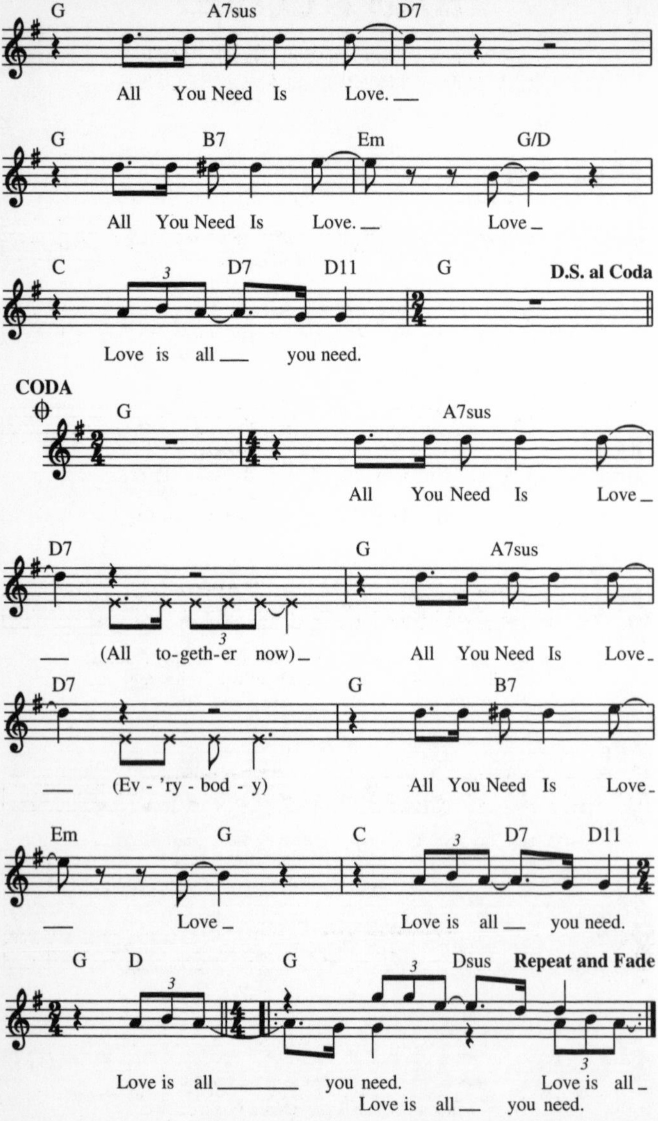
G A7sus D7
All You Need Is Love.
G B7 Em G/D
All You Need Is Love. Love
C D7 D11 G D.S. al Coda
Love is all you need.
CODA
G A7sus
All You Need Is Love
D7 G A7sus
(All to-geth-er now) All You Need Is Love
D7 G B7
(Ev - 'ry - bod - y) All You Need Is Love
Em G C D7 D11
Love Love is all you need.
G D G Dsus Repeat and Fade
Love is all you need. Love is all
Love is all you need.

BABY LOVE

Words and Music by BRIAN HOLLAND,
EDWARD HOLLAND and LAMONT DOZIER

Moderately
F
F7
Ba - by Love, my Ba - by Love, I
Ba - by Love, my Ba - by Love, why
me my love, my Ba - by Love, I
D7
Gm
need you oh how I need __ you.
must we sep - a - rate my love?
need ya oh how I need __ ya.
Bb6
F
But all you do is treat me bad, ______
All __ of my whole life through, __
Why you do me like you do, ______
Bb6
F
break my heart and leave me sad. ______
I nev - er loved no one but you. ______
af - ter I've been true to you. ______
Bb6
3
Wan - na know what did
Why ___ you do me
So _____ deep in

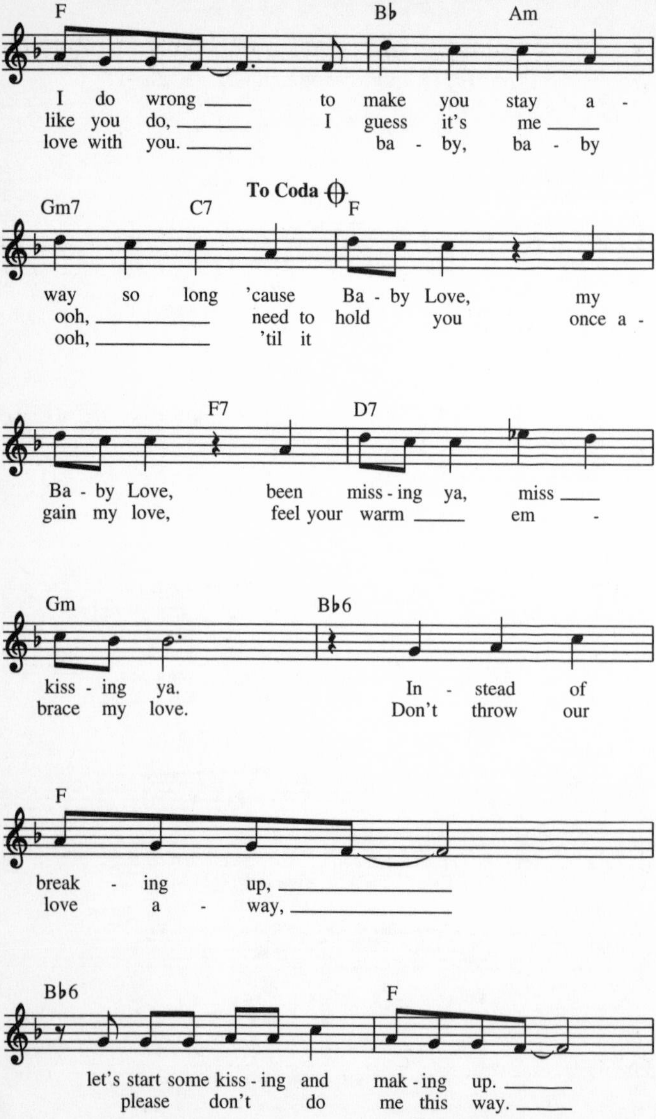
F
Bb
Am
I do wrong ____ to make you stay a -
like you do, ____ I guess it's me ____
love with you. ____ ba - by, ba - by
To Coda
Gm7
C7
F
way so long 'cause Ba - by Love, my
ooh, ____ need to hold you once a -
ooh, ____ 'til it
F7
D7
Ba - by Love, been miss - ing ya, miss ____
gain my love, feel your warm ____ em -
Gm
Bb6
kiss - ing ya. In - stead of
brace my love. Don't throw our
F
break - ing up, ____
love a - way, ____
Bb6
F
let's start some kiss - ing and mak - ing up. ____
please don't do me this way. ____

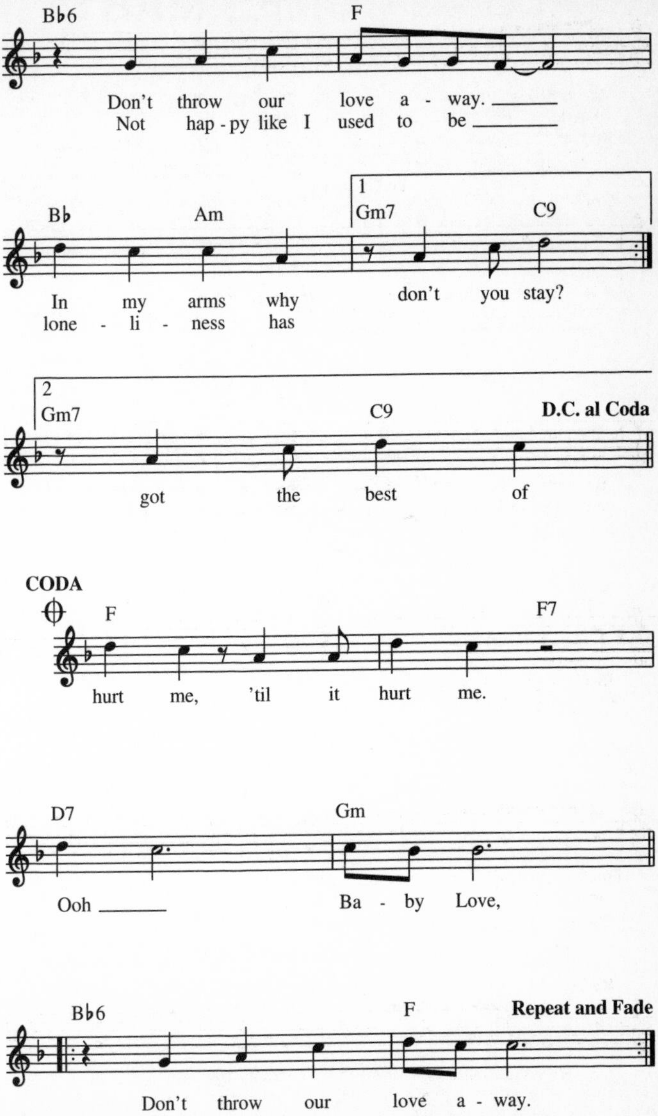
Bb6
F
Don't throw our love a - way.
Not hap - py like I used to be
1
Bb
Am
Gm7
C9
In my arms why don't you stay?
lone - li - ness has
2
Gm7
C9
D.C. al Coda
got the best of
CODA
F
F7
hurt me, 'til it hurt me.
D7
Gm
Ooh
Ba - by Love,
Bb6
F
Repeat and Fade
Don't throw our love a - way.

ALONG COMES MARY

Words and Music by
TANDYN ALMER

Moderately
Am D7
Ev - 'ry time I think that I'm the
sire is the fire in the
Am7 D7 Am D7
on - ly one who's lone - ly, some - one calls on me.
eyes of chicks whose sick - ness is the games they play.
Am7 D7 Am D7
And ev - 'ry now and then I spend my
And when the mas - quer - ade is played and neigh - bor
Am7 D7 Am D7
time at rhyme and verse and curse the faults in me.
folks make jokes at who is most to blame to - day.
Am7 D7 E A
But then a - long comes Mar - y,
And then a - long comes Mar - y,
E7 A E A
and does she wan - na give me kicks and be my
and does she wan - na set them free and make them

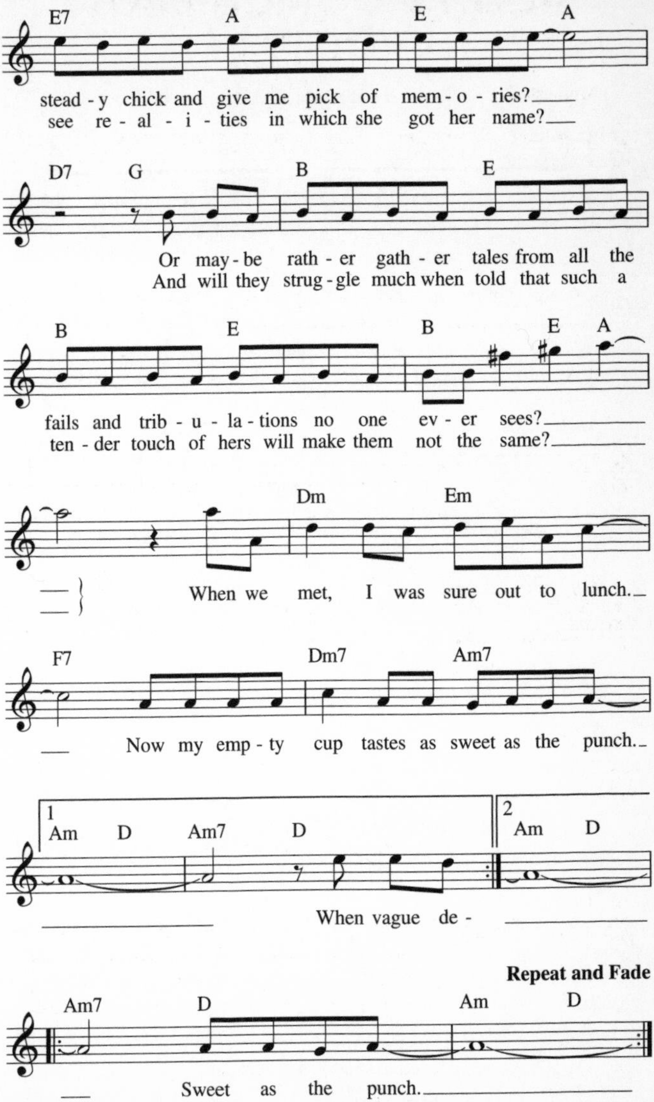
E7 A E A
stead - y chick and give me pick of mem - o - ries?
see re - al - i - ties in which she got her name?
D7 G B E
Or may - be rath - er gath - er tales from all the
And will they strug - gle much when told that such a
B E B E A
fails and trib - u - la - tions no one ev - er sees?
ten - der touch of hers will make them not the same?
Dm Em
When we met, I was sure out to lunch.
F7 Dm7 Am7
Now my emp - ty cup tastes as sweet as the punch.
1 Am D Am7 D
When vague de -
2 Am D
Repeat and Fade
Am7 D Am D
Sweet as the punch.

ARE YOU LONESOME TONIGHT?

Words and Music by ROY TURK
and LOU HANDMAN

Moderately
C
Are You Lone - some To - night, do you
miss me to - night, are you
B♭ A7
sor - ry we drift - ed a -
Dm A7 Dm G7
part? Does your mem - o - ry
stray to a bright sum - mer
day, when I kissed you and
C F Fm C
called you sweet - heart? Do the

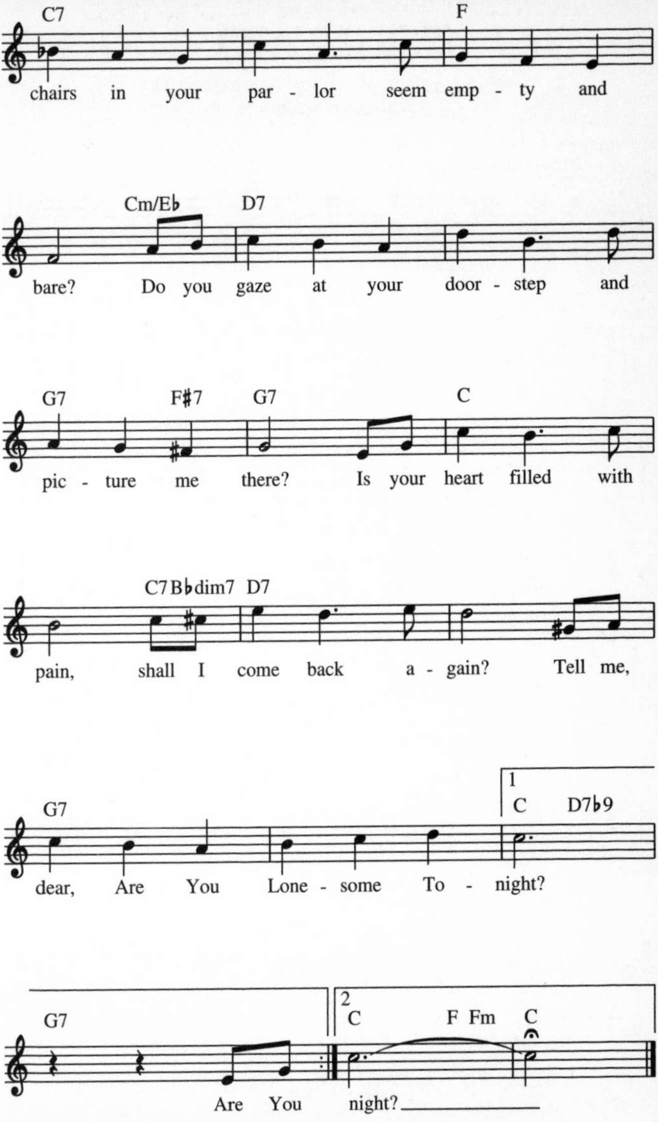
C7 F
chairs in your par - lor seem emp - ty and
Cm/E♭ D7
bare? Do you gaze at your door - step and
G7 F♯7 G7 C
pic - ture me there? Is your heart filled with
C7 B♭dim7 D7
pain, shall I come back a - gain? Tell me,
G7 1 C D7♭9
dear, Are You Lone - some To - night?
G7 2 C F Fm C
Are You night?

(It's A)

BEAUTIFUL MORNING

Words and Music by FELIX CAVALIERE
and EDWARD BRIGATI, JR.

Moderately
Eb
It's a beau - ti - ful morn - ing,
morn - ing,
Gm Fm7
Ah!
Ah!
I think I'll go
Each bird keeps sing -
Gm Fm7 Eb Cm Eb
out - side a - while and just smile.
ing his own song, So long,
Gm Fm7
Just take in some clean
I've got to be on
Gm Ab Bb Cm
fresh air 'cause no sense in
my way now, No good just
Fm Cm
stay-ing in - side If the weath - er's fine and
hang-ing a - round, I've got to cov - er ground you could - n't

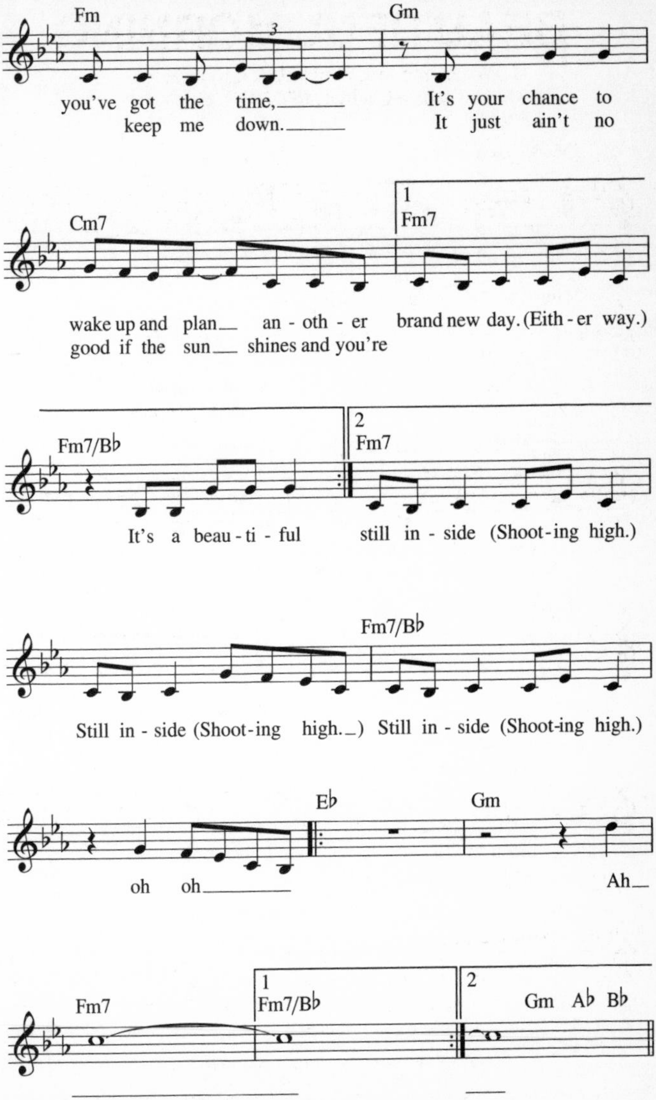
Fm
Gm
you've got the time,
It's your chance to
keep me down.
It just ain't no
Cm7
1
Fm7
wake up and plan an - oth - er
brand new day. (Eith - er way.)
good if the sun shines and you're
Fm7/B♭
2
Fm7
It's a beau - ti - ful
still in - side (Shoot - ing high.)
Fm7/B♭
Still in - side (Shoot - ing high.) Still in - side (Shoot-ing high.)
E♭
Gm
oh oh
Ah
Fm7
1
Fm7/B♭
2
Gm A♭ B♭

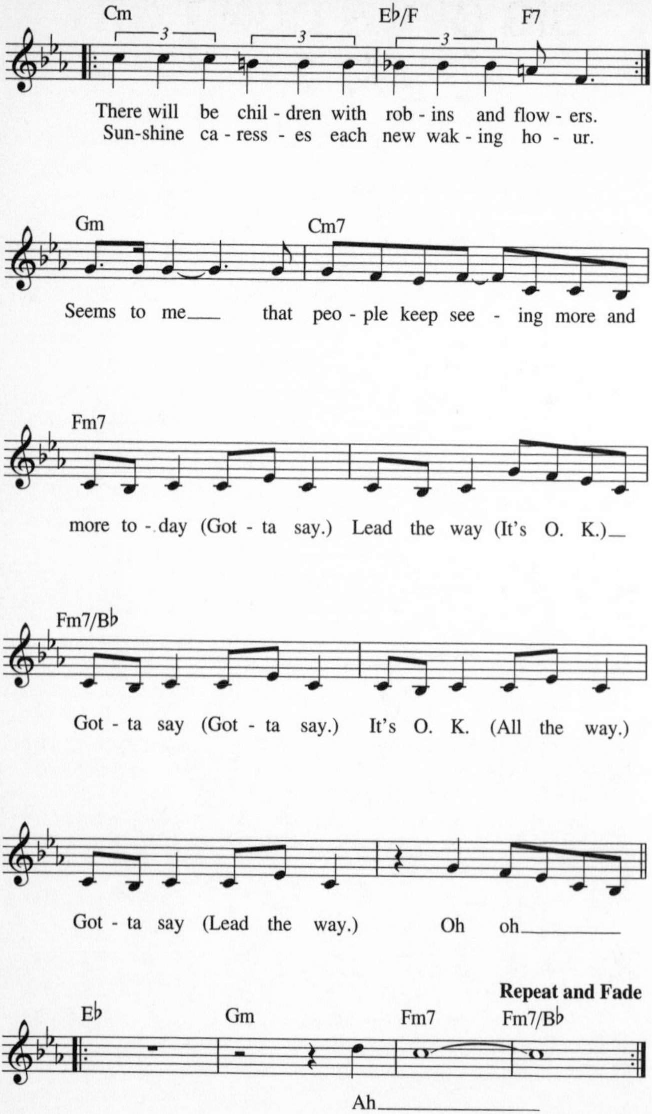
Cm
Eb/F
F7
There will be chil - dren with rob - ins and flow - ers.
Sun-shine ca - ress - es each new wak - ing ho - ur.
Gm
Cm7
Seems to me___ that peo - ple keep see - ing more and
Fm7
more to - day (Got - ta say.) Lead the way (It's O. K.)_
Fm7/Bb
Got - ta say (Got - ta say.) It's O. K. (All the way.)
Got - ta say (Lead the way.) Oh oh_________
Repeat and Fade
Eb
Gm
Fm7
Fm7/Bb
Ah_______________

BIG GIRLS DON'T CRY

Words and Music by BOB CREWE
and BOB GAUDIO

Moderately
Ab F7 Bbm7 Eb7 Ab F7
Big girls don't cry,
Bbm7 Eb7 Ab F7 Bbm7 Eb7
they don't cry. Big girls don't
Ab F7 Bbm7 Eb7
cry. (Who said they don't cry)
Ab F7 Bbm7 Eb7 Ab F7
My girl said good - bye,
Ba - by, I was true,
Bbm7 Eb7 Ab F7 Bbm7 Eb7
my, oh my, my girl did - n't
I was true, ba - by, I'm a

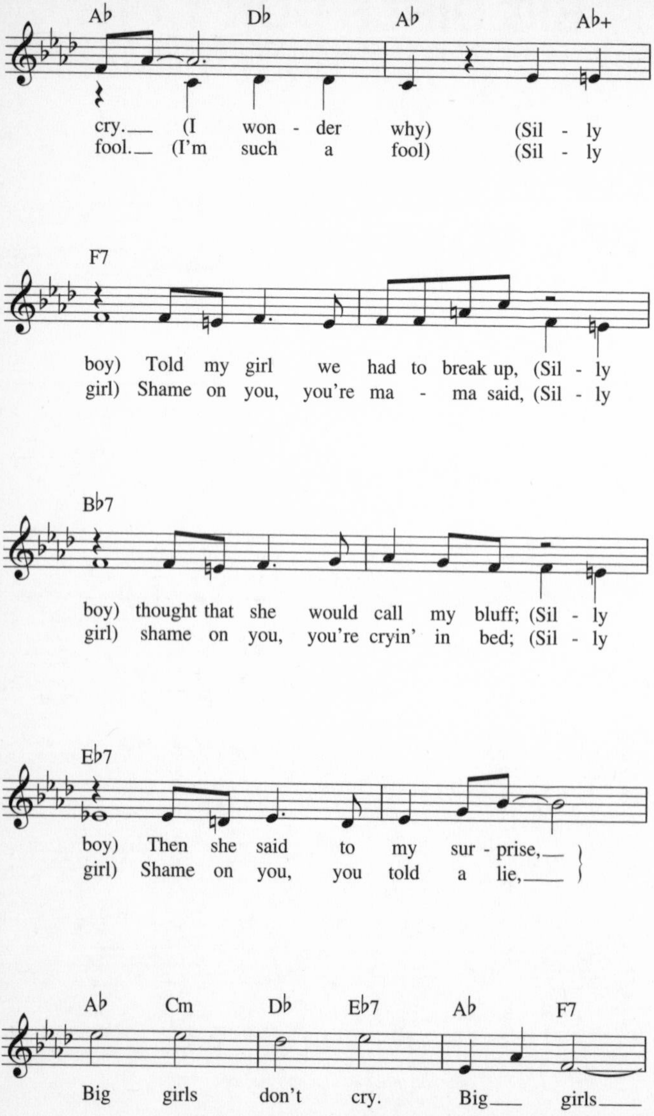
A♭ D♭ A♭ A♭+
cry. (I won - der why) (Sil - ly
fool. (I'm such a fool) (Sil - ly
F7
boy) Told my girl we had to break up, (Sil - ly
girl) Shame on you, you're ma - ma said, (Sil - ly
B♭7
boy) thought that she would call my bluff; (Sil - ly
girl) shame on you, you're cryin' in bed; (Sil - ly
E♭7
boy) Then she said to my sur - prise,
girl) Shame on you, you told a lie,
A♭ Cm D♭ E♭7 A♭ F7
Big girls don't cry. Big girls

Bbm7 Eb7 Ab F7
don't cry,
Bbm7 Eb7 Ab F7
they don't cry. Big girls
1
Bbm7 Eb7 Ab F7
don't cry. (Who said
2
Bbm7 Eb7 Ab F7
they don't cry) cry. (That's just an
Bbm7 Eb7 Ab Cm
al - i - bi) Big girls
Db Eb7 Ab Cm Db Eb7
don't cry. Big girls don't cry.

BOBBY'S GIRL

Words and Music by GARY KLEIN
and HENRY HOFFMAN

Moderately
C
When peo - ple ask of me
Each night I sit at home
Am
F
what would you like to be, now that you're
hop - ing that he will phone, but I know
Em
F
G
not a kid any - more?
Bob - by has some - one else.
C
I know just what to say,
Still in my heart I pray,
Am
F
I an - swer right a - way. There's just one
there soon will come a day when I will
Em
F6
G7 N.C.
thing I've been wish - ing for.
have him all to my - self.
I wan - na be

C
Bob - by's girl, I wan - na be
Am
Bob - by's girl.
F
That's the most im -
G
Dm7
G7
por - tant thing to me.
N.C.
C
And if I was Bob - by's girl;
if I was
F
Bob - by's girl,
G7
what a faith - ful, thank - ful girl I'd
C
1
2
be.

BREAD AND BUTTER

Words and Music by LARRY PARKS
and JAY TURNBOW

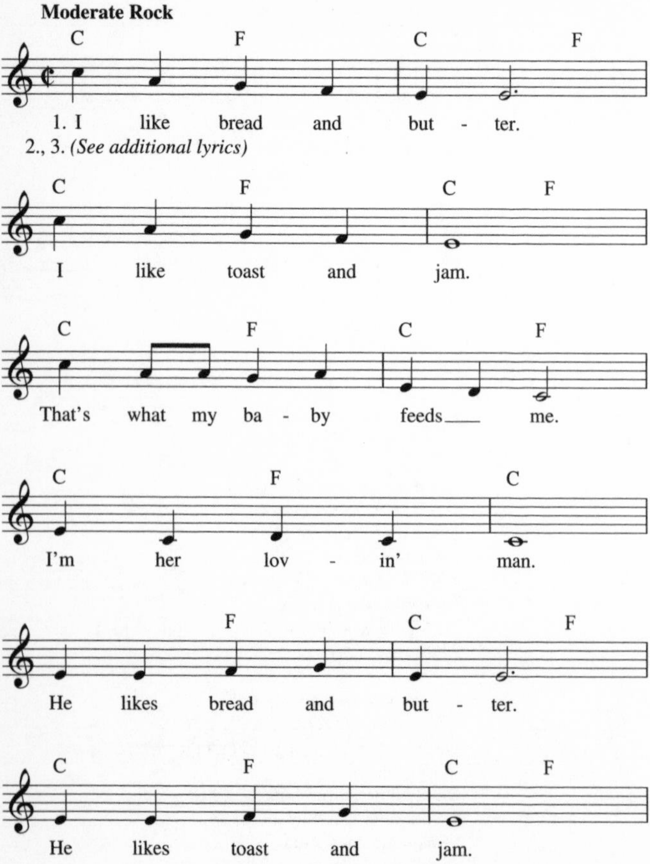
Moderate Rock
C F C F
1. I like bread and but - ter.
2., 3. (See additional lyrics)
C F C F
I like toast and jam.
C F C F
That's what my ba - by feeds___ me.
C F C
I'm her lov - in' man.
F C F
He likes bread and but - ter.
C F C F
He likes toast and jam.

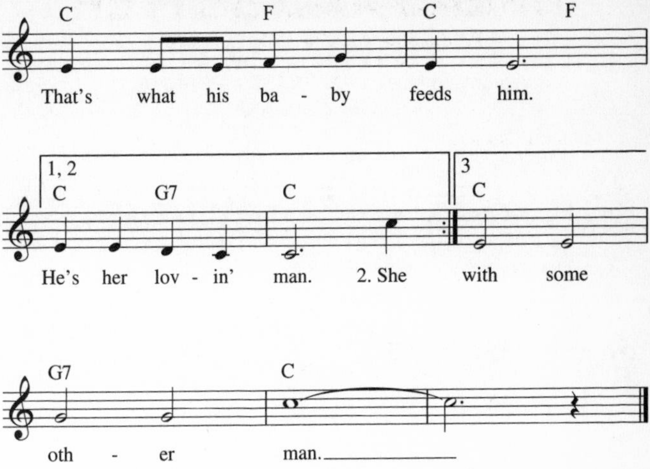
C F C F
That's what his ba - by feeds him.
1, 2
C G7 C
He's her lov - in' man. 2. She
3
C
with some
G7 C
oth - er man.

Additional Lyrics

2. She don't cook mashed potatoes,
   Don't cook T-bone steak.
   Don't feed me peanut butter.
   She knows that I can't take
   No more bread and butter,
   No more toast and jam.
   He found his baby eatin'
   With some other man.

3. Got home early one mornin'
   Much to my surprise,
   She was eatin' chicken and dumplin's
   With some other guy.
   No more bread and butter,
   No more toast and jam.
   I found my baby eatin'
   With some other man.

BREAKING UP IS HARD TO DO

Words and Music by HOWARD GREENFIELD
and NEIL SEDAKA

Rubato
F Ab7 C7 Bb6
You tell me that you're leav-ing, I can't be - lieve it's true,
Am7 Dm7 Gm7
girl, there's just no liv - ing with - out you.
Slowly
C7 F Dm7 Gm7 C7
Don't take your love a - way from me.
F Dm7 Gm7 C7
Don't you leave my heart in mis - er - y.
F Em9 A7 Dm7 G7
If you go, then I'll be blue,
Gm7 Am7 Bb Gm7 C7
break-ing up is hard to do. Re - mem - ber

F Dm7 Gm7 C7 F Dm7
3
when you held me tight, and you kissed me all
Gm7 C7 F Em9 A7
3
through the night. Think of all that
Dm7 G7 Gm7 Am7 B♭ C9
3
we've been through, break-ing up is hard to
F N.C. Fm7 B♭7 Fm7 B♭7
do. They say that break-ing up is hard to do.
E♭ A♭7
Now I know, I know that it's true.
E♭m7 A♭7 E♭m7 A♭7
Don't say that this is the end.
D♭
In - stead of break-ing up I wish that

C7 Db7
we were mak - ing up a - gain, we were mak - ing up a - gain.
C7 F Dm7 Gm7 Gm7/C C9
3
I beg_ of you, don't_ say_ good - bye._
F Dm7 Dm7/G C9
3
Can't we give our love___ a brand new try?_ Yeah,_
F Bm7b5/E A7#5 Dm7 Gm7
3
come on babe___ let's start a - new, 'cause
1
Am7 Bb6 C9 F N.C.
break ing up is hard to do.___ Don't take your
2
Am7 Bb6 C7 Cm6/Eb D7
break - ing up is hard to do,___ 'cause
Gm7 Gm9 Gm7/C C7 F Bb6 F
break - ing up is hard to do.___

DAYDREAM

Words and Music by
JOHN SEBASTIAN

Moderately
C
A7
What a day for a day - dream,
I've been hav - ing a sweet dream,
Whistle
Dm7
G7
3
what a day for a day - dream - in' boy.
I've been dream - in' since I woke up to - day.
Whistle
C
A7
And I'm lost in a day - dream,
It's star - ring me in my sweet dream,
Whistle
Dm7
G11
G7
dream - in' 'bout my bun - dle of joy.
'cause she's the one makes me feel this way.
Whistle
F
F♯dim
C
A7
3
3
And e - ven if time ain't real - ly on my side,
And e - ven if time is pass - ing me by a lot.
And you can be sure that if you're feel - in' right,

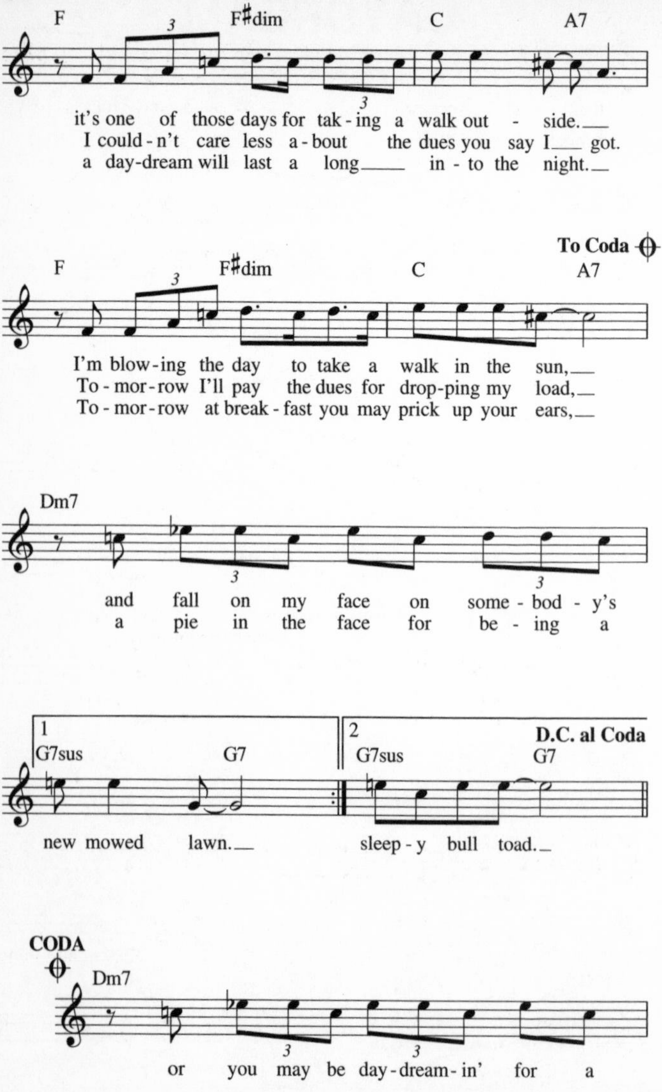
F
F#dim
C
A7
it's one of those days for tak - ing a walk out - side.
I could - n't care less a - bout the dues you say I got.
a day-dream will last a long in - to the night.
To Coda
F
F#dim
C
A7
I'm blow - ing the day to take a walk in the sun,
To - mor - row I'll pay the dues for drop - ping my load,
To - mor - row at break - fast you may prick up your ears,
Dm7
and fall on my face on some - bod - y's
a pie in the face for be - ing a
1
G7sus
G7
new mowed lawn.
2
D.C. al Coda
G7sus
G7
sleep - y bull toad.
CODA
Dm7
or you may be day - dream - in' for a

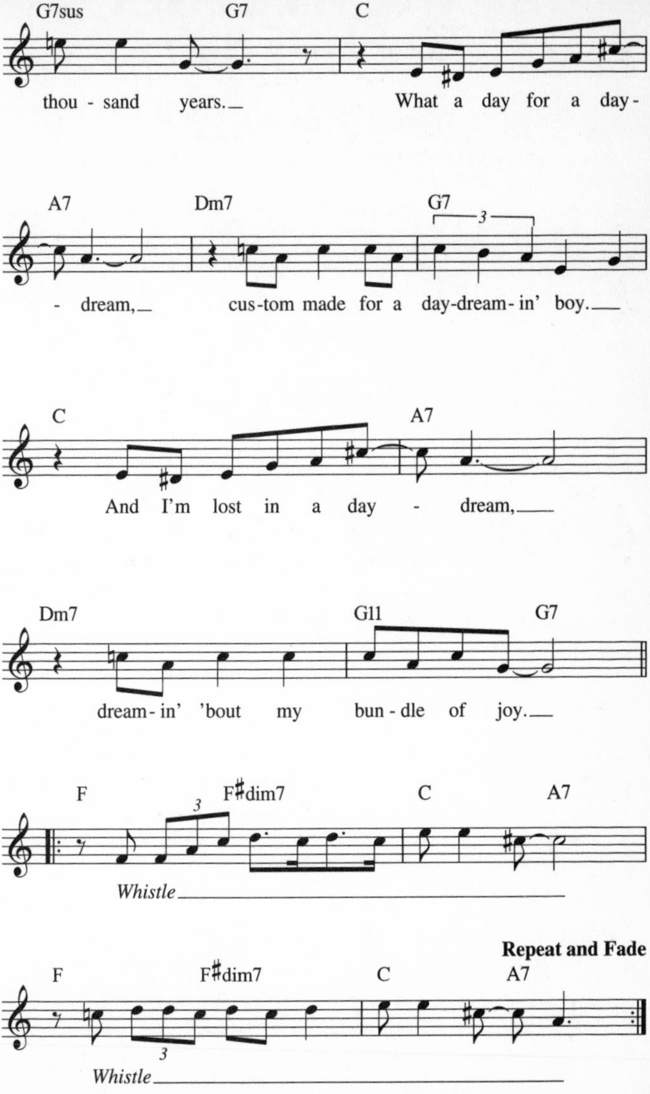
G7sus G7 C
thou - sand years. What a day for a day -
A7 Dm7 G7
- dream, cus-tom made for a day-dream- in' boy.
C A7
And I'm lost in a day - dream,
Dm7 G11 G7
dream - in' 'bout my bun - dle of joy.
F F♯dim7 C A7
Whistle
Repeat and Fade
F F♯dim7 C A7
Whistle

BY THE TIME I GET TO PHOENIX

Words and Music by
JIMMY WEBB

Gently
Gm7
By The Time I Get To
time I make Al - bu -
time I make Ok - la -
C7 Fmaj7
Phoe - nix she'll be ri - sin',
quer - que she'll be work - in'.
ho - ma she'll be sleep - in',
F6 Gm7
She'll find the note I left
She'll pro - 'bly stop at
She'll turn soft - ly and
C7 Fmaj7
hang - in' on her door.
lunch and give me a call.
call my name out low.
F7 B♭
She'll laugh when she reads the
But she'll just hear that
And cry just to

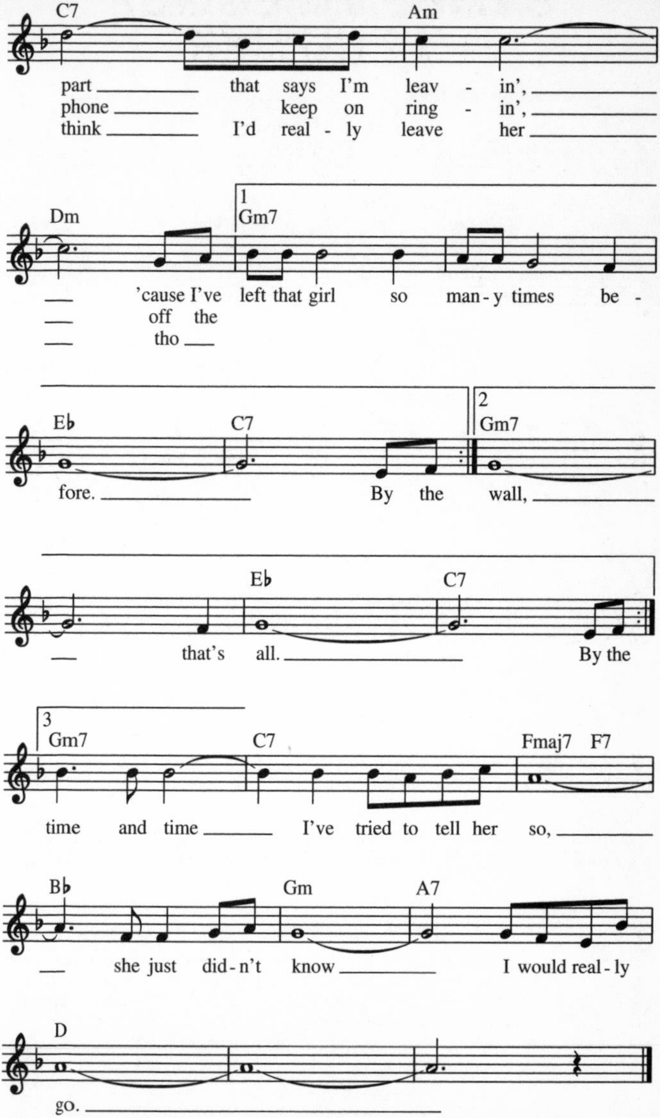
C7 Am
part that says I'm leav - in',
phone keep on ring - in',
think I'd real - ly leave her
Dm 1 Gm7
'cause I've left that girl so man - y times be -
off the
tho
Eb C7 2 Gm7
fore. By the wall,
Eb C7
that's all. By the
3 Gm7 C7 Fmaj7 F7
time and time I've tried to tell her so,
Bb Gm A7
she just did - n't know I would real - ly
D
go.

CALIFORNIA GIRLS

Words and Music by BRIAN WILSON
and MIKE LOVE

Moderate Shuffle Rock
B♭
Well, east coast girls are hip; I real - ly
west coast has the sun-shine and the
A♭/B♭
dig those styles they wear. ___ And the
girls all get so tan. ___ I dig a
E♭
south - ern girls _ with _ the way they talk, _ they knock me
French bi - ki - ni on Ha-wai - ian is-lands, dolls by a
F7
out when I'm down there. ___ The
palm tree in the sand. ___ I
B♭
A♭/B♭
mid-west farm-er's daugh-ters real - ly make you feel al -
been all a-round this great big world, and I've seen all kinds of
E♭
right, ___ and ___ north - ern girls _ with _ the
girls, ___ but I could - n't wait _ to ___ get
F7
way they kiss ___ they keep their boy - friends warm at night. _
back in the states _ back to the cut - est girls in the world. _

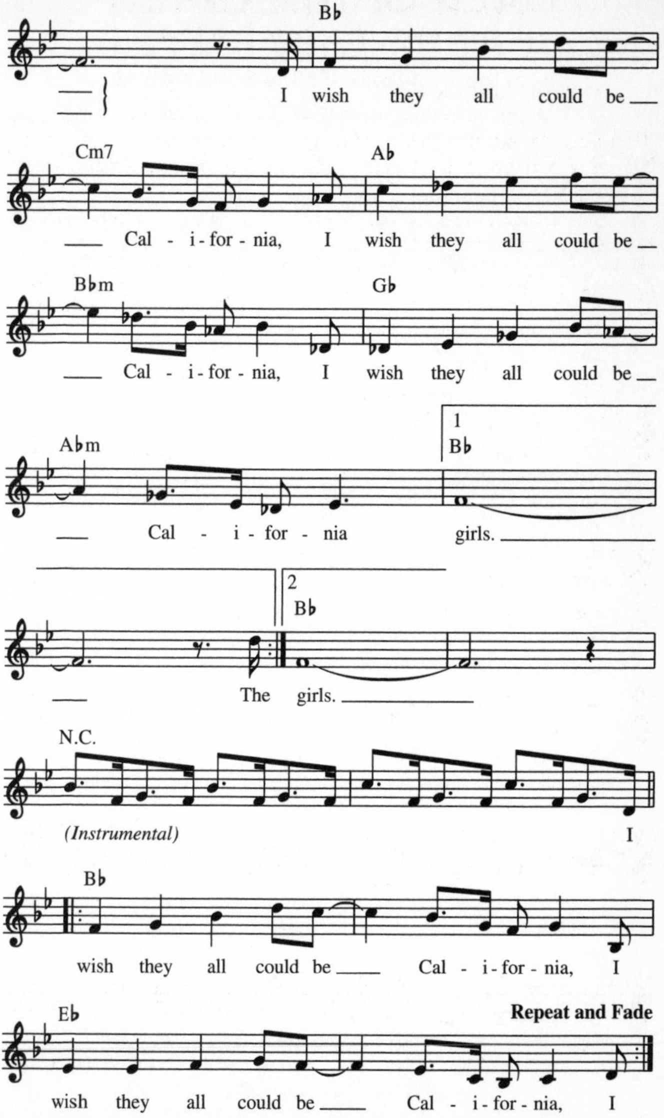
B♭
I wish they all could be
Cm7
A♭
Cal - i - for - nia, I wish they all could be
B♭m
G♭
Cal - i - for - nia, I wish they all could be
A♭m
1
B♭
Cal - i - for - nia girls.
2
B♭
The girls.
N.C.
(Instrumental)
I
B♭
wish they all could be Cal - i - for - nia, I
E♭
Repeat and Fade
wish they all could be Cal - i - for - nia, I

CAN'T HELP FALLING IN LOVE

from the Paramount Picture BLUE HAWAII

Words and Music by GEORGE DAVID WEISS,
HUGO PERETTI and LUIGI CREATORE

Moderately slow
F Am Dm
Wise men say on - ly
B♭ F C7
fools rush in, ___ but
B♭ C Dm Gm
I Can't Help Fall - ing In
3
F/C C7 F Am
Love with you. Shall I
Dm B♭ F
stay? Would it be a
C7 B♭ C
sin ___ if I Can't
Dm Gm F/C C7 F
Help Fall - ing In Love with you?
3

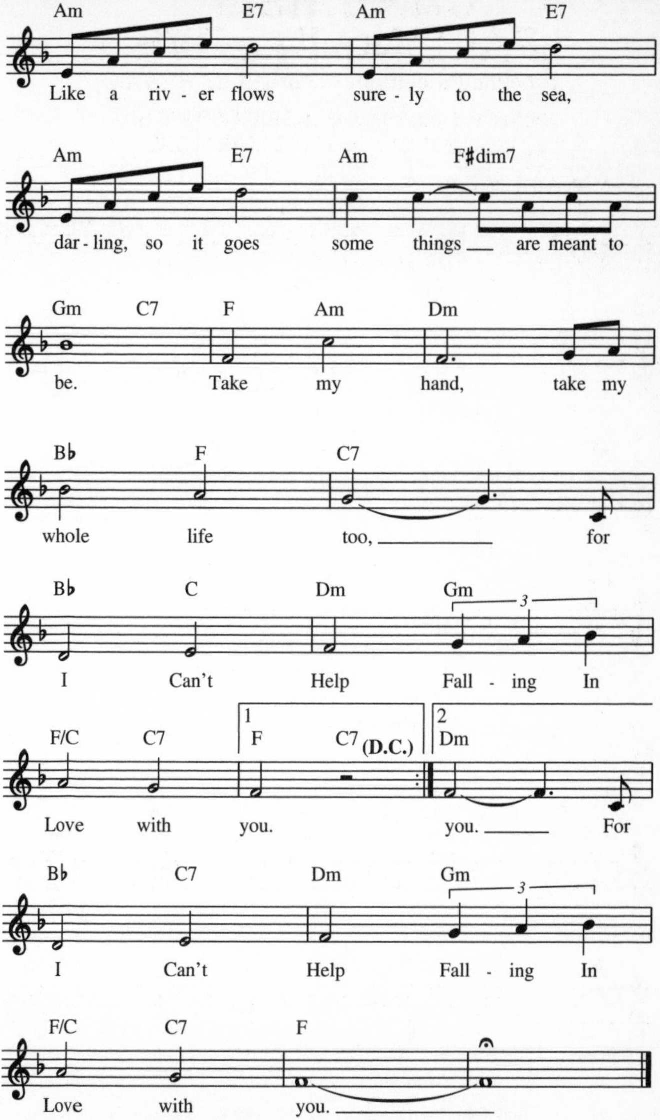
Am E7 Am E7
Like a riv - er flows sure - ly to the sea,
Am E7 Am F♯dim7
dar - ling, so it goes some things are meant to
Gm C7 F Am Dm
be. Take my hand, take my
B♭ F C7
whole life too, for
B♭ C Dm Gm
3
I Can't Help Fall - ing In
F/C C7
1
F C7 (D.C.)
2
Dm
Love with you. you. For
B♭ C7 Dm Gm
3
I Can't Help Fall - ing In
F/C C7 F
Love with you.

CHERISH

Words and Music by
TERRY KIRKMAN

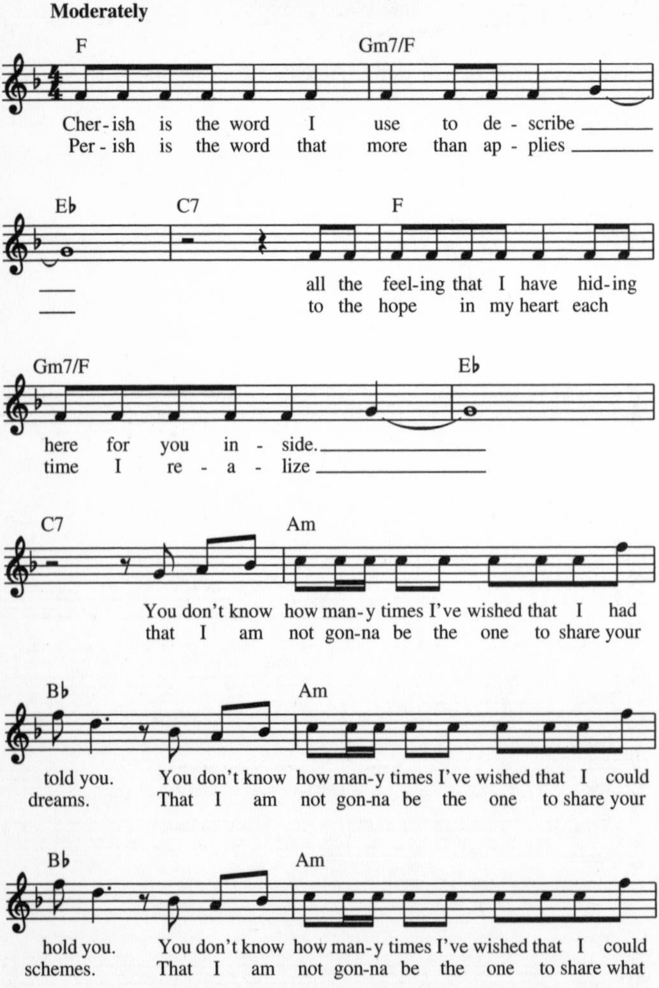
Moderately
F
Gm7/F
Cher-ish is the word I use to de - scribe
Per - ish is the word that more than ap - plies
E♭
C7
F
all the feel-ing that I have hid-ing
to the hope in my heart each
Gm7/F
E♭
here for you in - side.
time I re - a - lize
C7
Am
You don't know how man-y times I've wished that I had
that I am not gon-na be the one to share your
B♭
Am
told you. You don't know how man-y times I've wished that I could
dreams. That I am not gon-na be the one to share your
B♭
Am
hold you. You don't know how man-y times I've wished that I could
schemes. That I am not gon-na be the one to share what

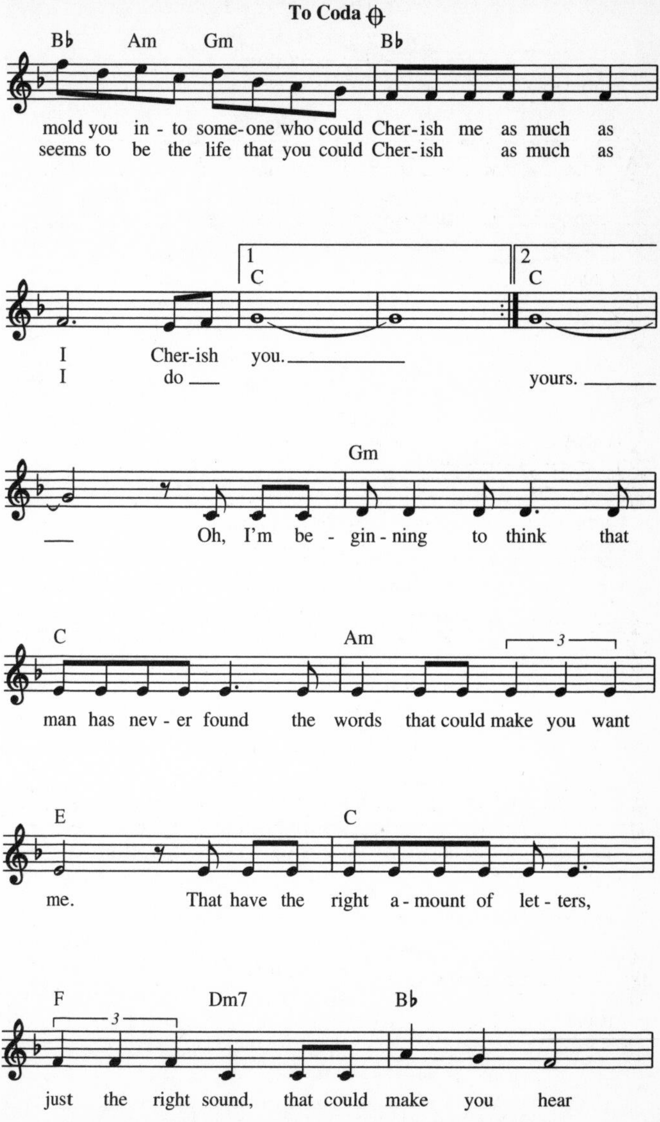
To Coda
B♭ Am Gm B♭
mold you in - to some-one who could Cher-ish me as much as
seems to be the life that you could Cher-ish as much as
1 C
2 C
I Cher-ish you.
I do
yours.
Gm
Oh, I'm be - gin - ning to think that
C Am
3
man has nev - er found the words that could make you want
E C
me. That have the right a - mount of let - ters,
F Dm7 B♭
3
just the right sound, that could make you hear

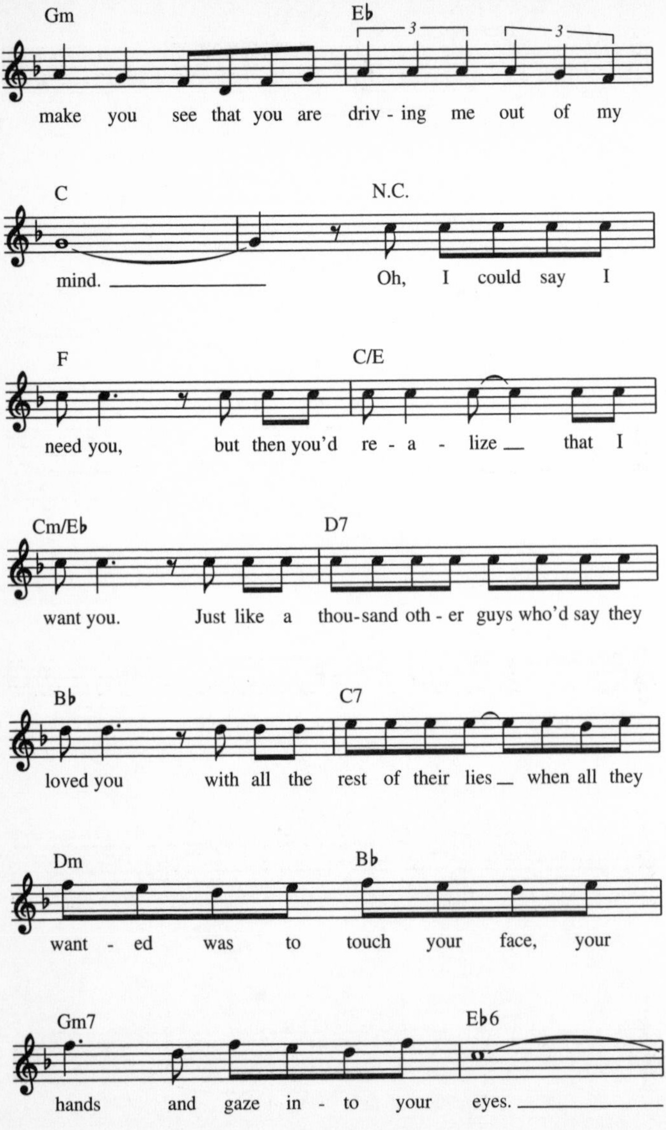
Gm
Eb
3
3
make you see that you are driv - ing me out of my
C
N.C.
mind. ___
Oh, I could say I
F
C/E
need you, but then you'd re - a - lize ___ that I
Cm/Eb
D7
want you. Just like a thou-sand oth - er guys who'd say they
Bb
C7
loved you with all the rest of their lies ___ when all they
Dm
Bb
want - ed was to touch your face, your
Gm7
Eb6
hands and gaze in - to your eyes. ___

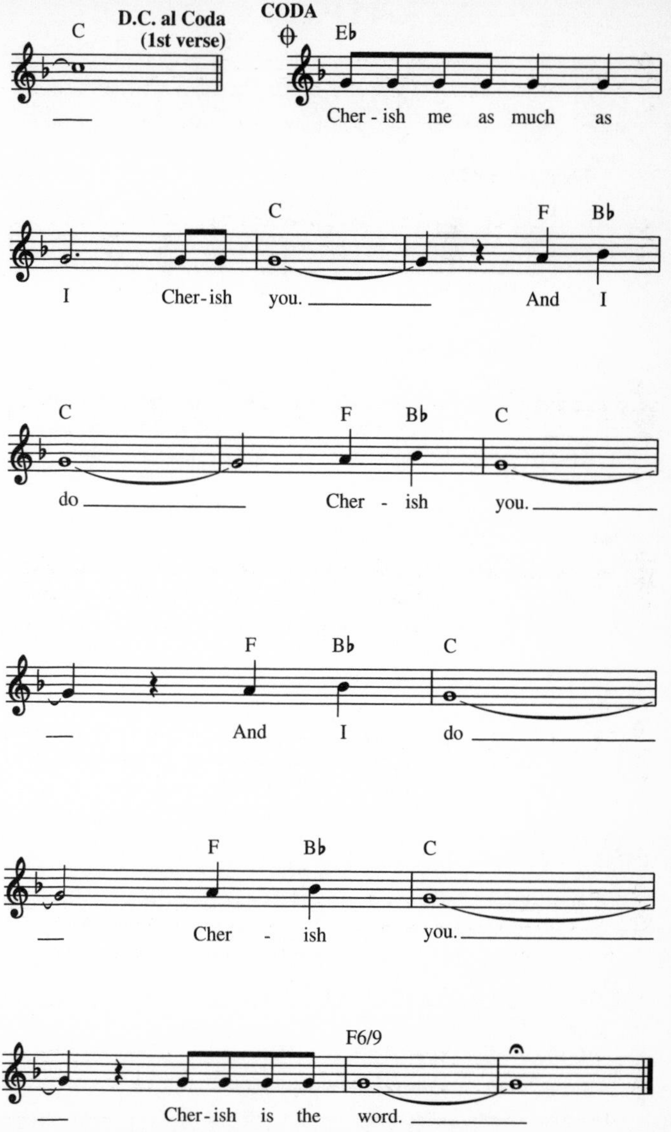
C
D.C. al Coda
(1st verse)
CODA
E♭
Cher - ish me as much as
C
F
B♭
I Cher-ish you.
And I
C
F
B♭
C
do
Cher - ish you.
F
B♭
C
And I do
F
B♭
C
Cher - ish you.
F6/9
Cher-ish is the word.

CRAZY

Words and Music by
WILLIE NELSON

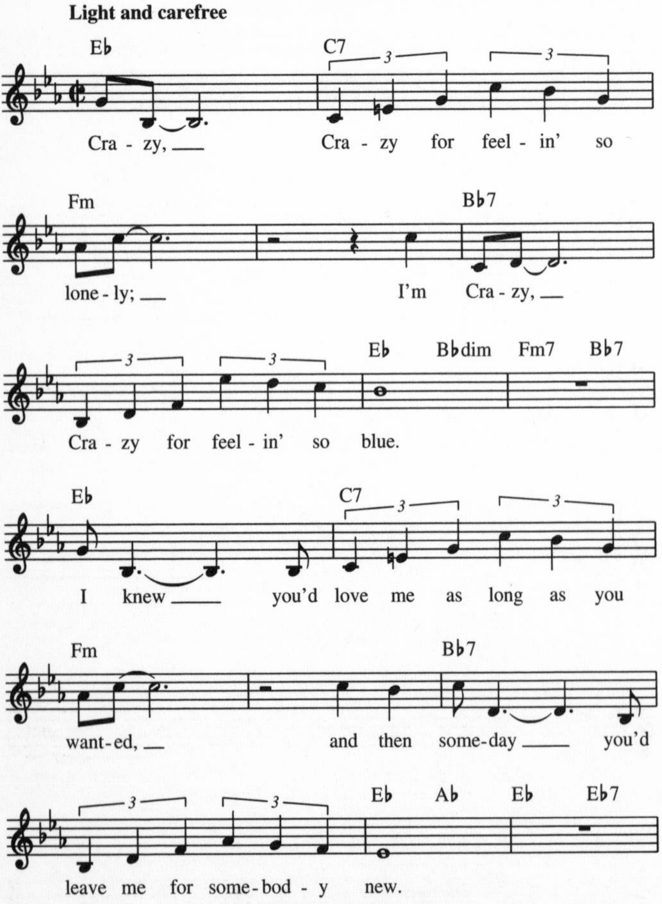
Light and carefree
Eb C7
Cra - zy, ___ Cra - zy for feel - in' so
Fm Bb7
lone - ly; ___ I'm Cra - zy, ___
Eb Bbdim Fm7 Bb7
Cra - zy for feel - in' so blue.
Eb C7
I knew ___ you'd love me as long as you
Fm Bb7
want - ed, ___ and then some - day ___ you'd
Eb Ab Eb Eb7
leave me for some - bod - y new.

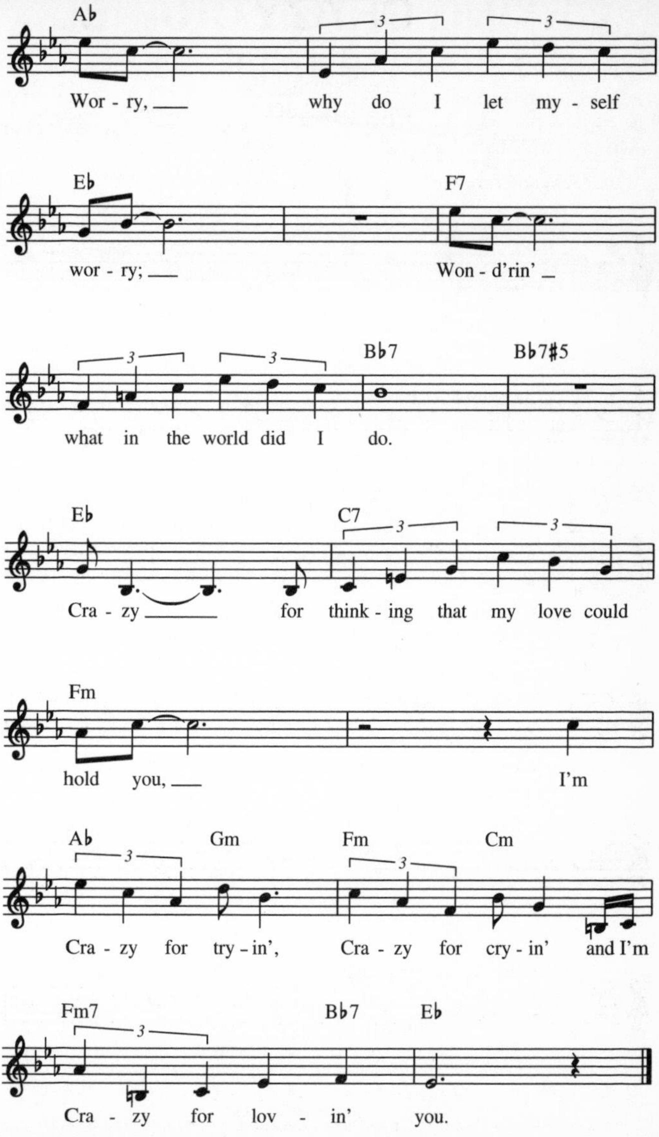
A♭
Wor - ry, why do I let my - self
E♭ F7
wor - ry; Won - d'rin'
B♭7 B♭7♯5
what in the world did I do.
E♭ C7
Cra - zy for think - ing that my love could
Fm
hold you, I'm
A♭ Gm Fm Cm
Cra - zy for try - in', Cra - zy for cry - in' and I'm
Fm7 B♭7 E♭
Cra - zy for lov - in' you.

CRYING IN THE CHAPEL

Words and Music by
ARTIE GLENN

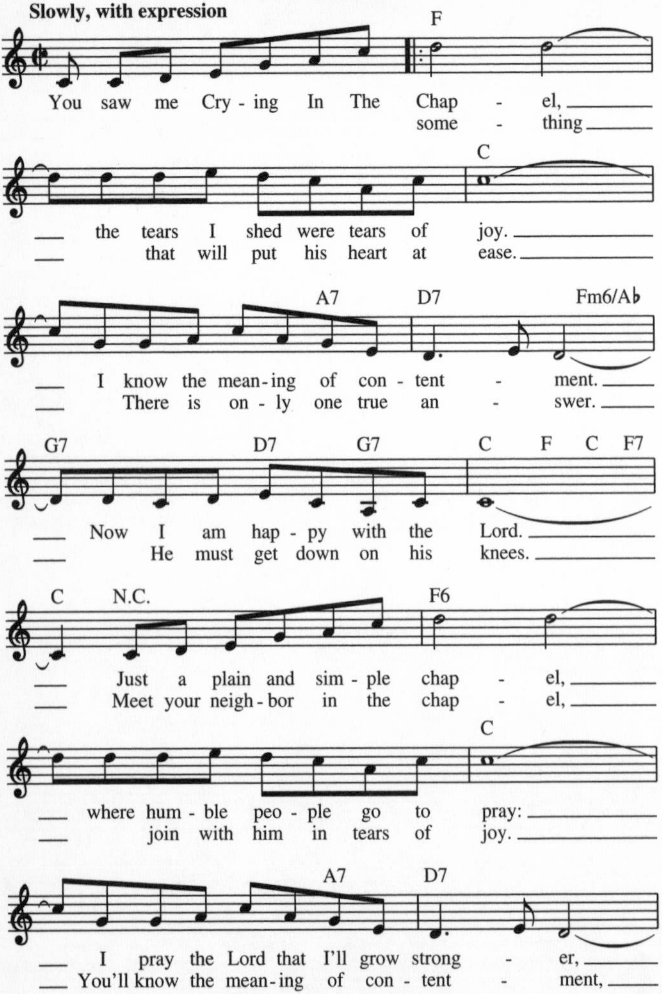
Slowly, with expression
F
You saw me Cry - ing In The Chap - el,
some - thing
C
the tears I shed were tears of joy.
that will put his heart at ease.
A7 D7 Fm6/A♭
I know the mean - ing of con - tent - ment.
There is on - ly one true an - swer.
G7 D7 G7 C F C F7
Now I am hap - py with the Lord.
He must get down on his knees.
C N.C. F6
Just a plain and sim - ple chap - el,
Meet your neigh - bor in the chap - el,
C
where hum - ble peo - ple go to pray:
join with him in tears of joy.
A7 D7
I pray the Lord that I'll grow strong - er,
You'll know the mean - ing of con - tent - ment,

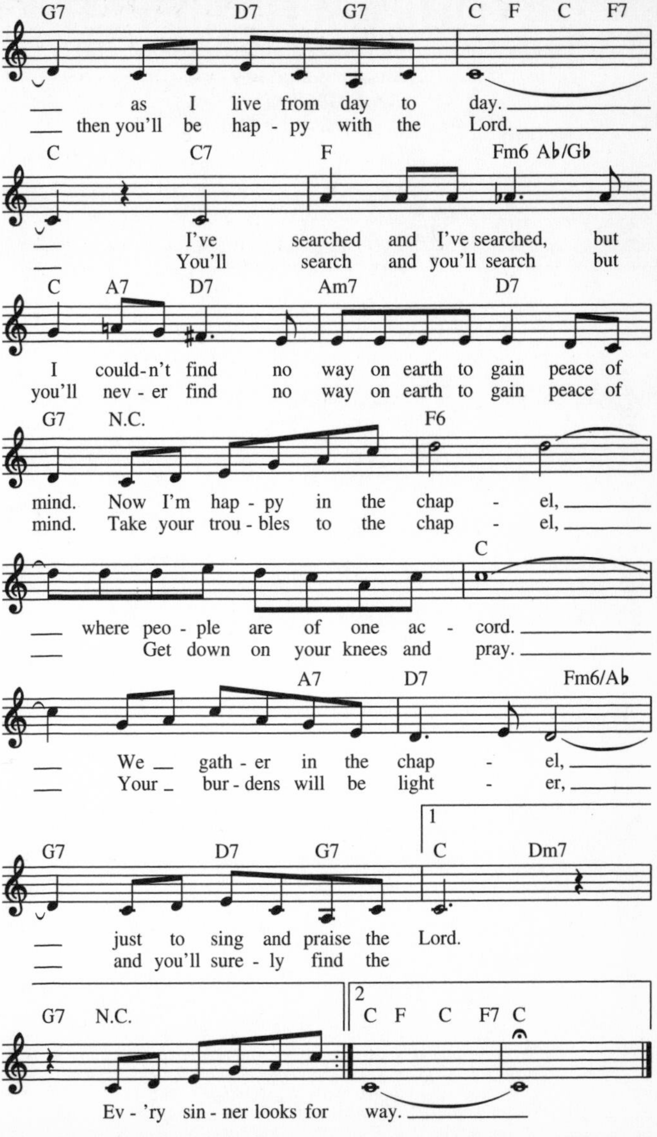
G7 D7 G7 C F C F7
as I live from day to day.
then you'll be hap - py with the Lord.
C C7 F Fm6 A♭/G♭
I've searched and I've searched, but
You'll search and you'll search but
C A7 D7 Am7 D7
I could-n't find no way on earth to gain peace of
you'll nev - er find no way on earth to gain peace of
G7 N.C. F6
mind. Now I'm hap - py in the chap - el,
mind. Take your trou - bles to the chap - el,
C
where peo - ple are of one ac - cord.
Get down on your knees and pray.
A7 D7 Fm6/A♭
We gath - er in the chap - el,
Your bur - dens will be light - er,
1
G7 D7 G7 C Dm7
just to sing and praise the Lord.
and you'll sure - ly find the
2
G7 N.C. C F C F7 C
Ev - 'ry sin - ner looks for way.

DAYDREAM BELIEVER

featured in the Television Series THE MONKEES

Words and Music by
JOHN STEWART

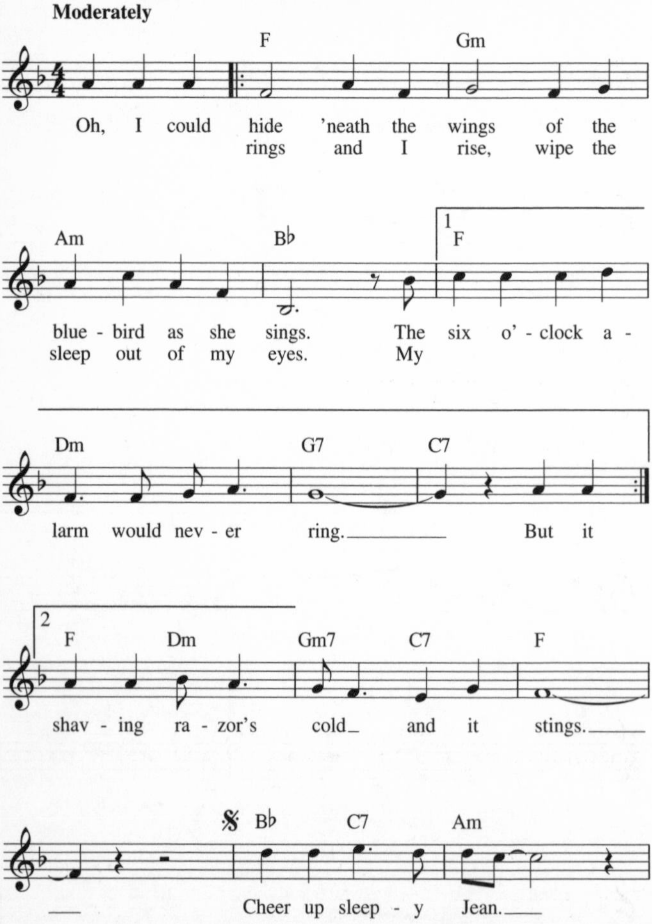
Moderately
F
Gm
Oh, I could hide 'neath the wings of the
rings and I rise, wipe the
Am
B♭
1
F
blue - bird as she sings. The six o' - clock a -
sleep out of my eyes. My
Dm
G7
C7
larm would nev - er ring.
But it
2
F
Dm
Gm7
C7
F
shav - ing ra - zor's cold and it stings.
B♭
C7
Am
Cheer up sleep - y Jean.

Bb C7 Dm Bb F
Oh, what can it mean to a day - dream be -
Bb F Dm
liev - er and a home - com - ing
G7 C7 F
queen.
You once thought of
good times start and
Gm Am Bb
me as a white knight on a steed.
end with - out dol - lar one to spend, but
1
F Dm
Now you know how hap - py I can
G7 C7
be.
Oh, and our
2
F Dm
how much, ba - by,
Gm7 C7 F
D.S. and Fade
do we real - ly need?

DUKE OF EARL

Words and Music by EARL EDWARDS,
EUGENE DIXON and BERNICE WILLIAMS

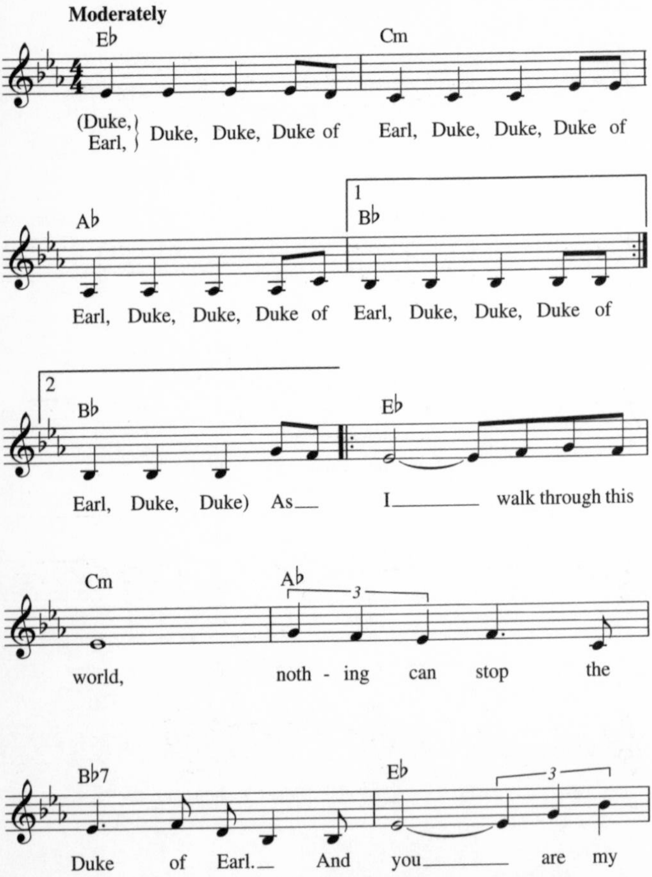
Moderately
Eb
Cm
(Duke, Earl,) Duke, Duke, Duke of Earl, Duke, Duke, Duke of
Ab
1
Bb
Earl, Duke, Duke, Duke of Earl, Duke, Duke, Duke of
2
Bb
Eb
Earl, Duke, Duke) As__ I______ walk through this
Cm
Ab
3
world, noth - ing can stop the
Bb7
Eb
3
Duke of Earl.__ And you______ are my

Cm
Ab
Bb7
girl, and no one can hurt you. Yes
Eb
Cm
I'm gon - na love you
Ab
let me hold you,
1
Bb
'cause I'm the Duke of Earl.
2
Bb
As Earl.
Eb
Cm
(Instrumental)
Ab
Bb
Eb

FUN, FUN, FUN

Words and Music by BRIAN WILSON
and MIKE LOVE

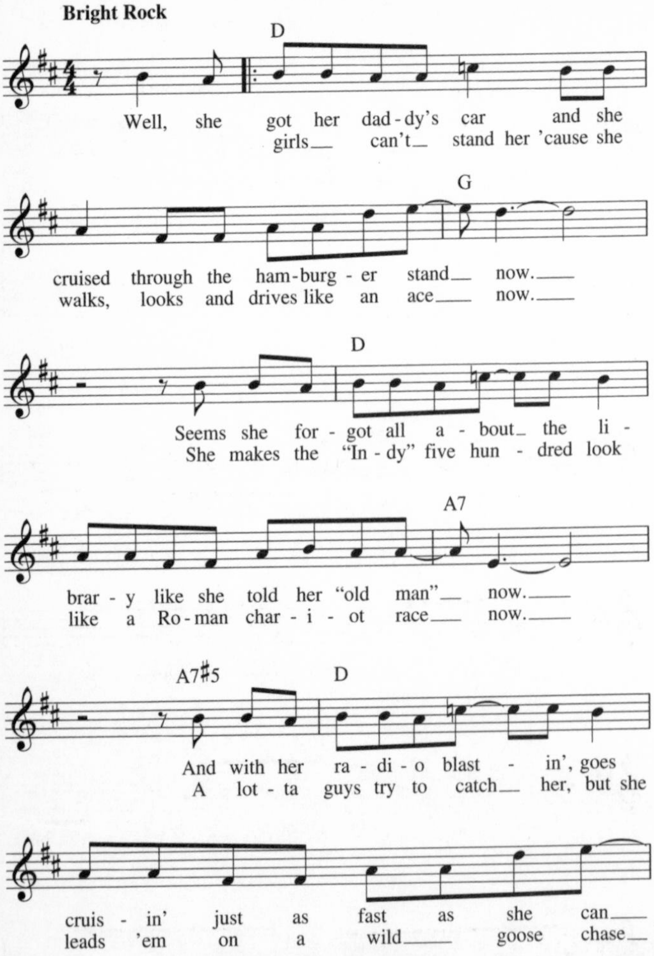
Bright Rock
D
Well, she got her dad - dy's car and she
girls can't stand her 'cause she
G
cruised through the ham-burg - er stand now.
walks, looks and drives like an ace now.
D
Seems she for - got all a - bout the li -
She makes the "In - dy" five hun - dred look
A7
brar - y like she told her "old man" now.
like a Ro - man char - i - ot race now.
A7♯5
D
And with her ra - di - o blast - in', goes
A lot - ta guys try to catch her, but she
cruis - in' just as fast as she can
leads 'em on a wild goose chase

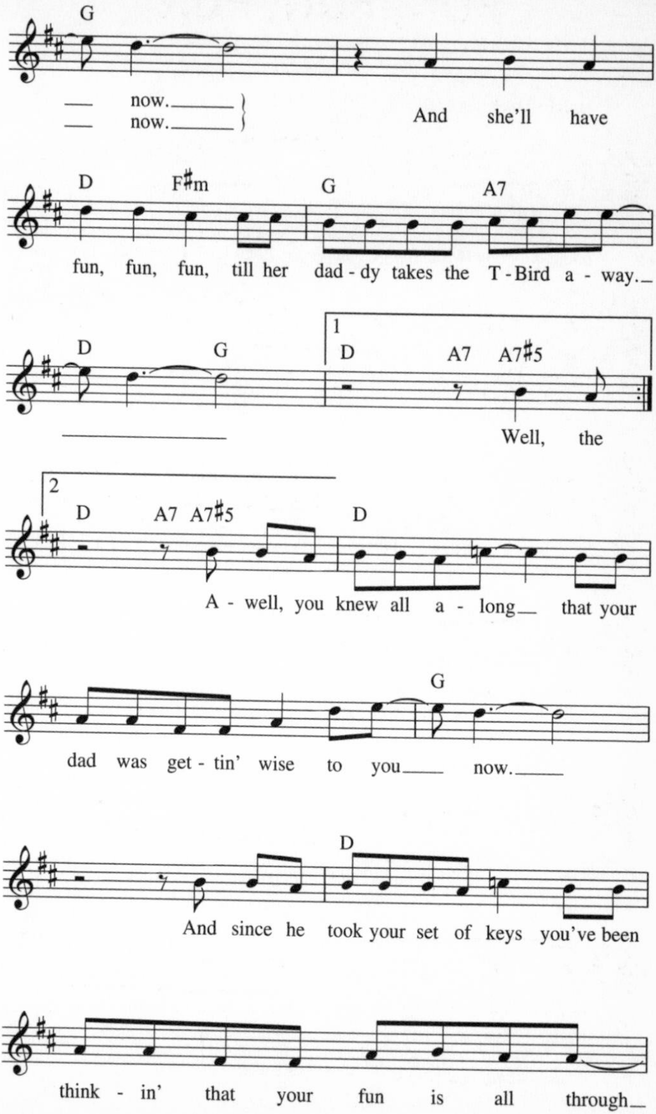
G
— now.
— now.
And she'll have
D F#m G A7
fun, fun, fun, till her dad - dy takes the T - Bird a - way.
D G
1
D A7 A7#5
Well, the
2
D A7 A7#5 D
A - well, you knew all a - long that your
G
dad was get - tin' wise to you now.
D
And since he took your set of keys you've been
think - in' that your fun is all through

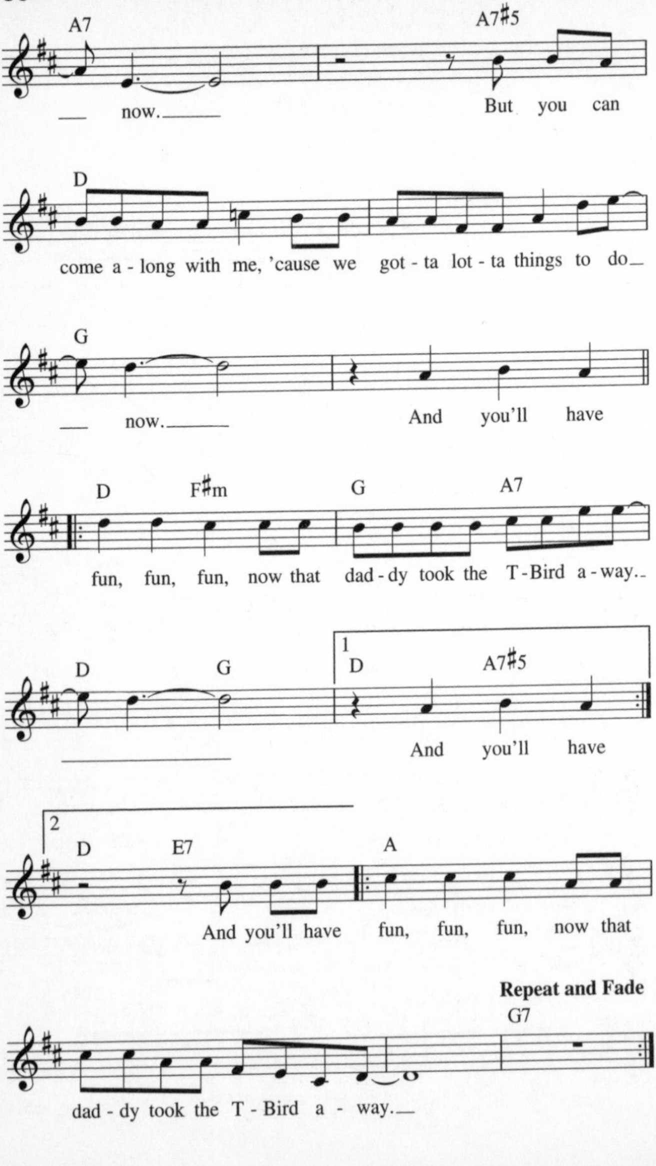
A7
A7#5
now.
But you can
D
come a - long with me, 'cause we got - ta lot - ta things to do
G
now.
And you'll have
D
F#m
G
A7
fun, fun, fun, now that dad - dy took the T - Bird a - way.
D
G
1
D
A7#5
And you'll have
2
D
E7
A
And you'll have fun, fun, fun, now that
Repeat and Fade
G7
dad - dy took the T - Bird a - way.

GEORGY GIRL

from GEORGY GIRL

Words by JIM DALE
Music by TOM SPRINGFIELD

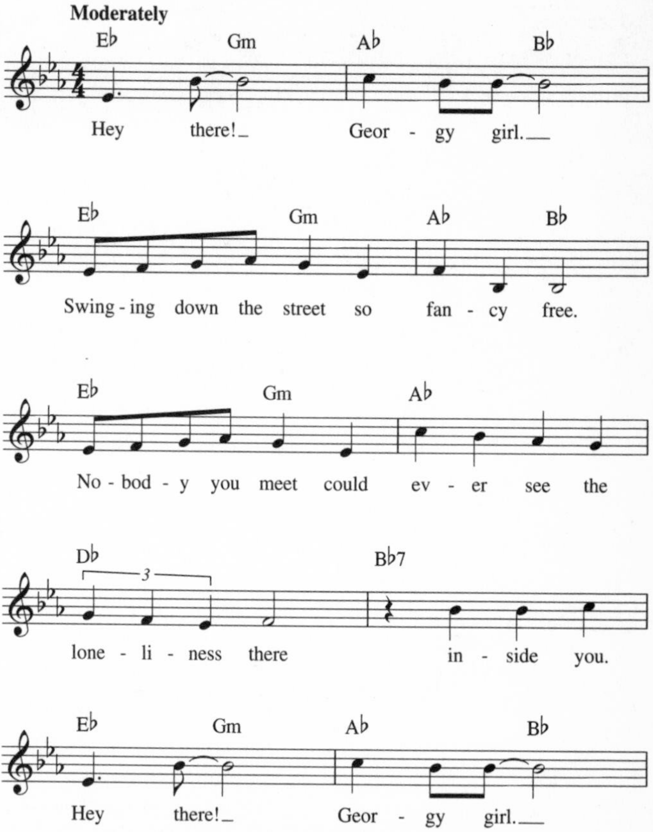
Moderately
Eb Gm Ab Bb
Hey there! Geor - gy girl.
Eb Gm Ab Bb
Swing - ing down the street so fan - cy free.
Eb Gm Ab
No - bod - y you meet could ev - er see the
Db Bb7
3
lone - li - ness there in - side you.
Eb Gm Ab Bb
Hey there! Geor - gy girl.

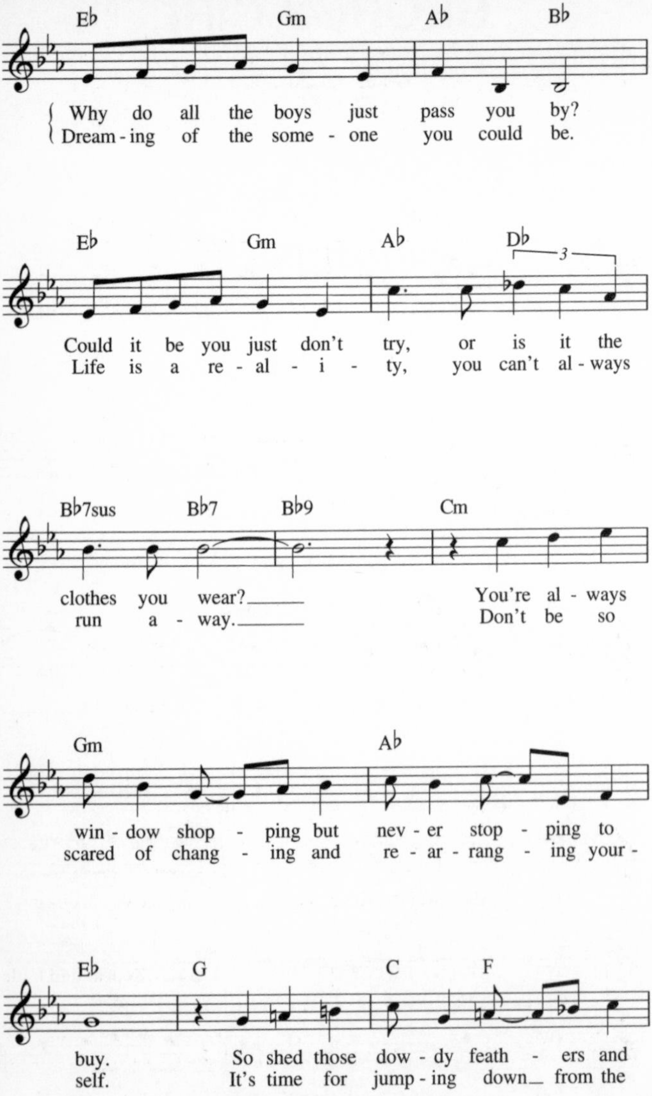
Eb Gm Ab Bb
Why do all the boys just pass you by?
Dream - ing of the some - one you could be.
Eb Gm Ab Db
3
Could it be you just don't try, or is it the
Life is a re - al - i - ty, you can't al - ways
Bb7sus Bb7 Bb9 Cm
clothes you wear?
run a - way.
You're al - ways
Don't be so
Gm Ab
win - dow shop - ping but nev - er stop - ping to
scared of chang - ing and re - ar - rang - ing your -
Eb G C F
buy.
self.
So shed those dow - dy feath - ers and
It's time for jump - ing down from the

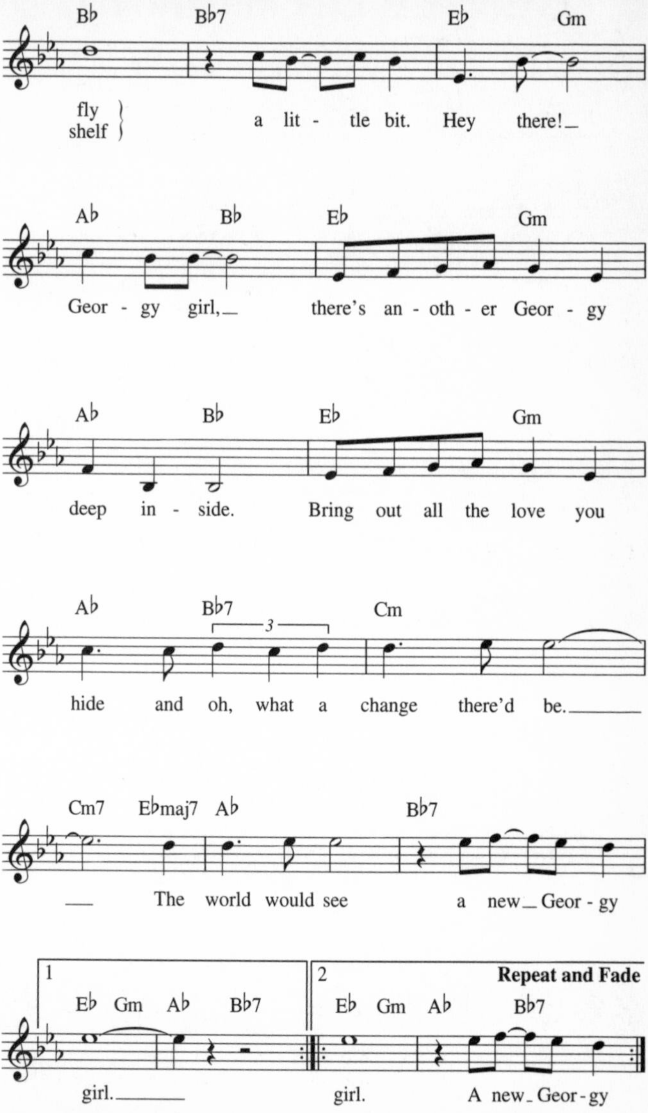
B♭ B♭7 E♭ Gm
fly / shelf a lit - tle bit. Hey there!
A♭ B♭ E♭ Gm
Geor - gy girl, there's an - oth - er Geor - gy
A♭ B♭ E♭ Gm
deep in - side. Bring out all the love you
A♭ B♭7 Cm
3
hide and oh, what a change there'd be.
Cm7 E♭maj7 A♭ B♭7
The world would see a new Geor - gy
1
E♭ Gm A♭ B♭7
girl.
2
Repeat and Fade
E♭ Gm A♭ B♭7
girl. A new Geor - gy

GENTLE ON MY MIND

Words and Music by
JOHN HARTFORD

Moderately bright
C Cmaj7 C6
1. It's know-ing that your door is al - ways o-pen and your
2.-4. (See additional lyrics)
Cmaj7 Dm
path is free to walk,
That makes me tend to leave my sleep - ing
Dm7 G7 C
bag rolled up and stashed be-hind your couch,
And it's know-ing I'm not
Cmaj7 C6 Cmaj7
shack-led by for - got-ten words and bonds__ And the
C Cmaj7 Dm
ink stains that have dried up - on some line,

That
Dm7 Dm6
keeps you in the back-roads by the riv-ers of my
Dm7 Dm Dmaj7 Dm7 G7
mem-'ry that keeps you ev-er Gen-tle On My
1-3
C
Mind. It's
4
C
Mind.

Additional Lyrics

2. It's not clinging to the rocks and ivy planted on their columns now that binds me
   Or something that somebody said because they thought we fit together walkin'.
   It's just knowing that the world will not be cursing or forgiving when I walk along
   Some railroad track and find
   That you're moving on the backroads by the rivers of my memory and for hours
   You're just Gentle On My Mind.

3. Though the wheat fields and the clothes lines and junkyards and the highways
   Come between us
   And some other woman crying to her mother 'cause she turned and I was gone.
   I still run in silence, tears of joy might stain my face and summer sun might
   Burn me 'til I'm blind
   But not to where I cannot see you walkin' on the backroads by the rivers flowing
   Gentle On My Mind.

4. I dip my cup of soup back from the gurglin' cracklin' cauldron in some train yard
   My beard a roughning coal pile and a dirty hat pulled low across my face.
   Through cupped hands 'round a tin can I pretend I hold you to my breast and find
   That you're waving from the backroads by the rivers of my memory ever smilin'
   Ever Gentle On My Mind.

GEORGIA ON MY MIND

Words by STUART GORRELL
Music by HOAGY CARMICHAEL

Slowly
F
A7
Dm
Geor-gia, __ Geor-gia, __ the whole day
Gm
B♭m
F
E7
Gm
C13
through, Just an old sweet song keeps Geor-gia __ on my
F
F♯dim7
Gm7
C7♯5
mind, Geor - gia on my mind.
F
A7
Dm
Geor-gia, __ Geor-gia, __ a song of
Gm
B♭m
F
E7
you Comes as sweet and clear as
Gm
C13
F
E♭9
F
A7
moon - light through the pines. __

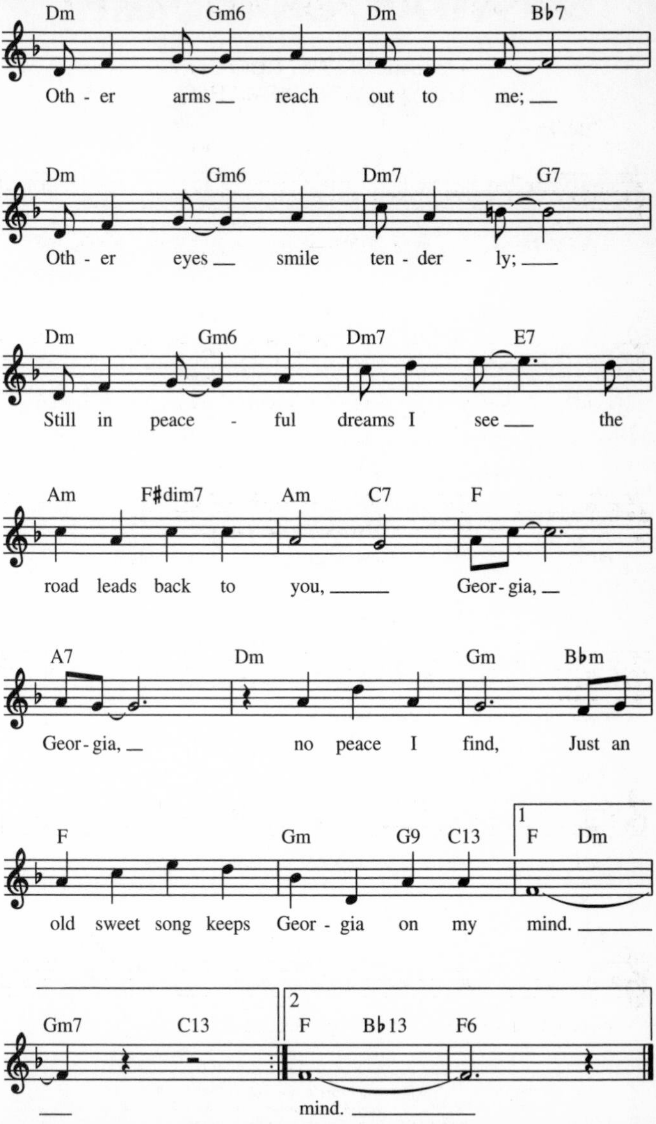
Dm Gm6 Dm B♭7
Oth - er arms reach out to me;
Dm Gm6 Dm7 G7
Oth - er eyes smile ten - der - ly;
Dm Gm6 Dm7 E7
Still in peace - ful dreams I see the
Am F♯dim7 Am C7 F
road leads back to you, Geor - gia,
A7 Dm Gm B♭m
Geor - gia, no peace I find, Just an
F Gm G9 C13 1 F Dm
old sweet song keeps Geor - gia on my mind.
Gm7 C13 2 F B♭13 F6
mind.

GO AWAY, LITTLE GIRL

Words and Music by GERRY GOFFIN and CAROLE KING

Moderately slow
G
Go a - way, lit - tle girl, go a -
Am7
way, lit - tle girl. I'm not sup - posed to
D7
G
be a - lone with you. I
Em
Em(maj7)
Em7
know that your lips are sweet, but our lips must nev - er
A7
D
D♯dim7
Em
A7
meet. I be - long to some - one else and I must be

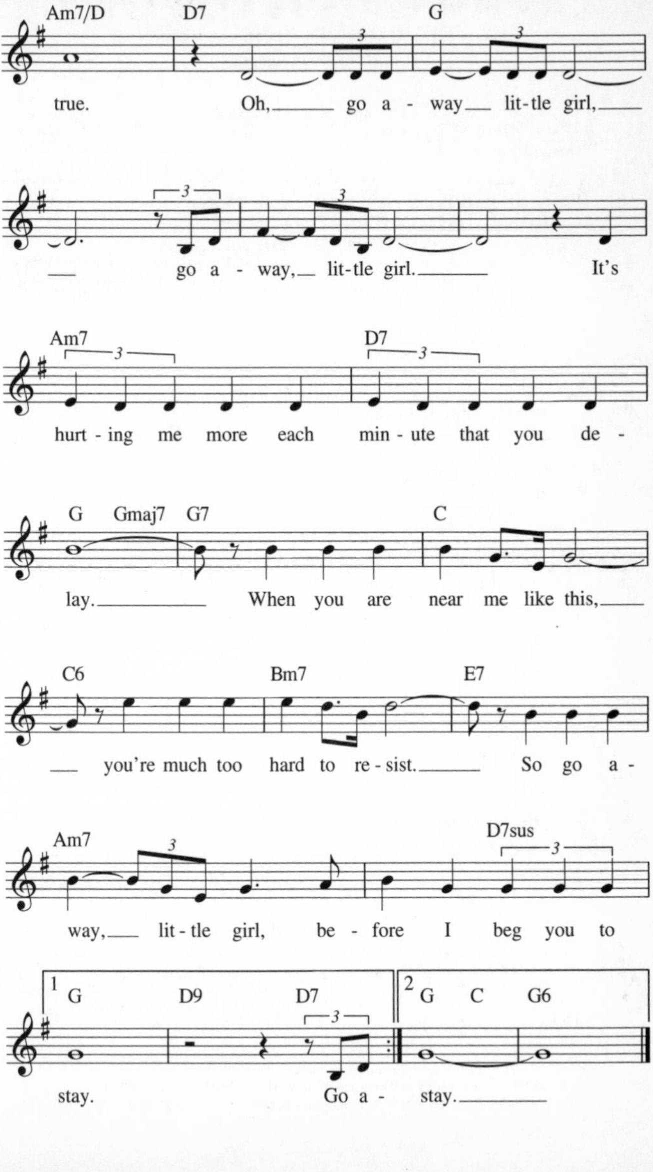
Am7/D D7 G
true. Oh, go a - way lit-tle girl,
go a - way, lit-tle girl. It's
Am7 D7
hurt - ing me more each min - ute that you de -
G Gmaj7 G7 C
lay. When you are near me like this,
C6 Bm7 E7
you're much too hard to re - sist. So go a -
Am7 D7sus
way, lit - tle girl, be - fore I beg you to
1 G D9 D7
stay. Go a -
2 G C G6
stay.

GOOD VIBRATIONS

Words and Music by BRIAN WILSON and MIKE LOVE

Light Rock

Dm
I, I love the col - or-ful
Close my eyes. She's some - how
C
clothes she wears, and the
clos - er now.
B♭
A
way the sun - light plays up - on her hair.
Soft - ly smile. I know she must be kind.
Dm
I hear the sound of a
Then I look
C
gen - tle word, on the
in her eyes. She goes
B♭
A
wind that lifts her per - fume through the air.
with me to a blos - som world.
C7
F
Cm7
F
Cm7
I'm pick - ing up good vi - bra - tions.

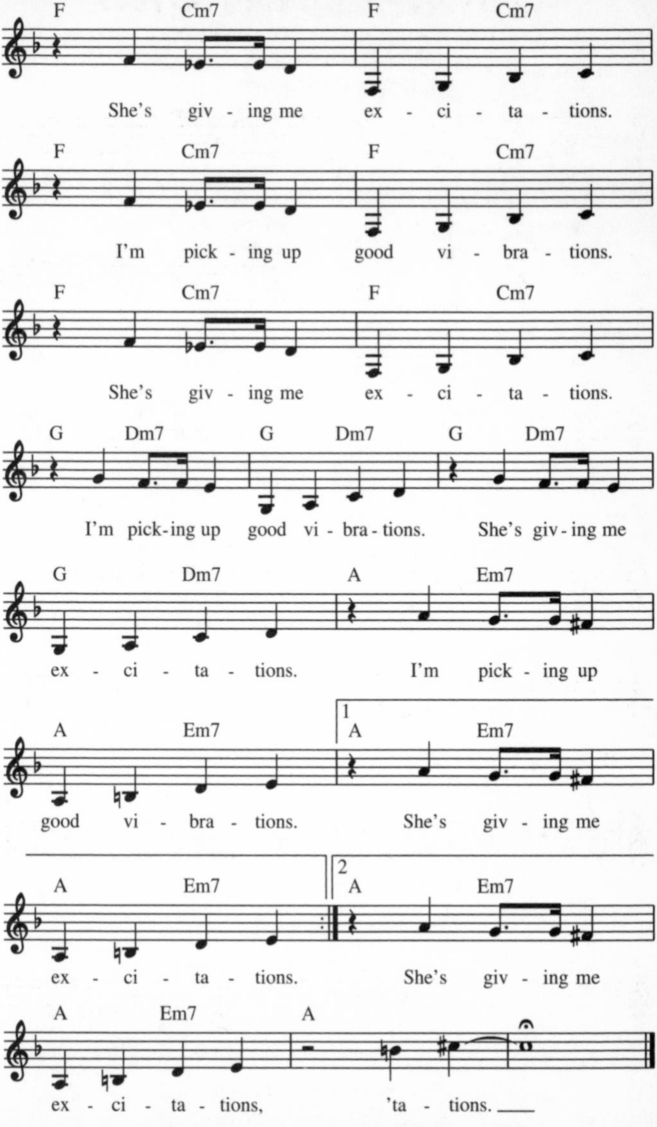
F Cm7 F Cm7
She's giv - ing me ex - ci - ta - tions.
F Cm7 F Cm7
I'm pick - ing up good vi - bra - tions.
F Cm7 F Cm7
She's giv - ing me ex - ci - ta - tions.
G Dm7 G Dm7 G Dm7
I'm pick-ing up good vi - bra - tions. She's giv - ing me
G Dm7 A Em7
ex - ci - ta - tions. I'm pick - ing up
1
A Em7 A Em7
good vi - bra - tions. She's giv - ing me
2
A Em7 A Em7
ex - ci - ta - tions. She's giv - ing me
A Em7 A
ex - ci - ta - tions, 'ta - tions.

GROOVIN'

Words and Music by FELIX CAVALIERE
and EDWARD BRIGATI, JR.

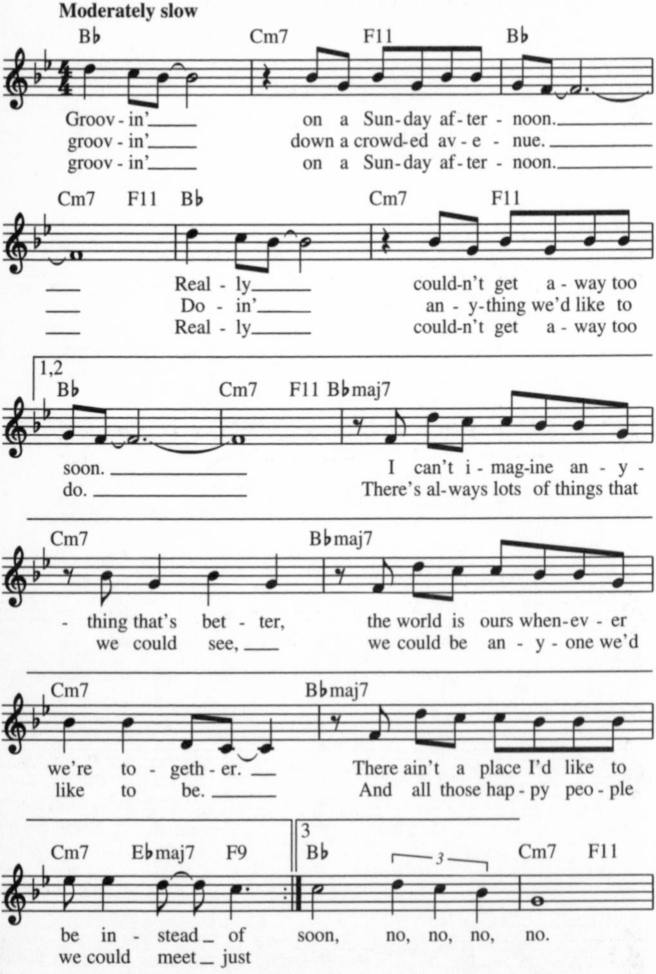
Moderately slow
Bb Cm7 F11 Bb
Groov - in' on a Sun-day af - ter - noon.
groov - in' down a crowd-ed av - e - nue.
groov - in' on a Sun-day af - ter - noon.
Cm7 F11 Bb Cm7 F11
Real - ly could-n't get a - way too
Do - in' an - y-thing we'd like to
Real - ly could-n't get a - way too
1,2
Bb Cm7 F11 Bbmaj7
soon. I can't i - mag-ine an - y -
do. There's al-ways lots of things that
Cm7 Bbmaj7
- thing that's bet - ter, the world is ours when-ev - er
we could see, we could be an - y - one we'd
Cm7 Bbmaj7
we're to - geth - er. There ain't a place I'd like to
like to be. And all those hap - py peo - ple
Cm7 Ebmaj7 F9
be in - stead of
we could meet just
3
Bb Cm7 F11
soon, no, no, no, no.

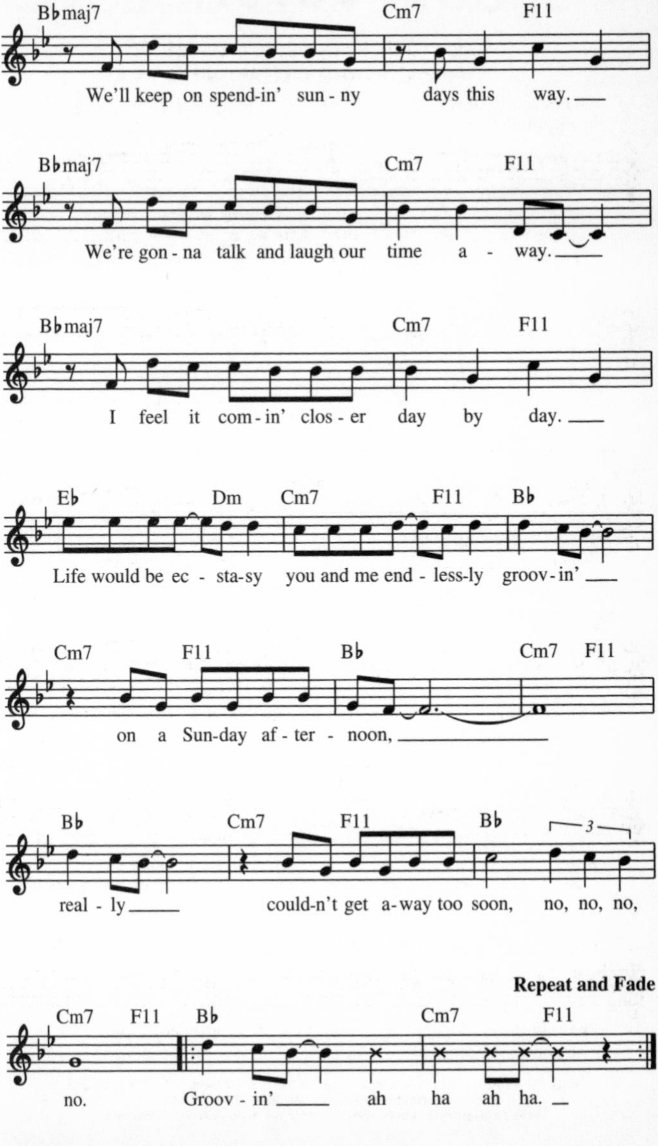
B♭maj7 Cm7 F11
We'll keep on spend-in' sun - ny days this way.
B♭maj7 Cm7 F11
We're gon - na talk and laugh our time a - way.
B♭maj7 Cm7 F11
I feel it com - in' clos - er day by day.
E♭ Dm Cm7 F11 B♭
Life would be ec - sta-sy you and me end - less-ly groov - in'
Cm7 F11 B♭ Cm7 F11
on a Sun-day af - ter - noon,
B♭ Cm7 F11 B♭
3
real - ly could-n't get a-way too soon, no, no, no,
Repeat and Fade
Cm7 F11 B♭ Cm7 F11
no. Groov - in' ah ha ah ha.

A GROOVY KIND OF LOVE

Words and Music by TONI WINE
and CAROLE BAYER SAGER

Moderately slow
G
When I'm feel - in' blue, all I have to
want to you can turn me
D7/G
G
do is take a look at you, then I'm not so
on to an - y - thing you want to, an - y - time at
Am7
blue. When you're close to me I can feel your
all. When I taste your lips oh, I start to
Bm7
Am7
heart beat I can hear you breath - ing in my
shiv - er can't con - trol the quiv - er - ing in -
D7
G
ear.
side.
Would-n't you a - gree, ba - by, you and
D7/G
G
me got A Groov - y Kind Of Love.

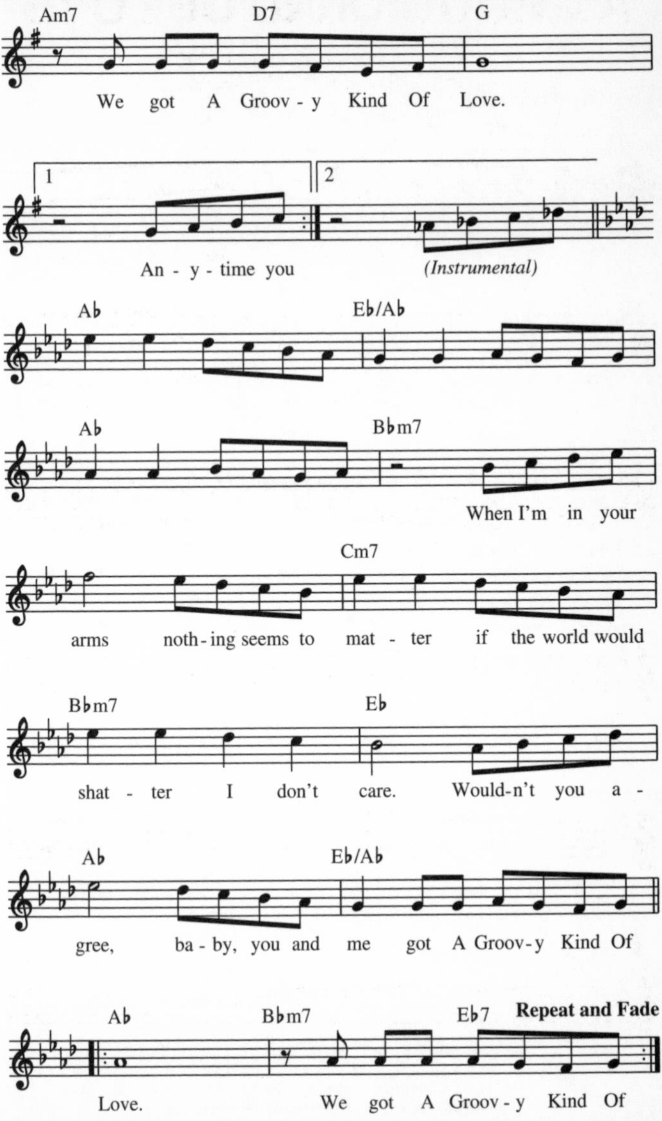
Am7 D7 G
We got A Groov - y Kind Of Love.
1
An - y - time you
2
(Instrumental)
Ab Eb/Ab
Ab Bbm7
When I'm in your
Cm7
arms noth - ing seems to mat - ter if the world would
Bbm7 Eb
shat - ter I don't care. Would-n't you a -
Ab Eb/Ab
gree, ba - by, you and me got A Groov-y Kind Of
Ab Bbm7 Eb7 Repeat and Fade
Love. We got A Groov - y Kind Of

HANG ON SLOOPY

Words and Music by WES FARRELL
and BERT RUSSELL

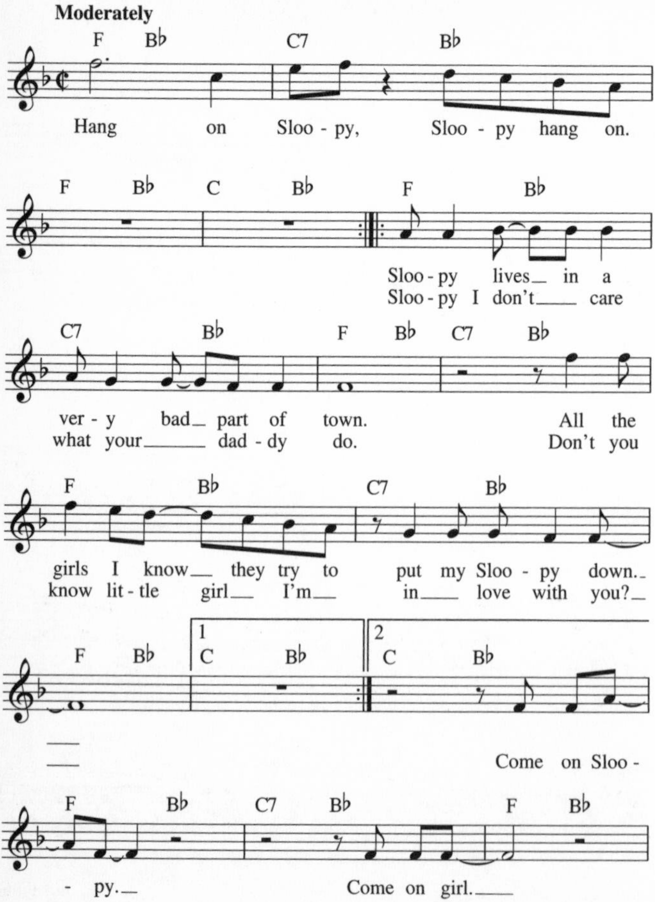
Moderately
F Bb C7 Bb
Hang on Sloo - py, Sloo - py hang on.
F Bb C Bb F Bb
Sloo - py lives in a
Sloo - py I don't care
C7 Bb F Bb C7 Bb
ver - y bad part of town. All the
what your dad - dy do. Don't you
F Bb C7 Bb
girls I know they try to put my Sloo - py down.
know lit - tle girl I'm in love with you?
1 2
F Bb C Bb C Bb
Come on Sloo -
F Bb C7 Bb F Bb
- py. Come on girl.

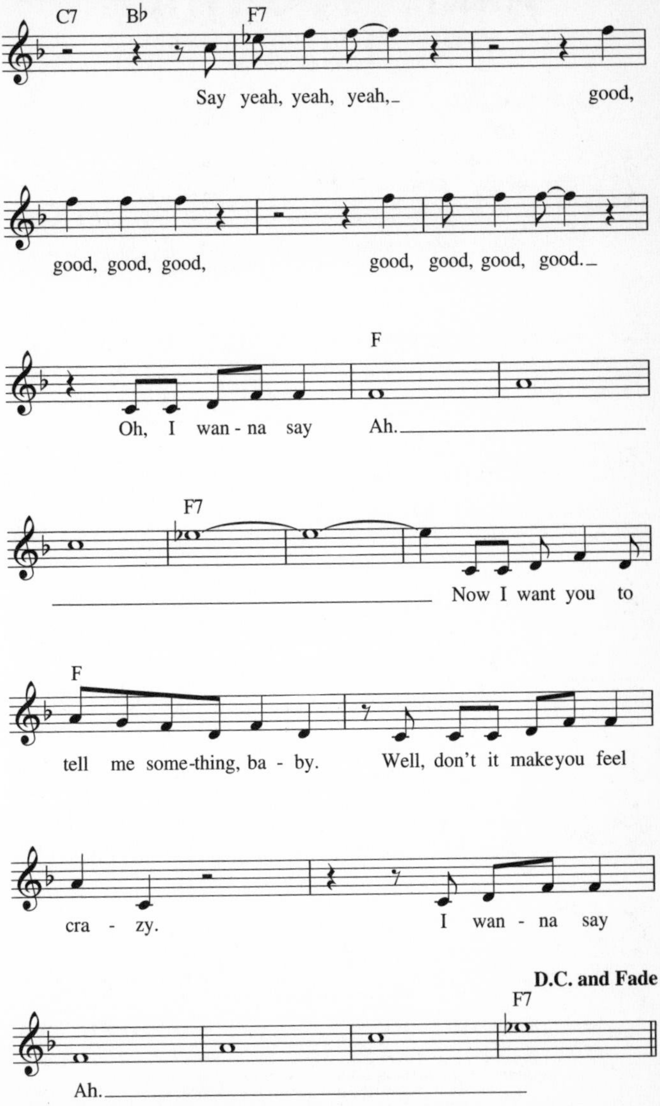
C7 B♭ F7
Say yeah, yeah, yeah,_ good,
good, good, good, good, good, good, good._
F
Oh, I wan - na say Ah._
F7
Now I want you to
F
tell me some-thing, ba - by. Well, don't it make you feel
cra - zy. I wan - na say
D.C. and Fade
F7
Ah._

HAPPY TOGETHER

Words and Music by GARY BONNER
and ALAN GORDON

Steady, solid beat
Em
I-mag-ine me and you. I do. I think a-bout you
call you up. In-vest a dime and you say you be-
D
day and night, it's on-ly right to think a-bout the
long to me and ease my mind, i-mag-ine how the
C
girl you love, and hold her tight, so hap-py to-
world would be so ver-y fine, so hap-py to-
1 B
geth-er. If I should
2 B
geth-er.
E
Bm7
I can see me lov-in' no-bod-y but
E
G
E
you for all my life. When you're with me,

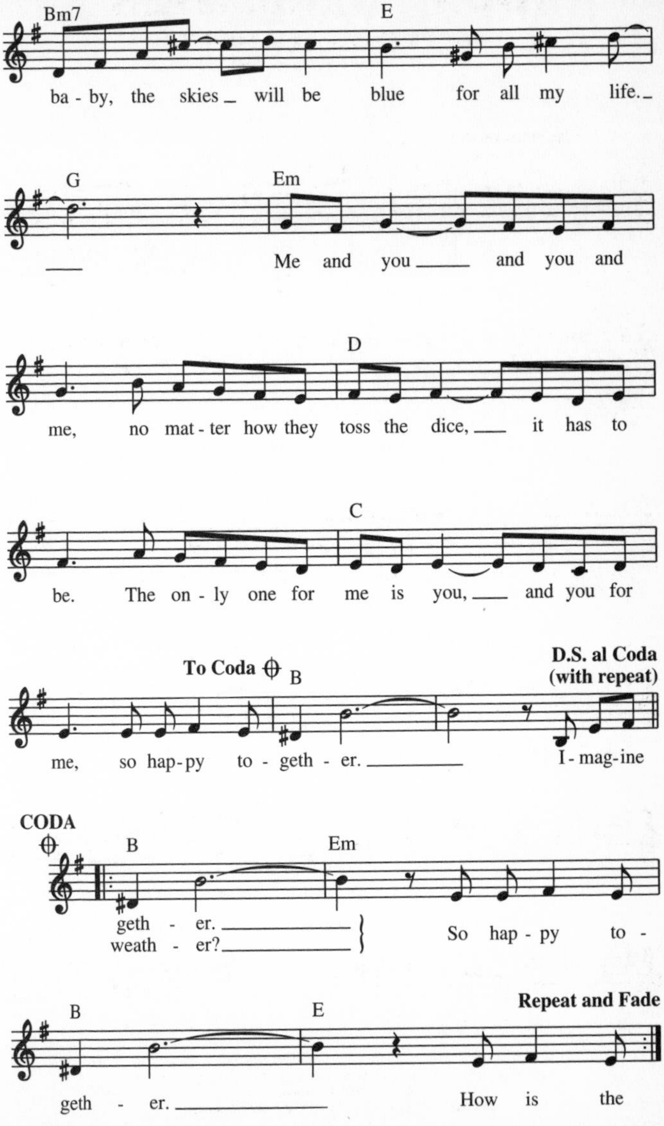
Bm7
E
ba - by, the skies_ will be blue for all my life._
G
Em
Me and you ___ and you and
D
me, no mat - ter how they toss the dice, ___ it has to
C
be. The on - ly one for me is you, ___ and you for
To Coda
B
D.S. al Coda (with repeat)
me, so hap - py to - geth - er. ___ I - mag - ine
CODA
B
Em
geth - er. ___
weath - er? ___
So hap - py to -
B
E
Repeat and Fade
geth - er. ___ How is the

HARPER VALLEY P.T.A.

Words and Music by
TOM T. HALL

Moderately
D
Dmaj7
1. I want to tell you all a sto - ry 'bout a
2.-5. (See additional lyrics)
D6
Dmaj7
D7
Har - per Val - ley wid - ow'd wife
G7
who had a teen - age daugh - ter who at -
tend - ed Har - per Val - ley Jun - ior High.
D
Dmaj7
Well, her daugh - ter came home one af - ter -

D6
Dmaj7
D
noon and did - n't e - ven stop to play.
D7
G7
She said, "Mom, I got_ a note here from the
A7
D
Har - per Val - ley P. T. A."

Additional Lyrics

2. The note said, Mrs. Johnson, you're wearing your dresses way too high –
It's reported you've been drinking and a-runnin' 'round with men and going wild.
We don't believe you ought to be a-bringing up your little girl this way –
It was signed by the secretary, Harper Valley P.T.A.

3. Well, it happened that the P.T.A. was gonna meet that very afternoon –
They were sure surprised when Mrs. Johnson wore her mini-skirt into the room.
As she walked up to the blackboard, I still recall the words she had to say.
She said, "I'd like to address this meeting of the Harper Valley P.T.A.

4. Well, there's Bobby Taylor sittin' there and seven times he's asked me for a date.
Mrs. Taylor sure seems to use a lot of ice whenever he's away.
And Mr. Baker, can you tell us why your secretary had to leave this town?
And shouldn't widow Jones be told to keep her window shades all pulled completely down?

5. Well, Mr. Harper couldn't be here 'cause he stayed too long at Kelly's Bar again.
And if you smell Shirley Thompson's breath, you'll find she's had a little nip of gin.
Then you have the nerve to tell me you think that as a mother I'm not fit.
Well, this is just a little Peyton Place and you're all Harper Valley hypocrites."
No, I wouldn't put you on, because it really did, it happened just this way,
The day my mama socked it to the Harper Valley P.T.A.

HE AIN'T HEAVY... HE'S MY BROTHER

Words and Music by BOB RUSSELL
and BOBBY SCOTT

Slowly
B♭
F/A
The road is long, with man - y a
go; his wel - fare is
E♭/G
Cm7/F
F7
wind - ing turn, that leads us to
my con - cern. No bur - den is
Gm
A♭
Cm7/F
who knows where, who knows where.
he to bear, we'll get there.
B♭maj7
F/A
But I'm strong, strong e - nough to
For I know he would not en -
E♭/G
Cm7/F
car - ry him;
cum - ber me;
He ain't heav - y,

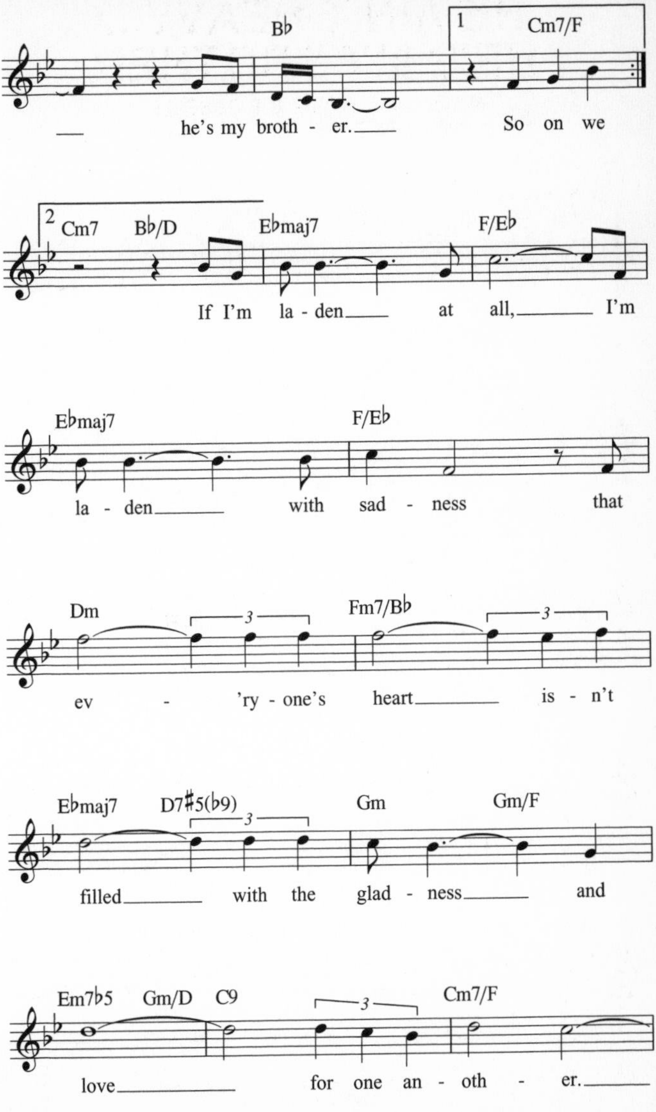
B♭
1
Cm7/F
he's my broth - er.
So on we
2
Cm7
B♭/D
E♭maj7
F/E♭
If I'm la - den at all, I'm
E♭maj7
F/E♭
la - den with sad - ness that
Dm
3
Fm7/B♭
3
ev - 'ry - one's heart is - n't
E♭maj7
D7♯5(♭9)
3
Gm
Gm/F
filled with the glad - ness and
Em7♭5
Gm/D
C9
3
Cm7/F
love for one an - oth - er.

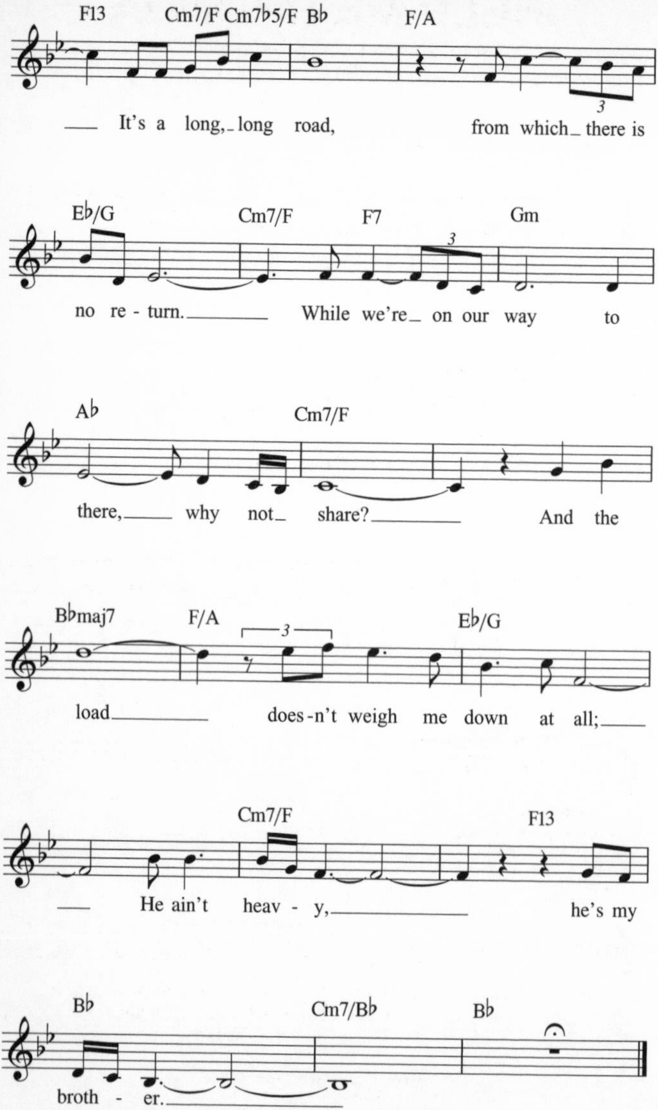
F13 Cm7/F Cm7♭5/F B♭ F/A
It's a long, long road, from which there is
E♭/G Cm7/F F7 Gm
no re - turn. While we're on our way to
A♭ Cm7/F
there, why not share? And the
B♭maj7 F/A E♭/G
load does - n't weigh me down at all;
Cm7/F F13
He ain't heav - y, he's my
B♭ Cm7/B♭ B♭
broth - er.

HELP ME RHONDA

Words and Music by BRIAN WILSON
and MIKE LOVE

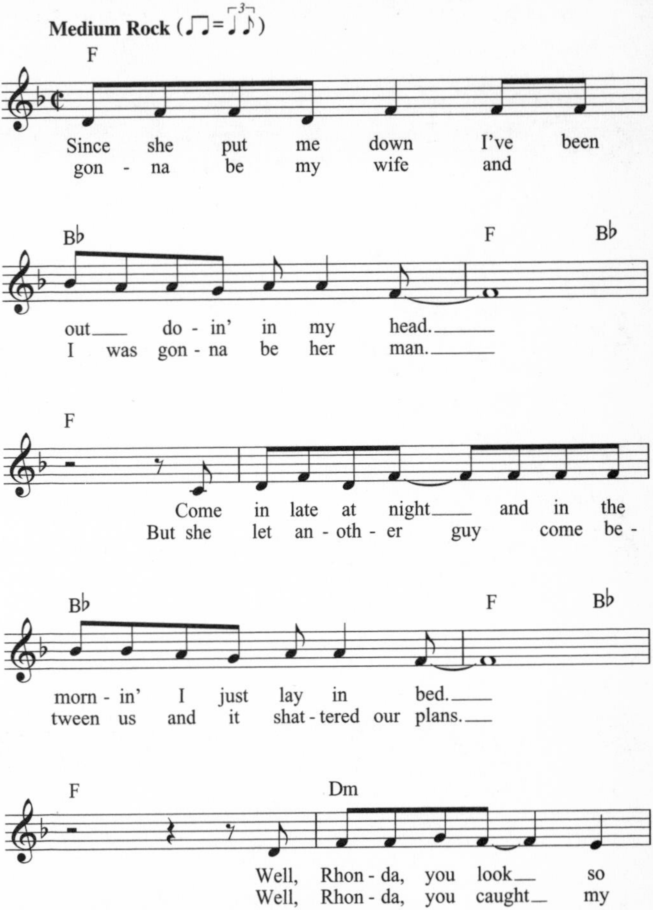
Medium Rock
F
Since she put me down I've been
gon - na be my wife and
B♭ F B♭
out do - in' in my head.
I was gon - na be her man.
F
Come in late at night and in the
But she let an - oth - er guy come be -
B♭ F B♭
morn - in' I just lay in bed.
tween us and it shat - tered our plans.
F Dm
Well, Rhon - da, you look so
Well, Rhon - da, you caught my

B♭
fine, and I know it would-n't take much
eye, and I'll give you lots of rea - sons
G7
F
time, for you to
why. You got - ta
help me, Rhon - da,
Gm7
C7
F
help me get her out of my heart.
C7
Help me, Rhon - da! Help, help me, Rhon - da!
F
Help me, Rhon - da! Help, help me, Rhon - da!
C7
Help me, Rhon - da! Help, help me, Rhon - da!

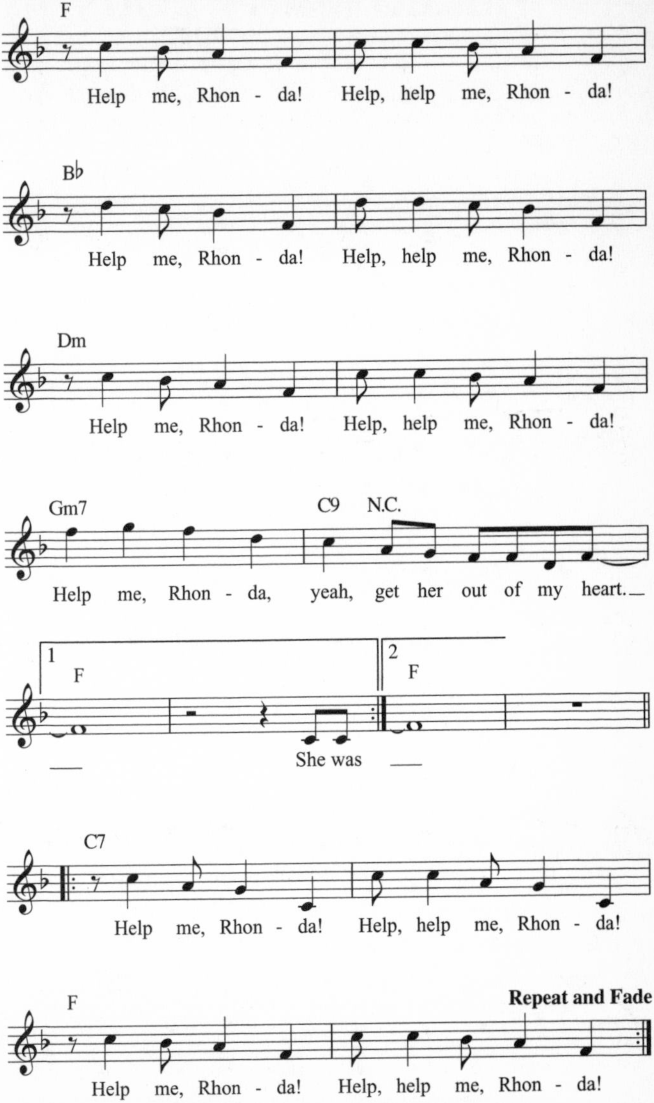
F
Help me, Rhon - da! Help, help me, Rhon - da!
B♭
Help me, Rhon - da! Help, help me, Rhon - da!
Dm
Help me, Rhon - da! Help, help me, Rhon - da!
Gm7
C9 N.C.
Help me, Rhon - da, yeah, get her out of my heart.
1
F
She was
2
F
C7
Help me, Rhon - da! Help, help me, Rhon - da!
F
Repeat and Fade
Help me, Rhon - da! Help, help me, Rhon - da!

HELLO MARY LOU

Words and Music by GENE PITNEY
and C. MANGIARACINA

Moderately
Bb Dm Gm Bb6
You passed me by one sun - ny day
saw your lips I heard your voice be -
Eb
flashed those big brown eyes my way and
lieve me I just had no choice, wild
Bb Bbdim7
ooh I want - ed you for - ev - er -
hors - es could - n't make me stay a -
F7 Bb Dm
more. Now I'm not one that
way. I thought a - bout a
Gm Bb Eb
gets a - round, I swear my feet stuck
moon - lit night, my arms a - bout you

Edim7 B♭ Gm Cm7 F7♭9
to the ground, and though I nev - er did meet you be -
good an' tight, that's all I had to see for me to
B♭ E♭ B♭ F7
fore.
say.
I said "Hel - lo Mar - y Lou
E♭ B♭
good - bye heart sweet Mar - y Lou I'm
C9 Am C7 F7
so in love with you. I
B♭ F9 B♭ D7 D+ D7
knew Mar - y Lou we'd nev - er
Gm C9 C7 C9 F7 Dm F7
part so hel - lo Mar - y Lou good - bye
1
B♭ F7
heart." I
2
B♭
heart."

I CAN'T STOP LOVING YOU

Words and Music by
DON GIBSON

Slowly
C
C7
Those hap - py hours that we once
F
C
knew, though long a - go,
D7
G7
still make me blue. They say that
C
C7
time heals a bro - ken
F
C
heart, but time has stood still
G7
C
F/G
C
C7
since we've been a - part.
I can't stop
I can't stop

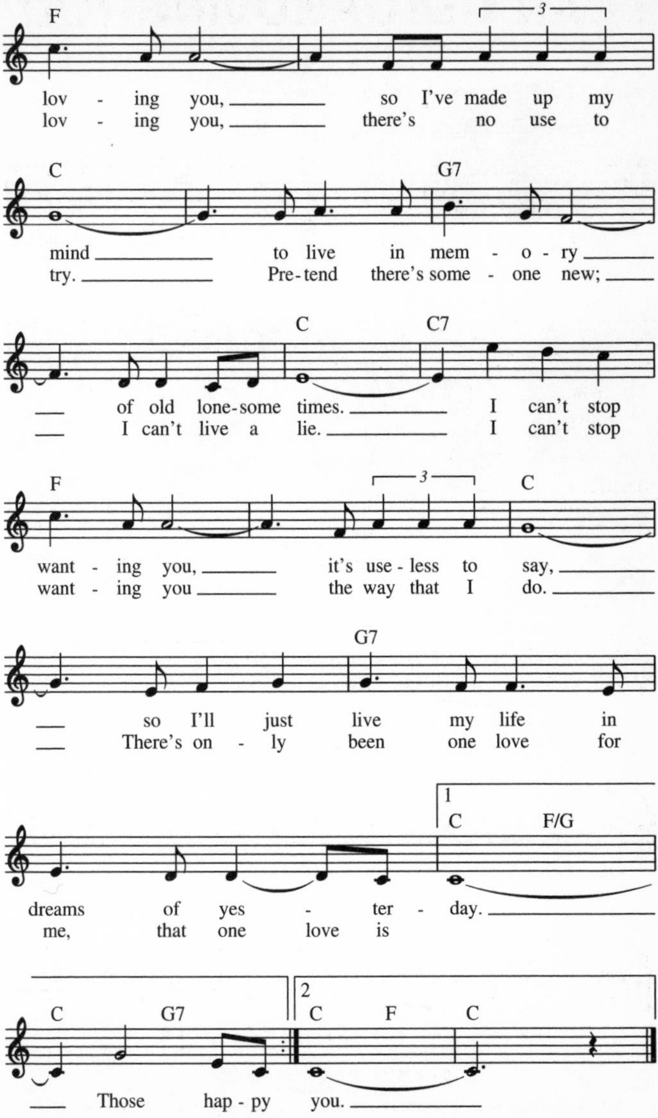
F
3
lov - ing you, so I've made up my
lov - ing you, there's no use to
C G7
mind to live in mem - o - ry
try. Pre-tend there's some - one new;
C C7
of old lone-some times. I can't stop
I can't live a lie. I can't stop
F 3 C
want - ing you, it's use-less to say,
want - ing you the way that I do.
G7
so I'll just live my life in
There's on - ly been one love for
1
C F/G
dreams of yes - ter - day.
me, that one love is
C G7
Those hap - py
2
C F C
you.

I GET AROUND

Words and Music by BRIAN WILSON
and MIKE LOVE

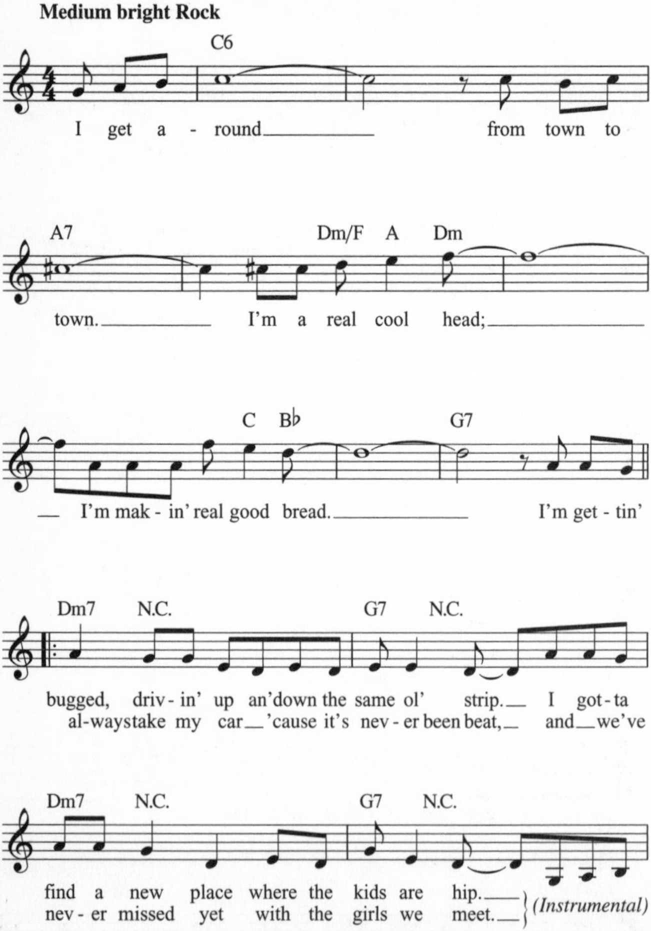
Medium bright Rock
C6
I get a - round from town to
A7 Dm/F A Dm
town. I'm a real cool head;
C B♭ G7
I'm mak - in' real good bread. I'm get - tin'
Dm7 N.C. G7 N.C.
bugged, driv - in' up an'down the same ol' strip. I got - ta
al-waystake my car 'cause it's nev - er been beat, and we've
Dm7 N.C. G7 N.C.
find a new place where the kids are hip.
nev - er missed yet with the girls we meet.
(Instrumental)

My
None of the
Dm7 N.C. G7 N.C.
bud-dies and me are get-tin' real well-known, yeah, the
guys go stead-y 'cause it would-n't be right to leave your
Dm7 N.C. G7 N.C.
bad guys know us and they leave us a-lone.
best girl home on a Sat-ur-day night.
I get a-
C6 A7
round from town to town.
Dm/F A Dm
I'm a real cool head;
C B♭
I'm mak-in' real good bread.
1 G7
2 G7 C
Repeat and Fade
Am
We

I HEARD IT THROUGH THE GRAPEVINE

Words and Music by NORMAN J. WHITFIELD
and BARRETT STRONG

Moderately
Em
Em
Mm. ___ I bet you're won-derin' how I knew
2. _ ain't sup-posed to cry,
3. (See additional lyrics)
B
A7
'bout your plans ___ to make me blue, ___
but these tears ___ I can't hold in - side. ___
Em
___ with some oth - er guy ___ you knew be - fore.
___ Los - in' you ___ would end my life you see,
B
Be - tween the two of us guys ___
'cause you mean ___
A7
___ you know I loved you more. ___ It took me by sur -
___ that much to me. ___ You could have told _
C#m
A7
prise ___ I must say ___ when I
___ me your - self ___ that you

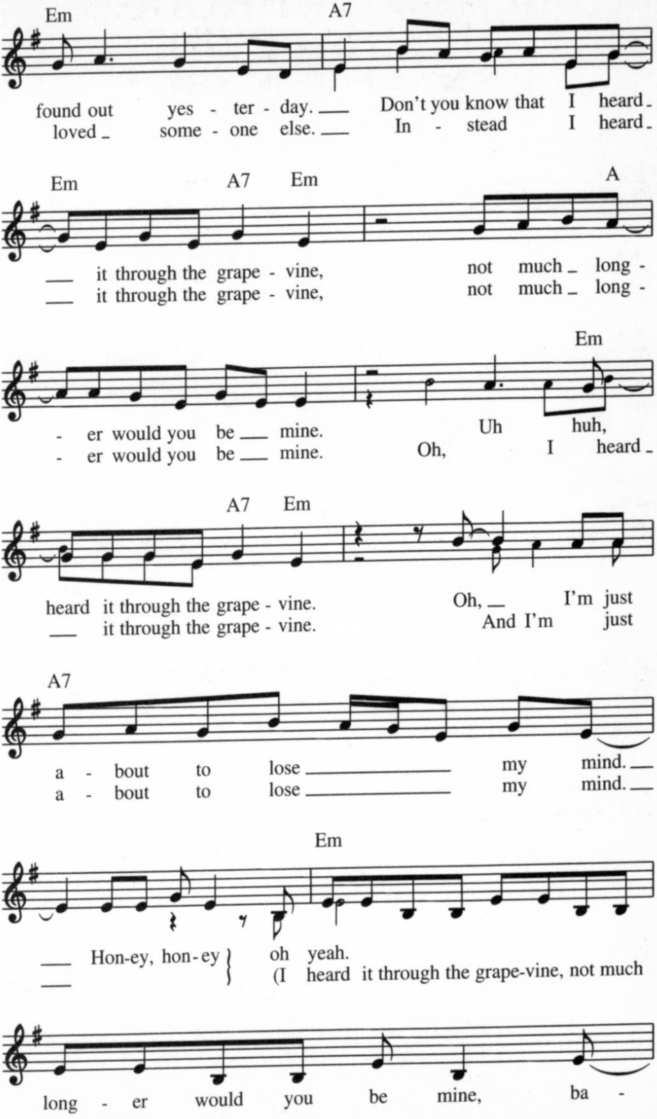
Em
A7
found out yes - ter - day. Don't you know that I heard
loved some - one else. In - stead I heard
Em
A7
Em
A
it through the grape - vine, not much long -
it through the grape - vine, not much long -
Em
- er would you be mine. Uh huh,
- er would you be mine. Oh, I heard
A7
Em
heard it through the grape - vine. Oh, I'm just
it through the grape - vine. And I'm just
A7
a - bout to lose my mind.
a - bout to lose my mind.
Em
Hon-ey, hon-ey oh yeah.
(I heard it through the grape-vine, not much
long - er would you be mine, ba -

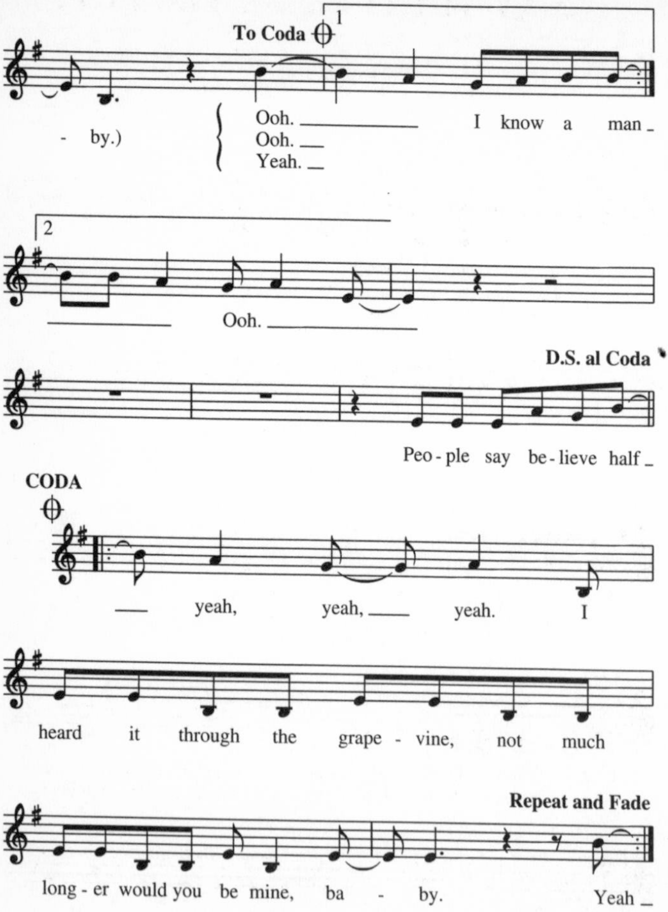
To Coda
1
- by.)
Ooh.
Ooh.
Yeah.
I know a man
2
Ooh.
D.S. al Coda
Peo - ple say be - lieve half
CODA
yeah, yeah, yeah. I
heard it through the grape - vine, not much
Repeat and Fade
long - er would you be mine, ba - by. Yeah

Additional Lyrics

3. People say believe half of what you see
   Oh, and none of what you hear;
   But I can't help but be confused
   If it's true please tell me dear.
   Do you plan to let me go
   For the other guy you loved before?

I SAY A LITTLE PRAYER

Lyric by HAL DAVID
Music by BURT BACHARACH

Moderately fast
Em7
Am7
(1.) The mo - ment I wake up,
(2.) I run for the bus, dear.
(D.S.) Instrumental solo
D
Gmaj7
be - fore I put on my make - up, I
While rid - ing, I think of us, dear. I
(I
F#m7
B
Say A Lit - tle Prayer for you.
Say A Lit - tle Prayer for you.
Say A Lit - tle Prayer for you.)
Em7
Am7
While comb - ing my hair now, and won - d'ring what
At work, I just take time, and all through my
D
Gmaj7
F#m7
dress to wear now,
cof - fee break time,
End solo
I Say A Lit - tle Prayer for you.
B
C
D/C
For - ev - er, for - ev - er, you'll

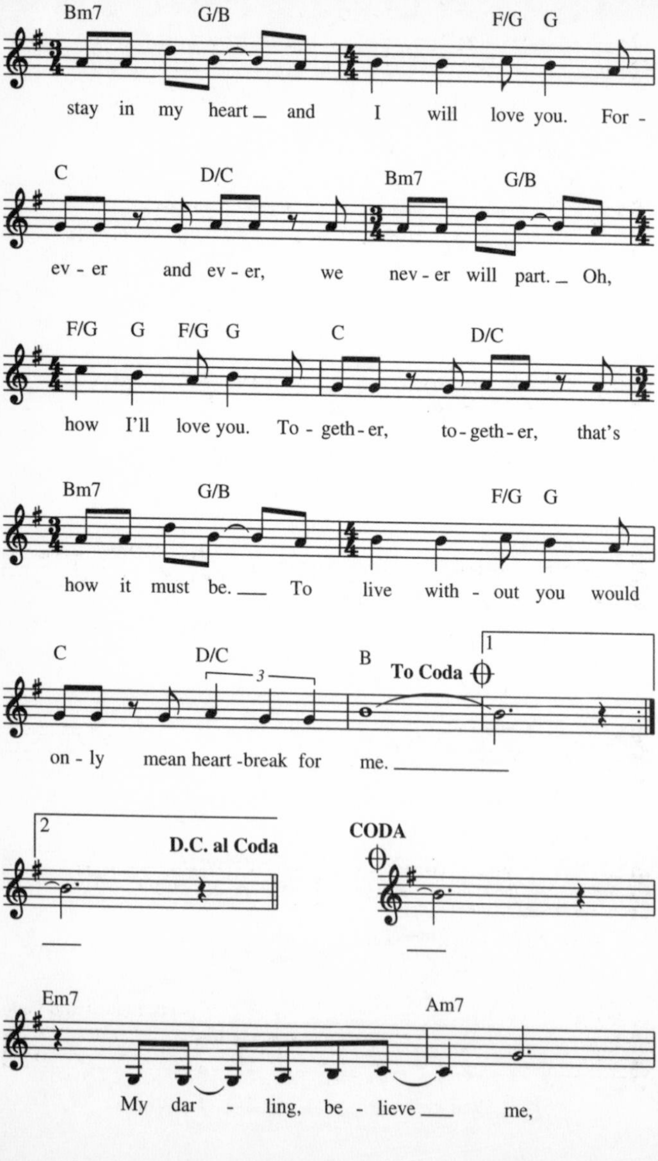
Bm7 G/B F/G G
stay in my heart _ and I will love you. For -
C D/C Bm7 G/B
ev - er and ev - er, we nev - er will part. _ Oh,
F/G G F/G G C D/C
how I'll love you. To - geth - er, to - geth - er, that's
Bm7 G/B F/G G
how it must be. ___ To live with - out you would
C D/C B
To Coda
1
3
on - ly mean heart -break for me. ________
2
D.C. al Coda
CODA
Em7 Am7
My dar - ling, be - lieve ___ me,

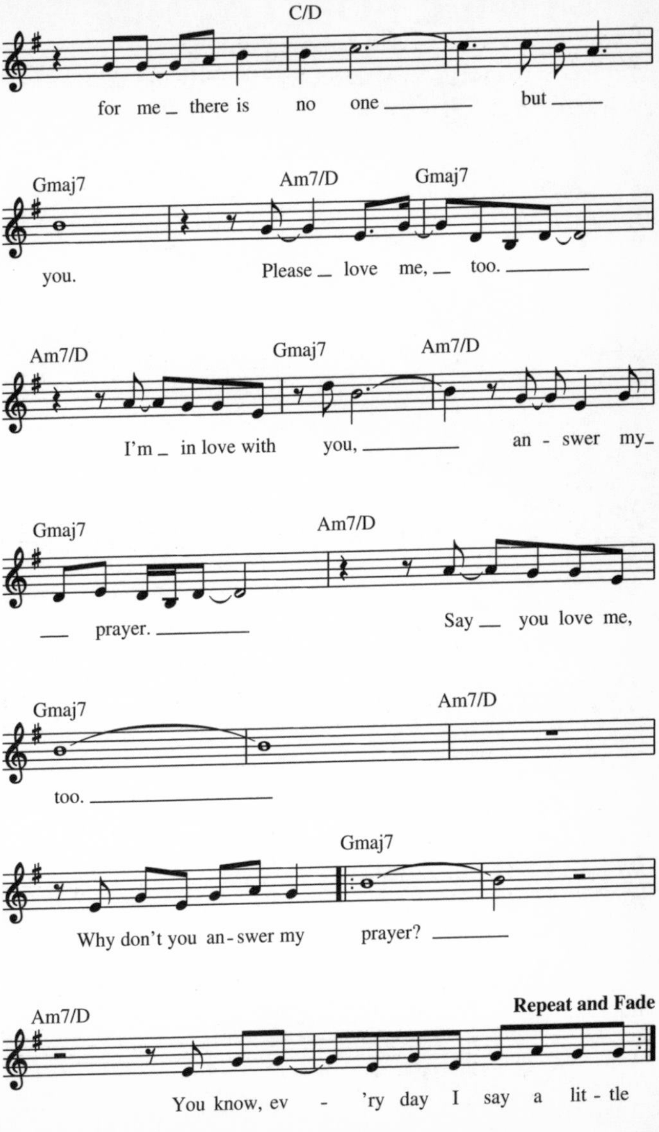
C/D
for me there is no one but
Gmaj7
Am7/D
Gmaj7
you. Please love me, too.
Am7/D
Gmaj7
Am7/D
I'm in love with you, an - swer my
Gmaj7
Am7/D
prayer. Say you love me,
Gmaj7
Am7/D
too.
Gmaj7
Why don't you an - swer my prayer?
Am7/D
Repeat and Fade
You know, ev - 'ry day I say a lit - tle

I WILL FOLLOW HIM

(I Will Follow You)

English Words by NORMAN GIMBEL and ARTHUR ALTMAN
French Words by JACQUES PLANTE
Music by J.W. STOLE and DEL ROMA

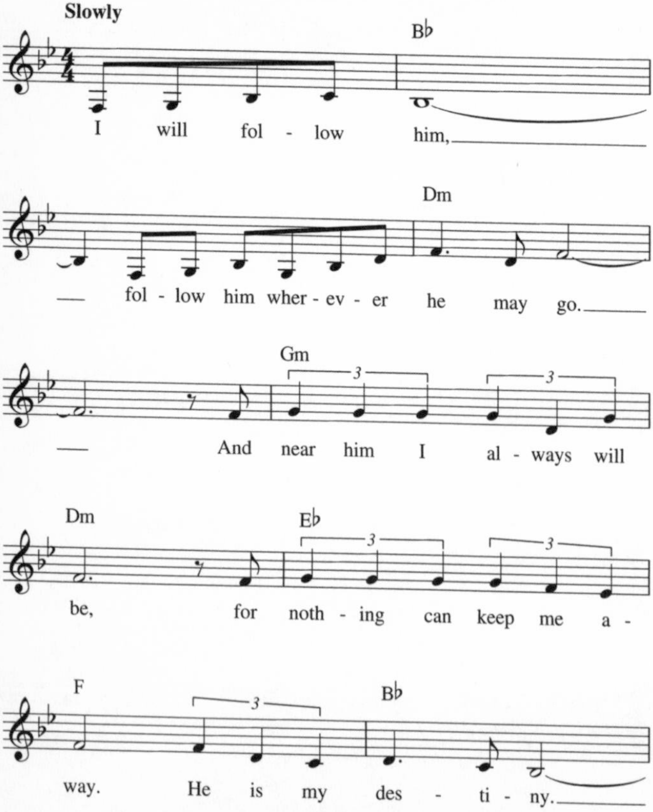
Slowly
B♭
I will fol - low him,
Dm
fol - low him wher - ev - er he may go.
Gm
3
3
And near him I al - ways will
Dm
E♭
3
3
be, for noth - ing can keep me a -
F
3
B♭
way. He is my des - ti - ny.

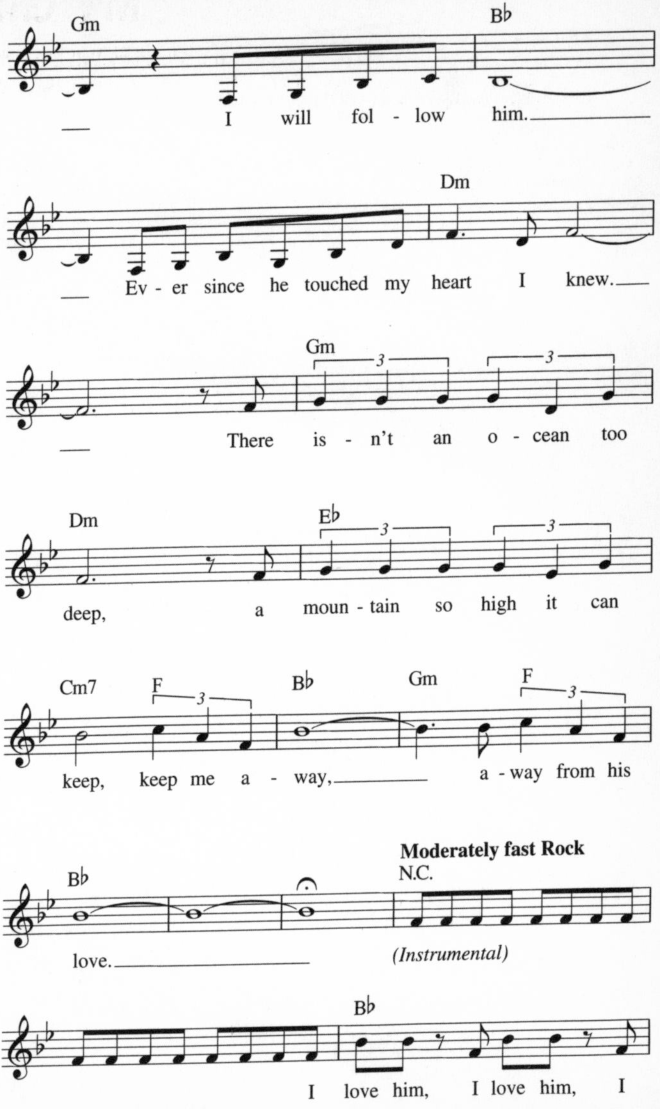
Gm
I will fol - low him.
Bb
Ev - er since he touched my heart I knew.
Dm
Gm
There is - n't an o - cean too
Dm
deep, a moun - tain so high it can
Eb
Cm7
F
Bb
Gm
F
keep, keep me a - way, a - way from his
Bb
love.
Moderately fast Rock
N.C.
(Instrumental)
Bb
I love him, I love him, I

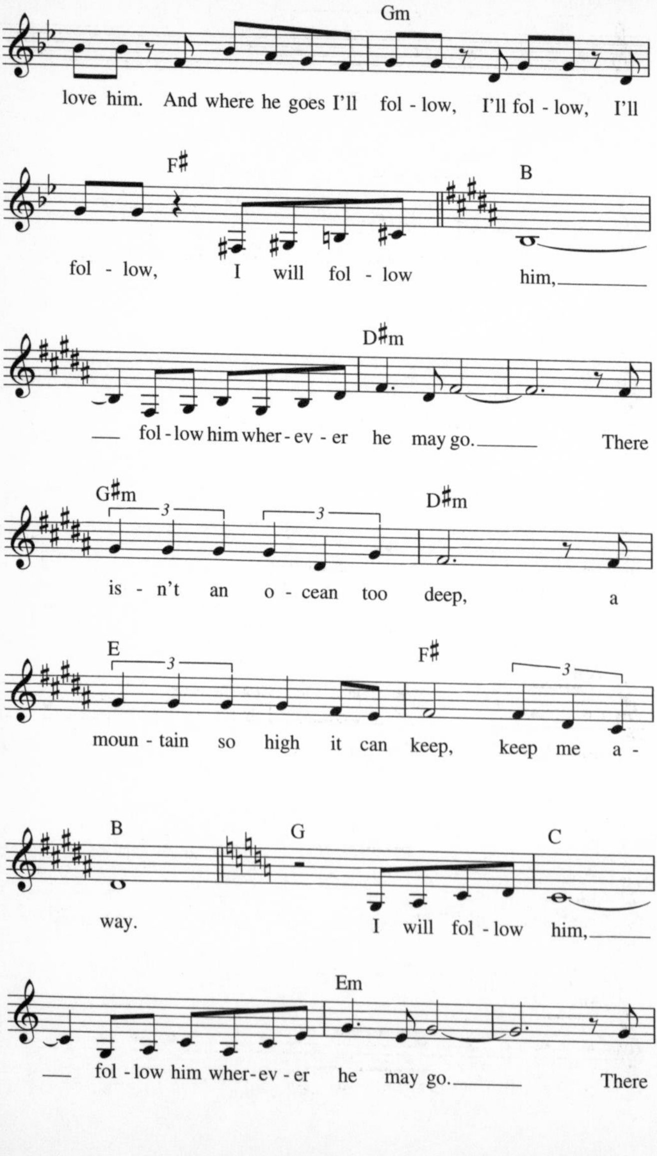
Gm
love him. And where he goes I'll fol - low, I'll fol - low, I'll
F♯
B
fol - low, I will fol - low him,
D♯m
fol - low him wher - ev - er he may go. There
G♯m
D♯m
is - n't an o - cean too deep, a
E
F♯
moun - tain so high it can keep, keep me a -
B
G
C
way. I will fol - low him,
Em
fol - low him wher - ev - er he may go. There

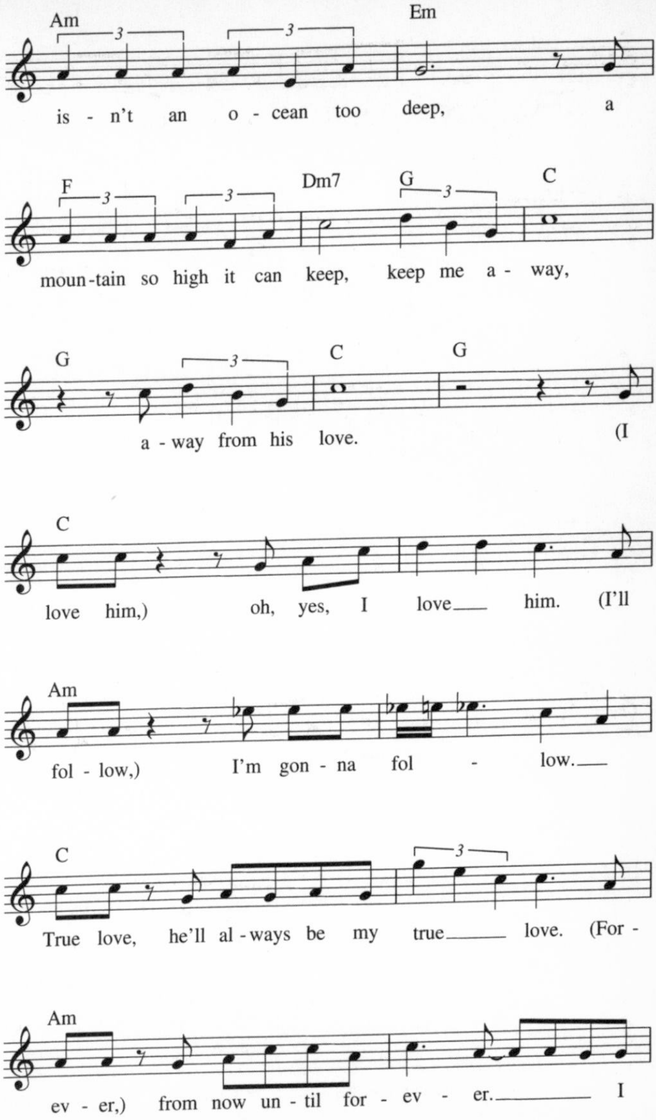
Am
Em
is - n't an o - cean too deep, a
F
Dm7
G
C
moun-tain so high it can keep, keep me a - way,
G
C
G
a - way from his love. (I
C
love him,) oh, yes, I love___ him. (I'll
Am
fol - low,) I'm gon - na fol - low.___
C
True love, he'll al - ways be my true___ love. (For -
Am
ev - er,) from now un - til for - ev - er.___ I

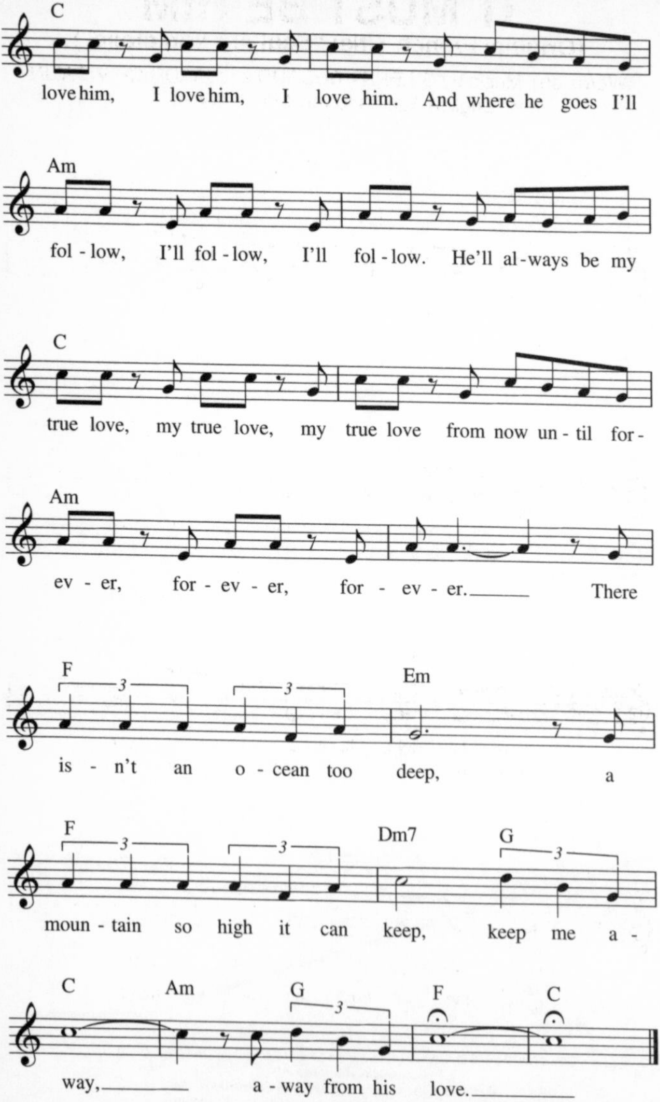
C
love him, I love him, I love him. And where he goes I'll
Am
fol - low, I'll fol - low, I'll fol - low. He'll al - ways be my
C
true love, my true love, my true love from now un - til for -
Am
ev - er, for - ev - er, for - ev - er. There
F
3
3
Em
is - n't an o - cean too deep, a
F
3
3
Dm7
G
3
moun - tain so high it can keep, keep me a -
C
Am
G
3
F
C
way, a - way from his love.

IT MUST BE HIM

(Original French Title: "Seul sur son etoile")

Words and Music by GILBERT BECAUD and MAURICE VIDALIN
English Adaptation by MACK DAVID

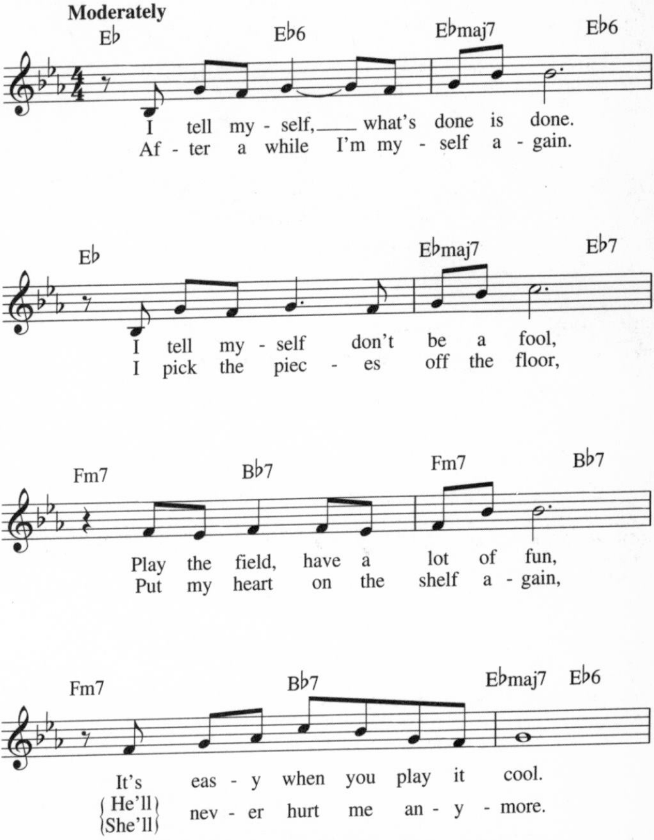
Moderately
Eb Eb6 Ebmaj7 Eb6
I tell my - self, what's done is done.
Af - ter a while I'm my - self a - gain.
Eb Ebmaj7 Eb7
I tell my - self don't be a fool,
I pick the piec - es off the floor,
Fm7 Bb7 Fm7 Bb7
Play the field, have a lot of fun,
Put my heart on the shelf a - gain,
Fm7 Bb7 Ebmaj7 Eb6
It's eas - y when you play it cool.
{He'll / She'll} nev - er hurt me an - y - more.

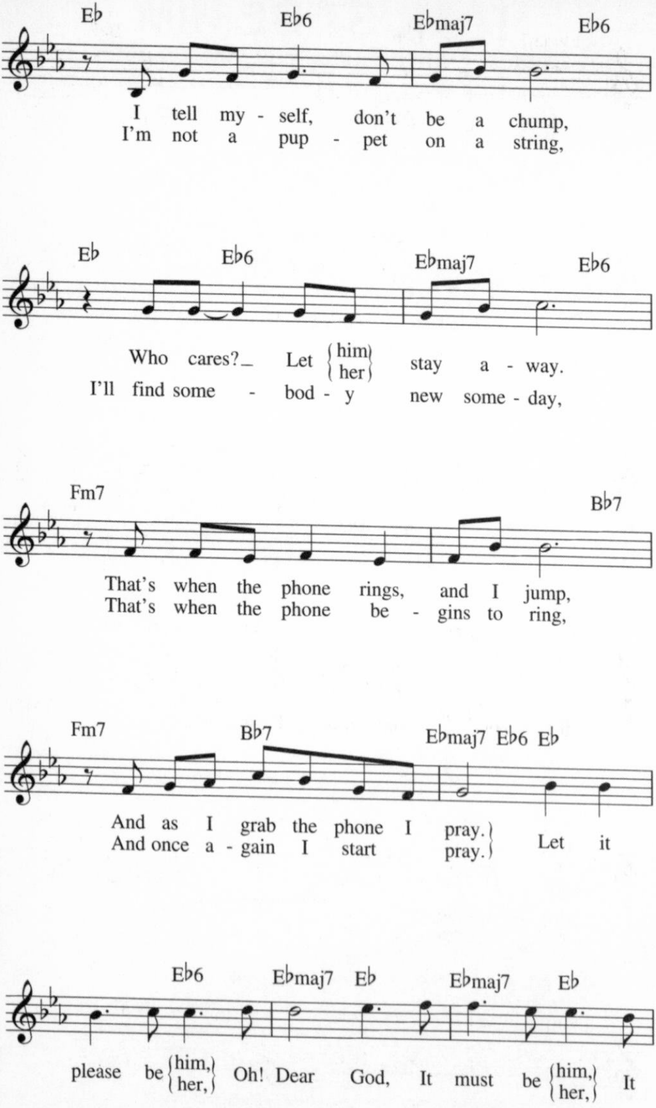
E♭ E♭6 E♭maj7 E♭6
I tell my - self, don't be a chump,
I'm not a pup - pet on a string,
E♭ E♭6 E♭maj7 E♭6
Who cares? Let {him / her} stay a - way.
I'll find some - bod - y new some - day,
Fm7 B♭7
That's when the phone rings, and I jump,
That's when the phone be - gins to ring,
Fm7 B♭7 E♭maj7 E♭6 E♭
And as I grab the phone I pray.
And once a - gain I start pray.
Let it
E♭6 E♭maj7 E♭ E♭maj7 E♭
please be {him, / her,} Oh! Dear God, It must be {him, / her,} It

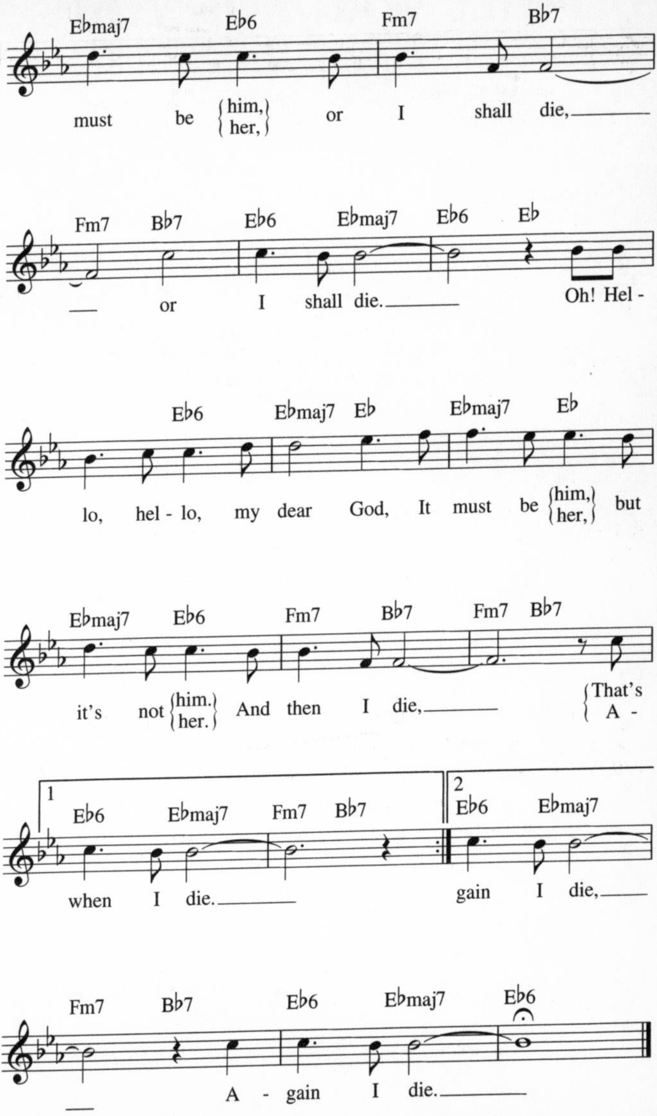
Ebmaj7 Eb6 Fm7 Bb7
must be {him, her,} or I shall die,
Fm7 Bb7 Eb6 Ebmaj7 Eb6 Eb
or I shall die. Oh! Hel -
Eb6 Ebmaj7 Eb Ebmaj7 Eb
lo, hel - lo, my dear God, It must be {him, her,} but
Ebmaj7 Eb6 Fm7 Bb7 Fm7 Bb7
it's not {him. her.} And then I die, {That's A -
1
Eb6 Ebmaj7 Fm7 Bb7
when I die.
2
Eb6 Ebmaj7
gain I die,
Fm7 Bb7 Eb6 Ebmaj7 Eb6
A - gain I die.

I WILL WAIT FOR YOU

from THE UMBRELLAS OF CHERBOURG

Music by MICHEL LEGRAND
Original French Text by JACQUES DEMY
English Words by NORMAN GIMBEL

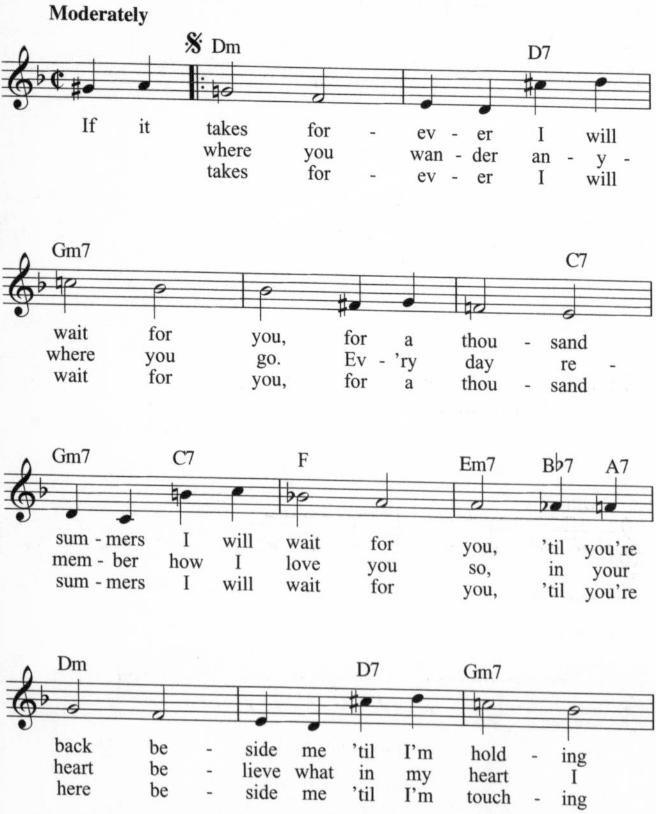
Moderately
Dm
D7
If it takes for - ev - er I will
where you wan - der an - y -
takes for - ev - er I will
Gm7
C7
wait for you, for a thou - sand
where you go. Ev - 'ry day re -
wait for you, for a thou - sand
Gm7 C7 F Em7 B♭7 A7
sum - mers I will wait for you, 'til you're
mem - ber how I love you so, in your
sum - mers I will wait for you, 'til you're
Dm D7 Gm7
back be - side me 'til I'm hold - ing
heart be - lieve what in my heart I
here be - side me 'til I'm touch - ing

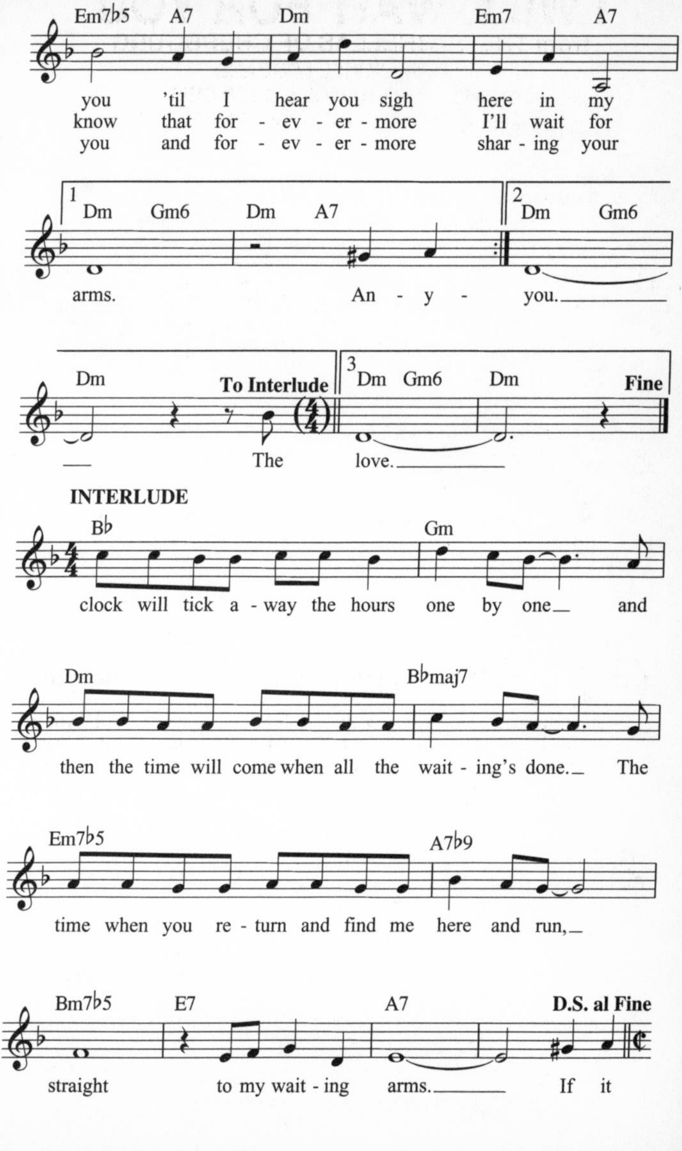

Em7♭5 A7 Dm Em7 A7
you 'til I hear you sigh here in my
know that for - ev - er - more I'll wait for
you and for - ev - er - more shar - ing your
1 Dm Gm6 Dm A7
arms. An - y -
2 Dm Gm6
you.
Dm
To Interlude
The
3 Dm Gm6 Dm
Fine
love.
INTERLUDE
B♭ Gm
clock will tick a - way the hours one by one and
Dm B♭maj7
then the time will come when all the wait - ing's done. The
Em7♭5 A7♭9
time when you re - turn and find me here and run,
Bm7♭5 E7 A7
D.S. al Fine
straight to my wait - ing arms. If it

I'M A BELIEVER

Words and Music by
NEIL DIAMOND

Moderately
E B7
I thought love was on - ly true in
I thought love was more or less a
E
fair - y tales, meant for some - one
giv - in' thing. Seems the more I
B7 E
else but not for me.
gave, the less I got.
A E A
Love was out to get me. That's the way it seemed.
What's the use in try - in'? All you get is pain.
E A E
Dis - ap - point - ment haunt - ed all my
When I need - ed sun - shine, I got
B7 E A
dreams.
rain.
Then I saw her face;
E A E A E A
now I'm A Be - liev - er! Not a

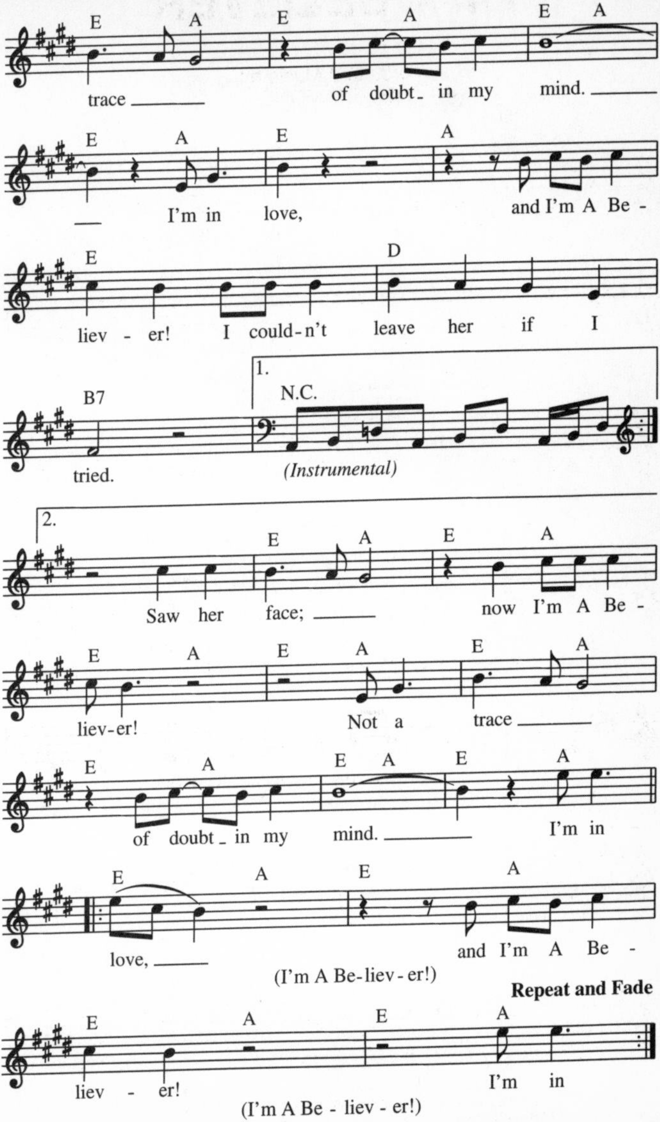
E A E A E A
trace of doubt in my mind.
E A E A
I'm in love, and I'm A Be -
E D
liev - er! I could-n't leave her if I
B7
tried.
1.
N.C.
(Instrumental)
2.
E A E A
Saw her face; now I'm A Be -
E A E A E A
liev-er! Not a trace
E A E A E A
of doubt in my mind. I'm in
E A E A
love, and I'm A Be -
(I'm A Be-liev - er!)
Repeat and Fade
E A E A
liev - er! I'm in
(I'm A Be - liev - er!)

IF I HAD A HAMMER

(The Hammer Song)

Words and Music by LEE HAYS
and PETE SEEGER

Moderately
D
1. If I had a ham - mer,
2. bell,
3.,4. (See additional lyrics)
A7
D
I'd ham - mer in the morn - ing,
I'd ring it in the morn - ing,
I'd ham - mer in the eve - ning
I'd ring it in the eve - ning
D7
A7
all o - ver this land; I'd ham-mer out
all o - ver this land; I'd ring out
D
dan - ger, I'd ham - mer out a
dan - ger, I'd ring out a

Bm G
warn - ing, I'd ham - mer out
warn - ing, I'd ring out
D G D A7
love be - tween my broth - ers and my sis - ters,
love be - tween my broth - ers and my sis - ters,
D G D A7
All o - ver this
All o - ver this
1-3 D G D
4 D G D
land. If I had a land.
land. If I had a

Additional Lyrics

3. If I had a song,
I'd sing it in the morning,
I'd sing it in the evening
All over this land;
I'd sing out danger,
I'd sing out warning,
I'd sing out love between my
Brothers and my sisters,
All over this land.

4. Well, I got a hammer,
And I've got a bell
And I've got a song to sing
All over this land;
It's the hammer of justice,
It's the bell of freedom,
It's the song about love
Between my brothers and my sisters,
All over this land.

IT'S MY PARTY

Words and Music by HERB WIENER,
WALLY GOLD and JOHN GLUCK, JR.

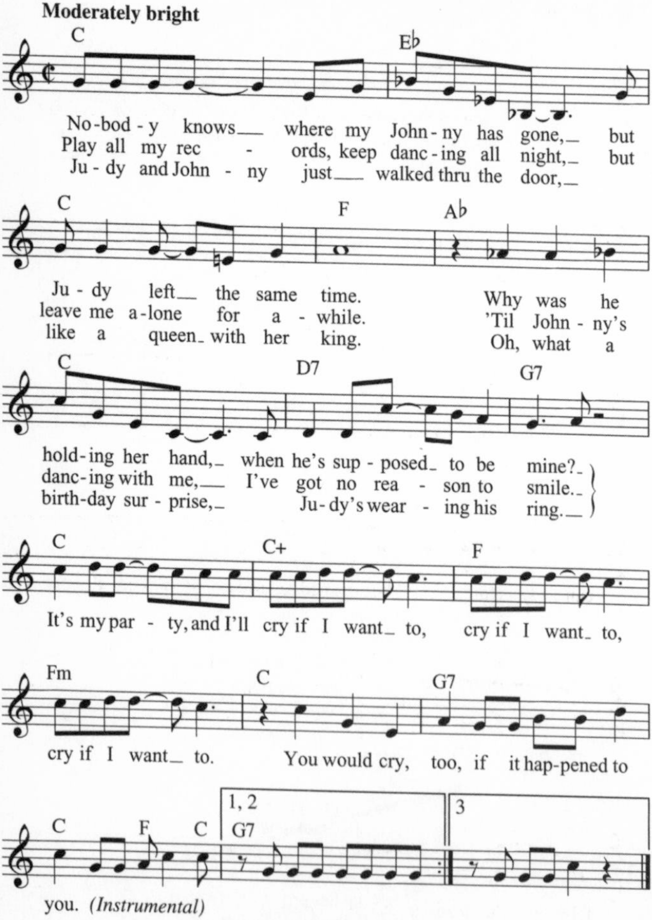
Moderately bright
C Eb
No-bod-y knows where my John-ny has gone, but
Play all my rec-ords, keep danc-ing all night, but
Ju-dy and John-ny just walked thru the door,
C F Ab
Ju-dy left the same time. Why was he
leave me a-lone for a-while. 'Til John-ny's
like a queen with her king. Oh, what a
C D7 G7
hold-ing her hand, when he's sup-posed to be mine?
danc-ing with me, I've got no rea-son to smile.
birth-day sur-prise, Ju-dy's wear-ing his ring.
C C+ F
It's my par-ty, and I'll cry if I want to, cry if I want to,
Fm C G7
cry if I want to. You would cry, too, if it hap-pened to
C F C
1, 2
G7
3
you. (Instrumental)

LEADER OF THE PACK

Words and Music by GEORGE MORTON,
JEFF BARRY and ELLIE GREENWICH

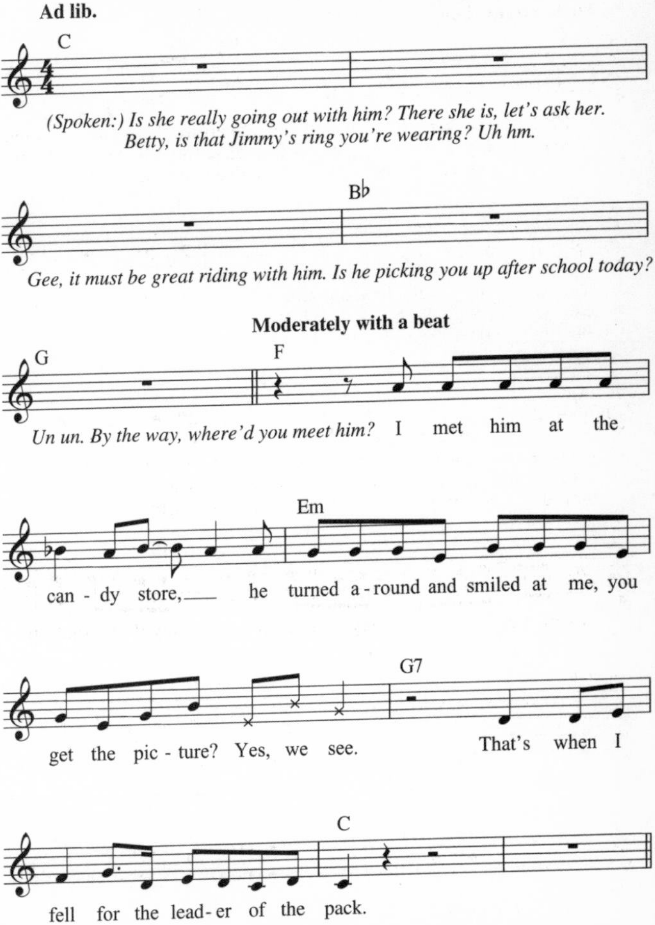
Ad lib.
C
(Spoken:) Is she really going out with him? There she is, let's ask her.
Betty, is that Jimmy's ring you're wearing? Uh hm.
B♭
Gee, it must be great riding with him. Is he picking you up after school today?
Moderately with a beat
G
F
Un un. By the way, where'd you meet him? I met him at the
Em
can - dy store, he turned a - round and smiled at me, you
G7
get the pic - ture? Yes, we see. That's when I
C
fell for the lead - er of the pack.

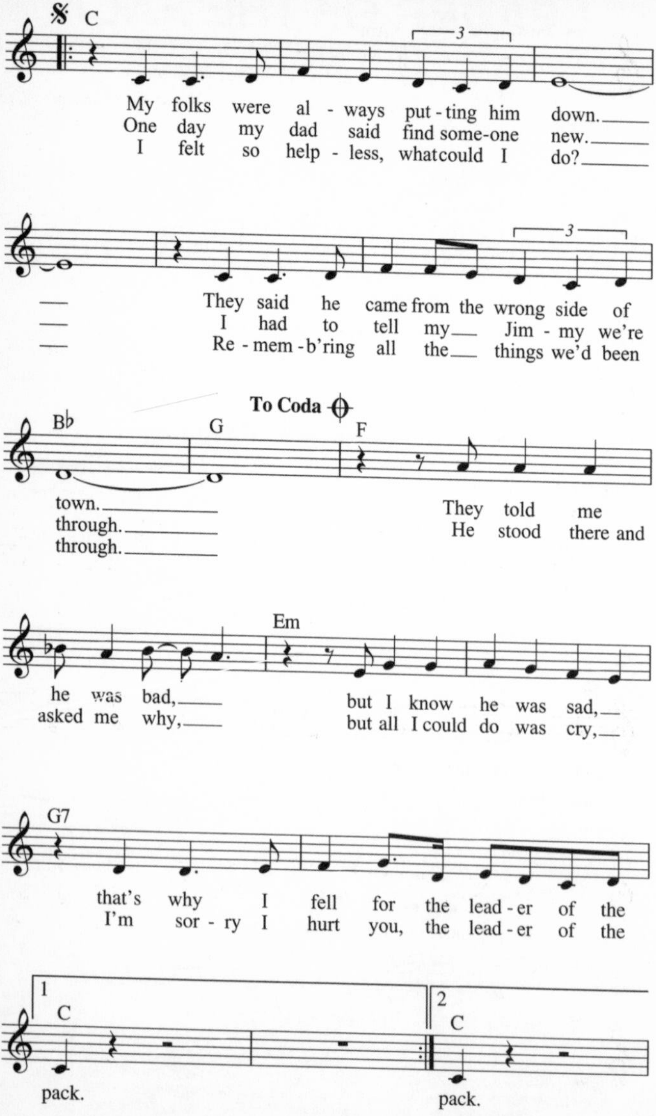
C
3
My folks were al - ways put - ting him down.
One day my dad said find some-one new.
I felt so help - less, what could I do?
3
They said he came from the wrong side of
I had to tell my Jim - my we're
Re - mem - b'ring all the things we'd been
To Coda
B♭
G
F
town.
through.
through.
They told me
He stood there and
Em
he was bad,
asked me why,
but I know he was sad,
but all I could do was cry,
G7
that's why I fell for the lead - er of the
I'm sor - ry I hurt you, the lead - er of the
1
C
pack.
2
C
pack.

Bm
Am
(Spoken:) He sort of smiled and kissed me goodbye,
but the tears were beginning to show as he drove away on that rainy night.
D.S. al Coda
I begged him to go slow, but whether he heard, I'll never know.
CODA
F
In school they all stop and stare, I
Em
can't hide the tears, but I don't care.
G7
I'll nev - er for - get him, the lead - er of the
C
pack.

IT'S NOW OR NEVER

Words and Music by AARON SCHROEDER
and WALLY GOLD

Moderately
N.C.
Eb
Cdim
It's Now Or Nev-er; come hold me
Fm7
Bb7
Fm7
tight. Kiss me, my dar - lin';
Bb7
Eb
be mine to - night. To -
Abm
Eb
mor - row will be too late.
Ebdim
Bb7
1, 2
It's Now Or Nev-er; my love won't
Eb
To Interlude
3
wait.
1. When I first
2. Just like a
my love won't

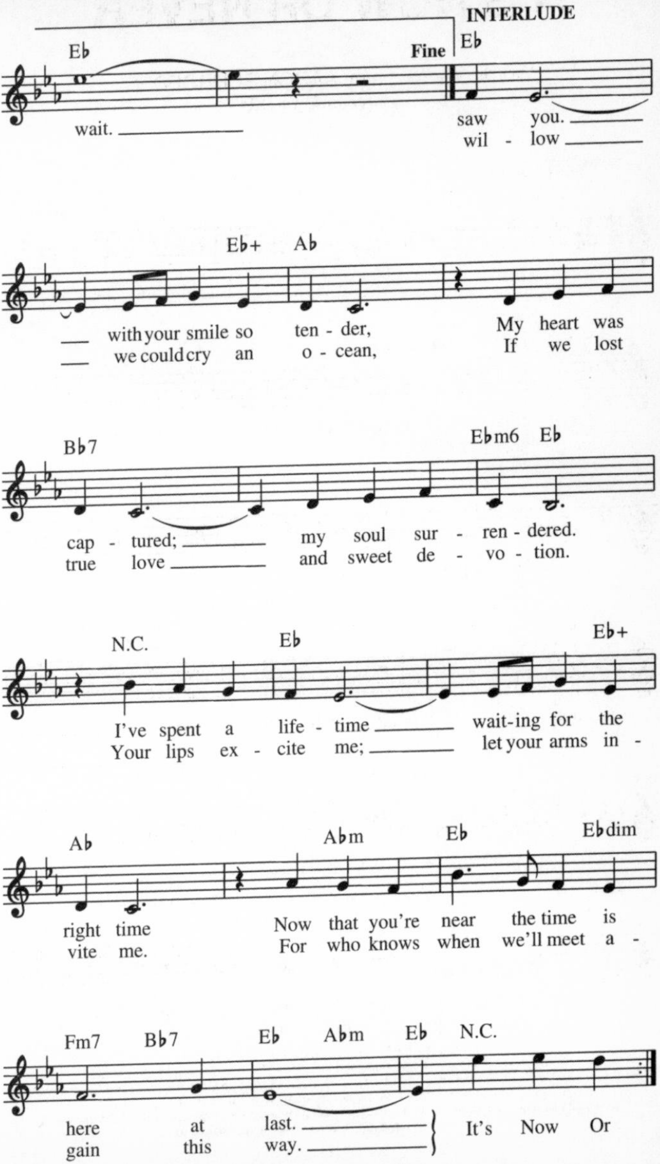
INTERLUDE
Eb Fine Eb
wait. saw you.
wil - low
Eb+ Ab
with your smile so ten - der, My heart was
we could cry an o - cean, If we lost
Bb7 Ebm6 Eb
cap - tured; my soul sur - ren - dered.
true love and sweet de - vo - tion.
N.C. Eb Eb+
I've spent a life - time wait-ing for the
Your lips ex - cite me; let your arms in -
Ab Abm Eb Ebdim
right time Now that you're near the time is
vite me. For who knows when we'll meet a -
Fm7 Bb7 Eb Abm Eb N.C.
here at last. It's Now Or
gain this way.

KING OF THE ROAD

Words and Music by
ROGER MILLER

Carefree
C
F
Trail - er for sale or rent,
Third box car mid - night train,
G
C
rooms ___ to let ___ fif - ty cents,
des - ti - na - tion Bang - or, Maine.
F
No phone, no pool, no pets
Old worn out suit and shoes,
G
I ain't got no ci - ga - rettes, Ah, but
I don't pay no u - nion dues I smoke
C
F
two hours of push - ing broom buys a
old sto - gies I have found
G
C
eight ___ by twelve ___ four - bit room
short ___ but not too big a - round
I'm a

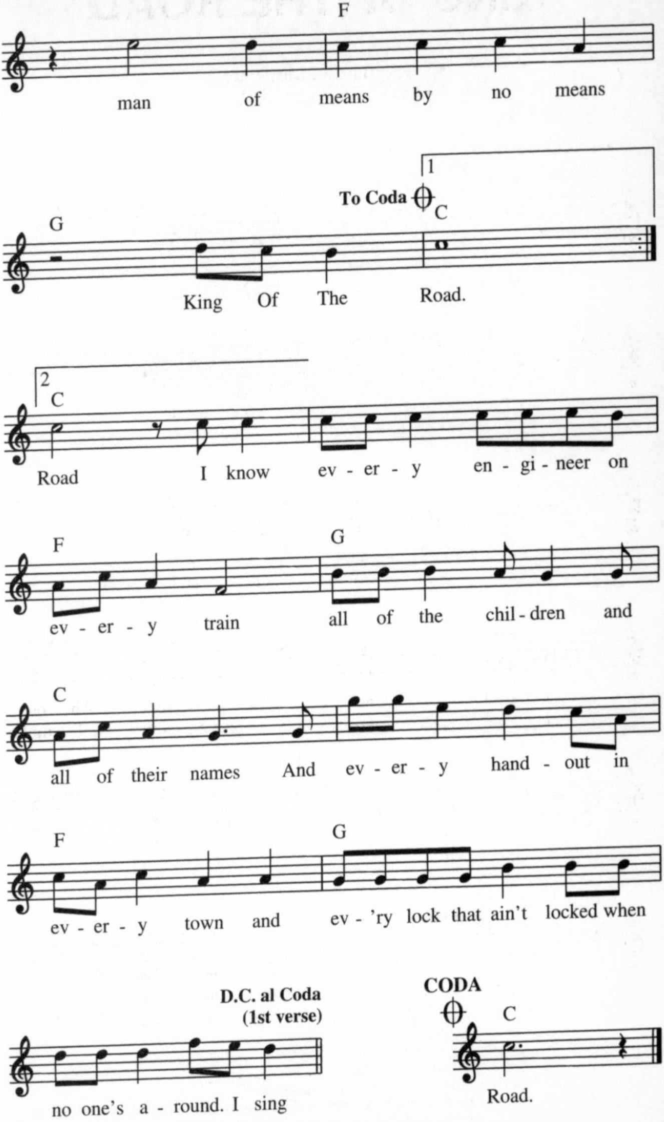
F
man of means by no means
G
To Coda
1
C
King Of The Road.
2
C
Road I know ev - er - y en - gi - neer on
F
G
ev - er - y train all of the chil - dren and
C
all of their names And ev - er - y hand - out in
F
G
ev - er - y town and ev - 'ry lock that ain't locked when
D.C. al Coda
(1st verse)
no one's a - round. I sing
CODA
C
Road.

LEAVING ON A JET PLANE

Words and Music by
JOHN DENVER

Moderately
G
C
All my bags are packed,_ I'm read-y to go, I'm
man - y times___ I've let you down, so
Now the time___ has come to leave you,
G
C
stand - ing here_ out - side your door,_ I
man - y times_ I've played a - round;_ I
one more time_ let me kiss___ you then
G
C
hate to wake_ you up to say___ good -
tell you now_ they don't mean_ a
close your eyes_ I'll be on___ my
D
G
bye.___ But the dawn is break - in', it's
thing.___ Ev - 'ry place I go___ I'll
way.___ Dream a - bout___ the
C
G
ear - ly morn,_ the tax - i's wait-in' he's
think of you,_ ev - 'ry song I sing I'll
days to come_ when I won't have to

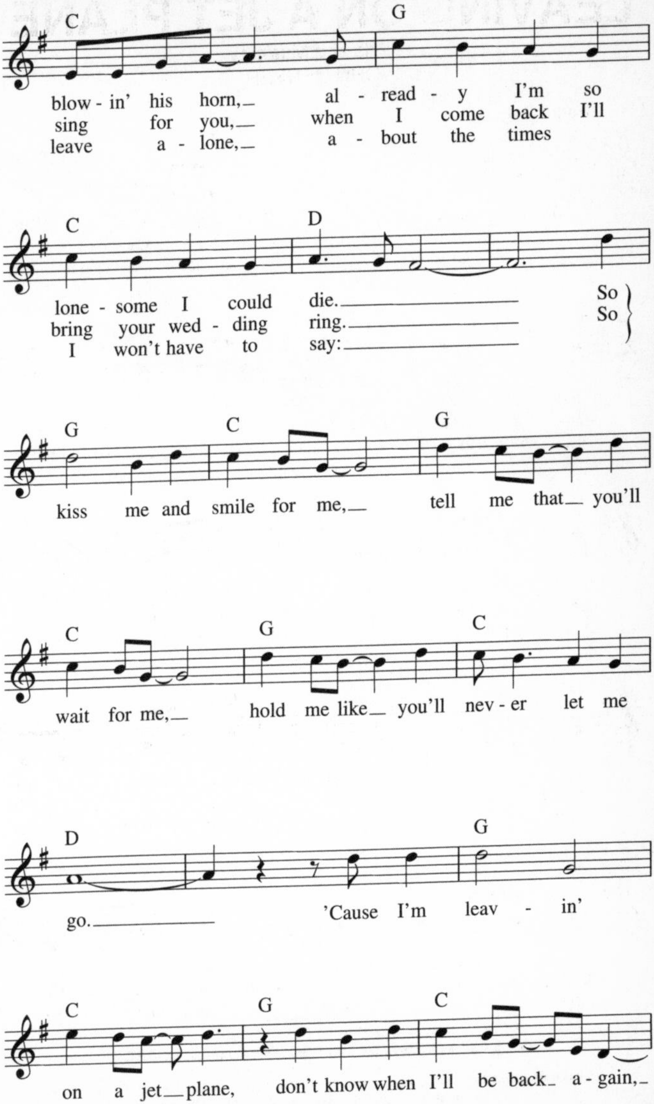
C G
blow - in' his horn, al - read - y I'm so
sing for you, when I come back I'll
leave a - lone, a - bout the times
C D
lone - some I could die. So
bring your wed - ding ring. So
I won't have to say:
G C G
kiss me and smile for me, tell me that you'll
C G C
wait for me, hold me like you'll nev - er let me
D G
go. 'Cause I'm leav - in'
C G C
on a jet plane, don't know when I'll be back a - gain,

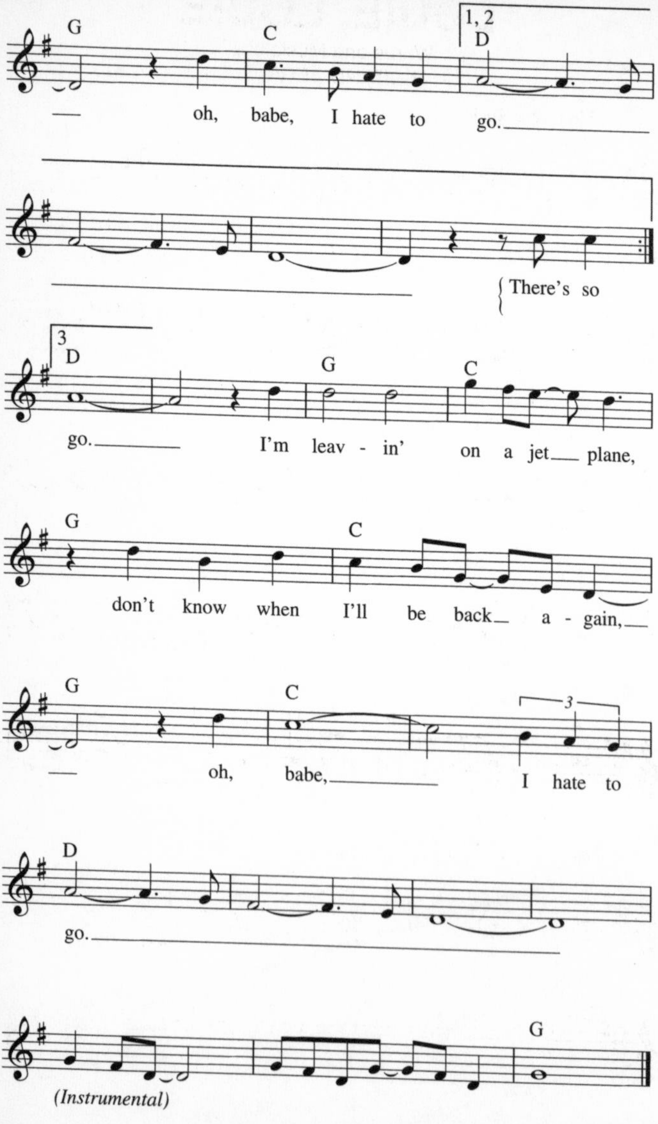
G C 1, 2 D
— oh, babe, I hate to go.
There's so
3 D G C
go. I'm leav - in' on a jet plane,
G C
don't know when I'll be back a - gain,
G C 3
— oh, babe, I hate to
D
go.
G
(Instrumental)

LOUIE, LOUIE

Words and Music by
RICHARD BERRY

Moderate Rock
A D Em D A D
Em D A D Em D
To Coda
A D Em D A D
Em D A D Em D
A D Em D A D
Last Time,
D.C. al Coda
CODA
Em D Em D A D
Em D A D Em D A

LET'S HANG ON

Words and Music by BOB CREWE,
DENNY RANDELL and SANDY LINZER

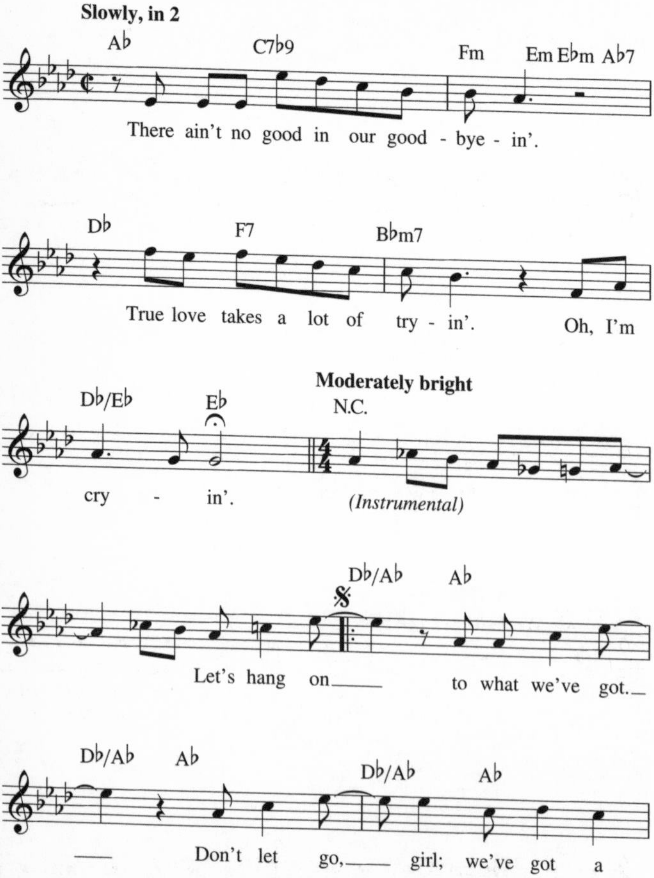
Slowly, in 2
Ab
C7b9
Fm
Em Ebm Ab7
There ain't no good in our good - bye - in'.
Db
F7
Bbm7
True love takes a lot of try - in'. Oh, I'm
Db/Eb
Eb
Moderately bright
N.C.
cry - in'.
(Instrumental)
Db/Ab
Ab
Let's hang on to what we've got.
Db/Ab
Ab
Db/Ab
Ab
Don't let go, girl; we've got a

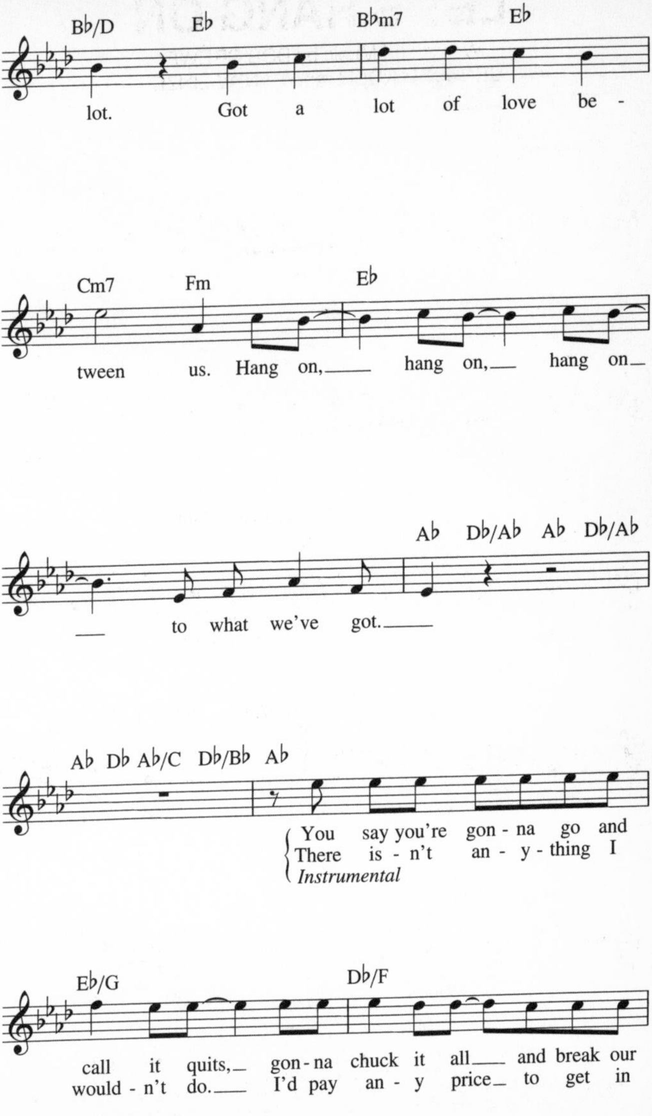
Bb/D Eb Bbm7 Eb
lot. Got a lot of love be -
Cm7 Fm Eb
tween us. Hang on, hang on, hang on
Ab Db/Ab Ab Db/Ab
to what we've got.
Ab Db Ab/C Db/Bb Ab
You say you're gon - na go and
There is - n't an - y - thing I
Instrumental
Eb/G Db/F
call it quits, gon - na chuck it all and break our
would - n't do. I'd pay an - y price to get in

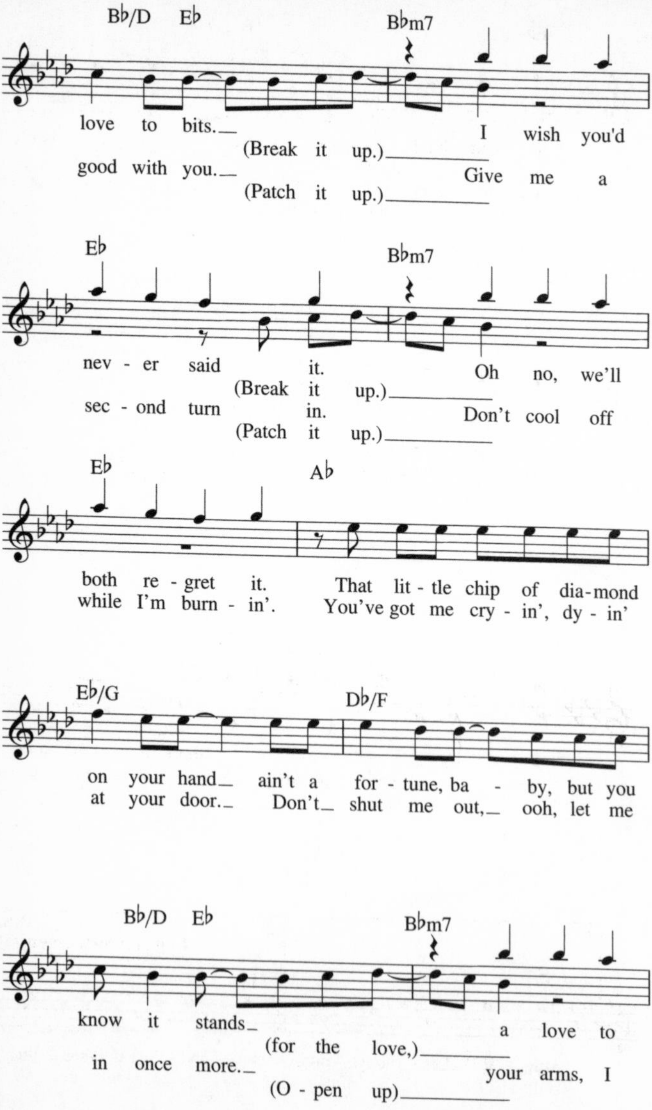
Bb/D Eb
Bbm7
love to bits.
I wish you'd
(Break it up.)
good with you.
Give me a
(Patch it up.)
Eb
Bbm7
nev - er said it.
Oh no, we'll
(Break it up.)
sec - ond turn in.
Don't cool off
(Patch it up.)
Eb
Ab
both re - gret it.
That lit - tle chip of dia-mond
while I'm burn - in'.
You've got me cry - in', dy - in'
Eb/G
Db/F
on your hand ain't a for - tune, ba - by, but you
at your door. Don't shut me out, ooh, let me
Bb/D Eb
Bbm7
know it stands
a love to
(for the love,)
in once more.
your arms, I
(O - pen up)

Eb
Bbm7
tie and bind ya. We just can't
(such a love.)
need to hold you. your heart, oh
(O - pen up)
Eb
Ab/Eb
leave be - hind us.
girl, I love you.
Ba - by,
(Don't you know?)
Bb/Eb
Bbm7
ba - by;
(Don't you go.)
(think it o - ver and
1
Eb
N.C.
stay - ay!) Let's hang on
2
D.S.
(Fade on instrumental)
Eb
N.C.
stay - ay!) Let's hang on

LIMBO ROCK

Words and Music by BILLY STRANGE
and JON SHELDON

Bright Latin Rock
G
Ev - 'ry lim - bo boy __ and girl
spread your lim - bo feet,
self a lim - bo girl,
D7 G
all a - round the lim - bo world,
then you move to lim - bo beat.
give that chick a lim - bo whirl.
gon - na do the Lim - bo Rock
Lim - bo an - kle, lim - bo knee;
There's a lim - bo moon, _ a - bove,
D7 G
all a - round the lim - bo clock.
bend back, like the lim - bo tree.
you will fall in lim - bo love.
C
Jack be lim - bo, Jack __ be quick,

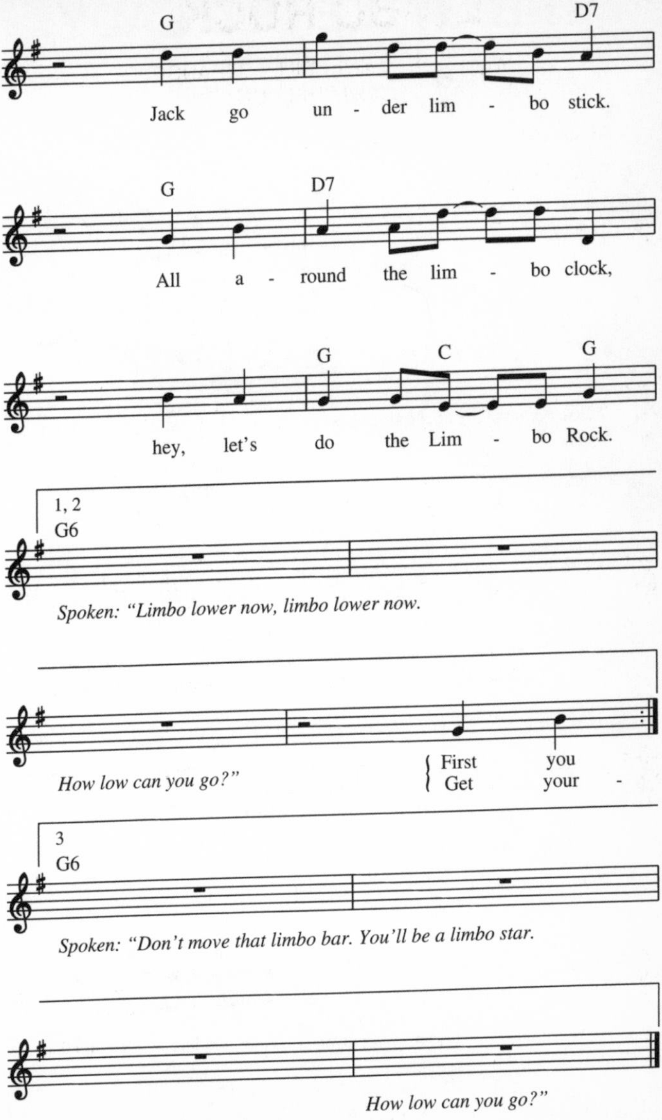
G
D7
Jack go un - der lim - bo stick.
G
D7
All a - round the lim - bo clock,
G
C
G
hey, let's do the Lim - bo Rock.
1, 2
G6
Spoken: "Limbo lower now, limbo lower now.
How low can you go?"
First you
Get your -
3
G6
Spoken: "Don't move that limbo bar. You'll be a limbo star.
How low can you go?"

THE LITTLE OLD LADY
(From Pasadena)

Words and Music by DON ALTFELD
and ROGER CHRISTIAN

Moderately, with a beat

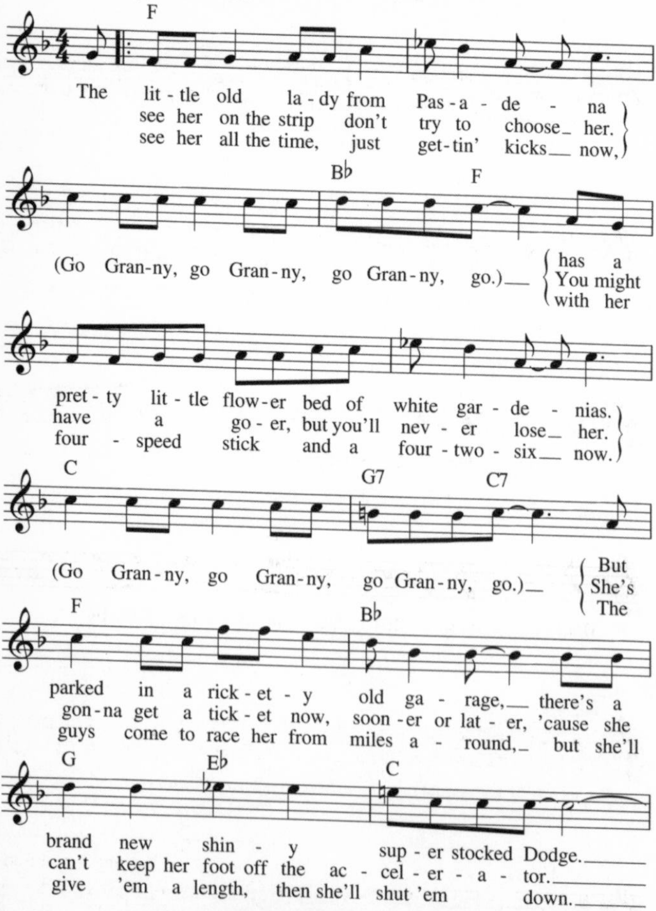
F
The lit - tle old la - dy from Pas - a - de - na
see her on the strip don't try to choose_ her.
see her all the time, just get-tin' kicks__ now,
Bb F
(Go Gran-ny, go Gran-ny, go Gran-ny, go.)__
has a
You might
with her
pret - ty lit - tle flow-er bed of white gar - de - nias.
have a go - er, but you'll nev - er lose_ her.
four - speed stick and a four - two - six__ now.
C G7 C7
(Go Gran-ny, go Gran-ny, go Gran-ny, go.)_
But
She's
The
F Bb
parked in a rick - et - y old ga - rage,__ there's a
gon-na get a tick - et now, soon -er or lat - er, 'cause she
guys come to race her from miles a - round,_ but she'll
G Eb C
brand new shin - y sup - er stocked Dodge.
can't keep her foot off the ac - cel - er - a - tor.
give 'em a length, then she'll shut 'em down.

F
And ev - 'ry - bod - y's say - in' that there's
no - bod - y mean - er than the lit - tle old la - dy from
Bb7
Pas - a - de - na. She drives real fast and she
F
drives real hard. She's the ter - ror of Col - o - ra - do
Ab
Boul - e - vard. It's the lit - tle old la - dy from
C7
1, 2
3
Pas - a - de - na!
If you
You'll
The
F
Repeat and Fade
lit - tle old la - dy from Pas - a - de - na. The

THE LOCO-MOTION

Words and Music by GERRY GOFFIN
and CAROLE KING

Moderately
Eb Cm
Ev-'ry-bod-y's do - in' a brand new dance_ now.
Eb Cm
C'm on, ba-by, do___ The Lo-co-mo-tion. I
Eb Cm
know you'll get to like it if you give it a chance_ now.
Eb Cm
C'm on, ba-by, do___ The Lo-co-mo-tion. My
Ab Fm
lit-tle ba-by sis - ter can do it with ease,_ It's
Ab F7
eas-i-er than learn - in' your A B C's,_ So
Eb Bb9
come on, come on, do___ The Lo-co-mo-tion with

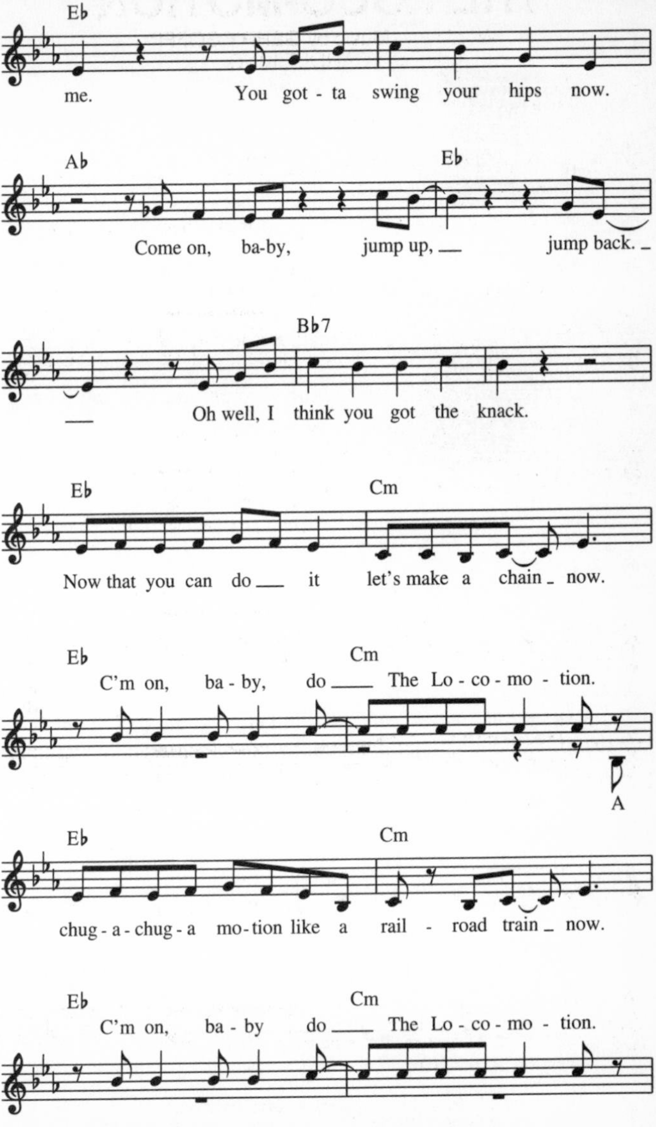
Eb
me. You got - ta swing your hips now.
Ab Eb
Come on, ba-by, jump up, jump back.
Bb7
Oh well, I think you got the knack.
Eb Cm
Now that you can do it let's make a chain now.
Eb Cm
C'm on, ba - by, do The Lo - co - mo - tion.
A
Eb Cm
chug - a - chug - a mo - tion like a rail - road train now.
Eb Cm
C'm on, ba - by do The Lo - co - mo - tion.

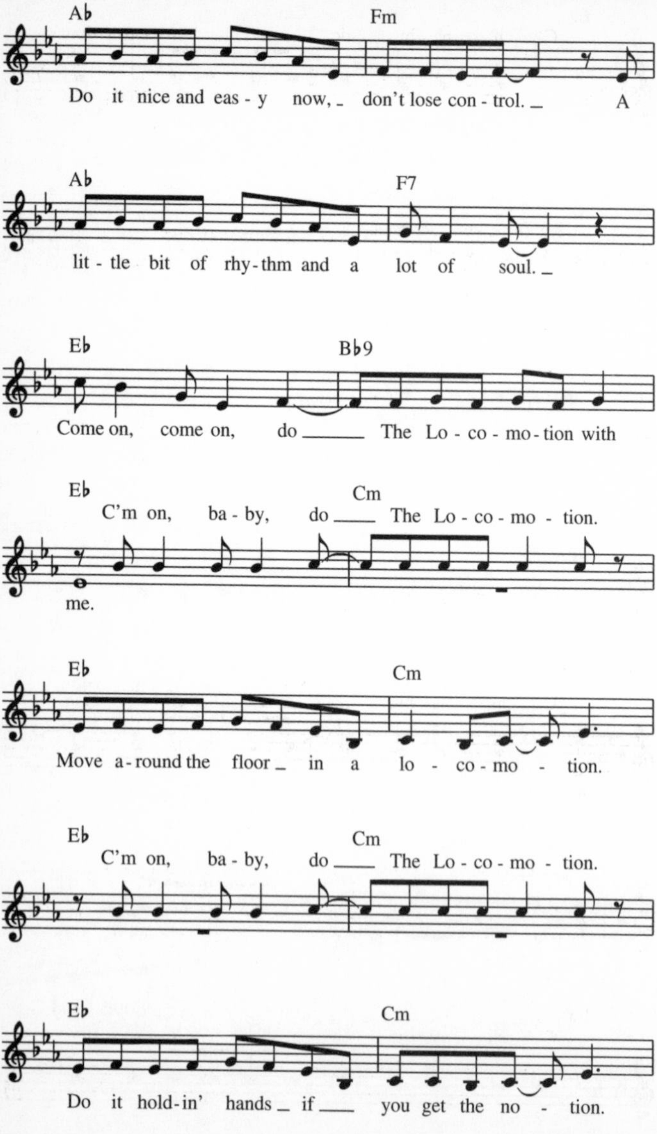
A♭ Fm
Do it nice and eas - y now, _ don't lose con - trol. _ A
A♭ F7
lit - tle bit of rhy - thm and a lot of soul. _
E♭ B♭9
Come on, come on, do ___ The Lo - co - mo - tion with
E♭ Cm
C'm on, ba - by, do ___ The Lo - co - mo - tion.
me.
E♭ Cm
Move a - round the floor _ in a lo - co - mo - tion.
E♭ Cm
C'm on, ba - by, do ___ The Lo - co - mo - tion.
E♭ Cm
Do it hold - in' hands _ if ___ you get the no - tion.

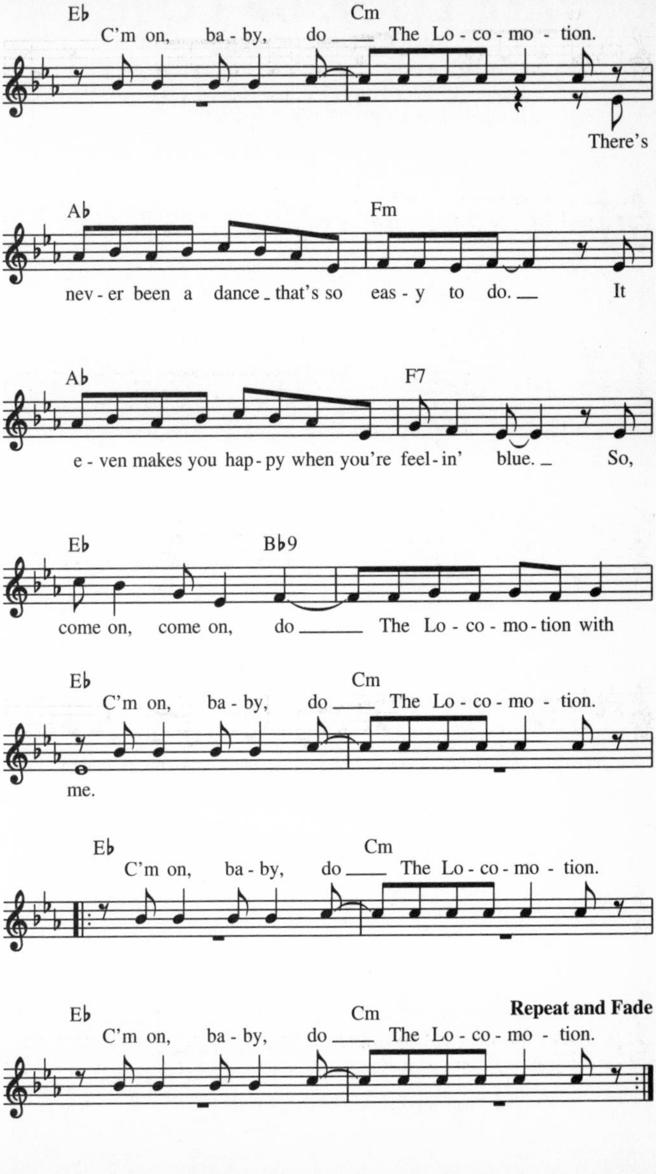
Eb
Cm
C'm on, ba - by, do The Lo - co - mo - tion.
There's
Ab
Fm
nev - er been a dance that's so eas - y to do.
It
Ab
F7
e - ven makes you hap - py when you're feel - in' blue.
So,
Eb
Bb9
come on, come on, do The Lo - co - mo - tion with
Eb
Cm
C'm on, ba - by, do The Lo - co - mo - tion.
me.
Eb
Cm
C'm on, ba - by, do The Lo - co - mo - tion.
Eb
Cm
Repeat and Fade
C'm on, ba - by, do The Lo - co - mo - tion.

THE LOOK OF LOVE

from CASINO ROYALE

Words by HAL DAVID
Music by BURT BACHARACH

Medium Rock ballad
Dm7(add4)
The Look ___ Of Love ___ is in ___
___ Of Love ___ it's on ___
Am7
Bb
___ your eyes ___ a look ___ your smile ___
___ your face ___ a look ___ that time ___
Bb6
A7sus
A7
___ can't dis - guise; ___ The Look ___
___ can't e - rase. ___ Be mine ___
Dm7(add4)
D7sus
D7
Bb6
___ Of Love ___ it's say-ing so ___
___ to - night ___ let this be just ___
Bbm6
___ much more ___ than just words could ev - er say. ___
___ the start ___ of so man - y nights ___ like this. ___
Fmaj7
F7
Bbmaj7
And what my heart ___
Let's take a lov -

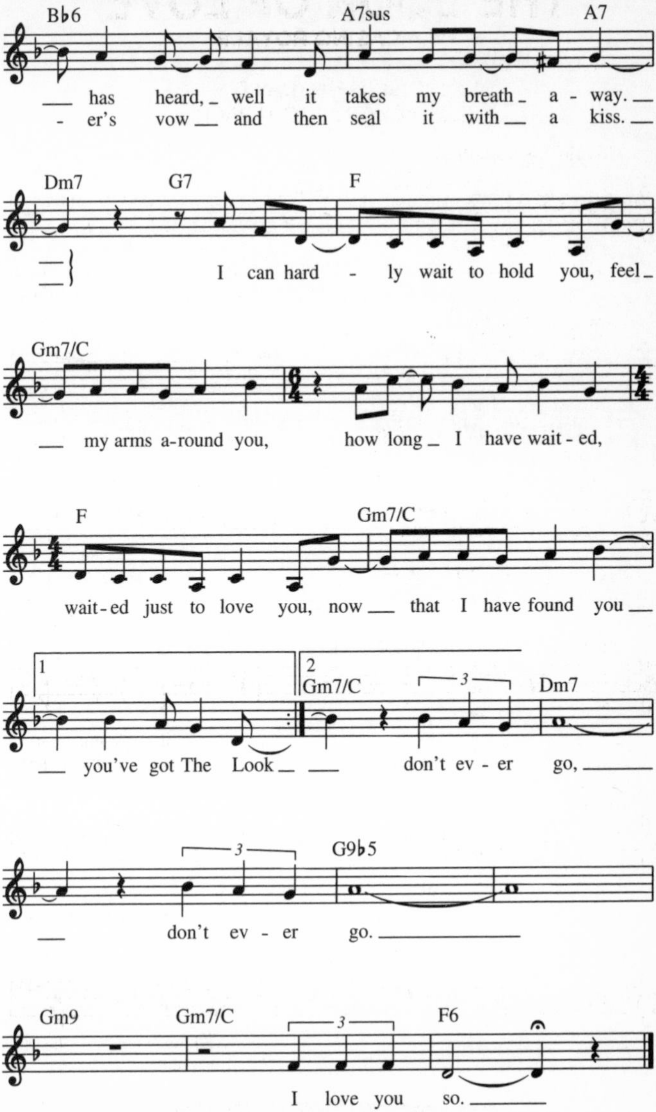
B♭6 A7sus A7
__ has heard, _ well it takes my breath _ a - way. __
- er's vow __ and then seal it with __ a kiss. __
Dm7 G7 F
I can hard - ly wait to hold you, feel _
Gm7/C
__ my arms a-round you, how long _ I have wait - ed,
F Gm7/C
wait - ed just to love you, now __ that I have found you __
1 2
Gm7/C 3 Dm7
__ you've got The Look __ __ don't ev - er go, ______
3 G9♭5
__ don't ev - er go. ______
Gm9 Gm7/C 3 F6
I love you so. ______

MUSIC TO WATCH GIRLS BY

By SID RAMIN

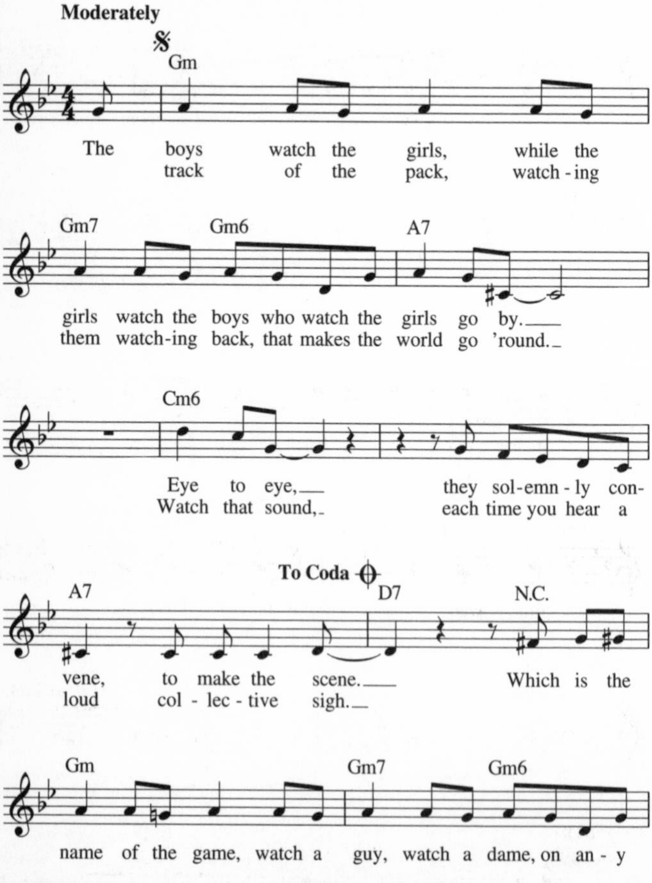
Moderately
Gm
The boys watch the girls, while the
track of the pack, watch - ing
Gm7 Gm6 A7
girls watch the boys who watch the girls go by.
them watch-ing back, that makes the world go 'round.
Cm6
Eye to eye, they sol-emn - ly con-
Watch that sound, each time you hear a
To Coda
A7 D7 N.C.
vene, to make the scene. Which is the
loud col - lec - tive sigh.
Gm Gm7 Gm6
name of the game, watch a guy, watch a dame, on an - y

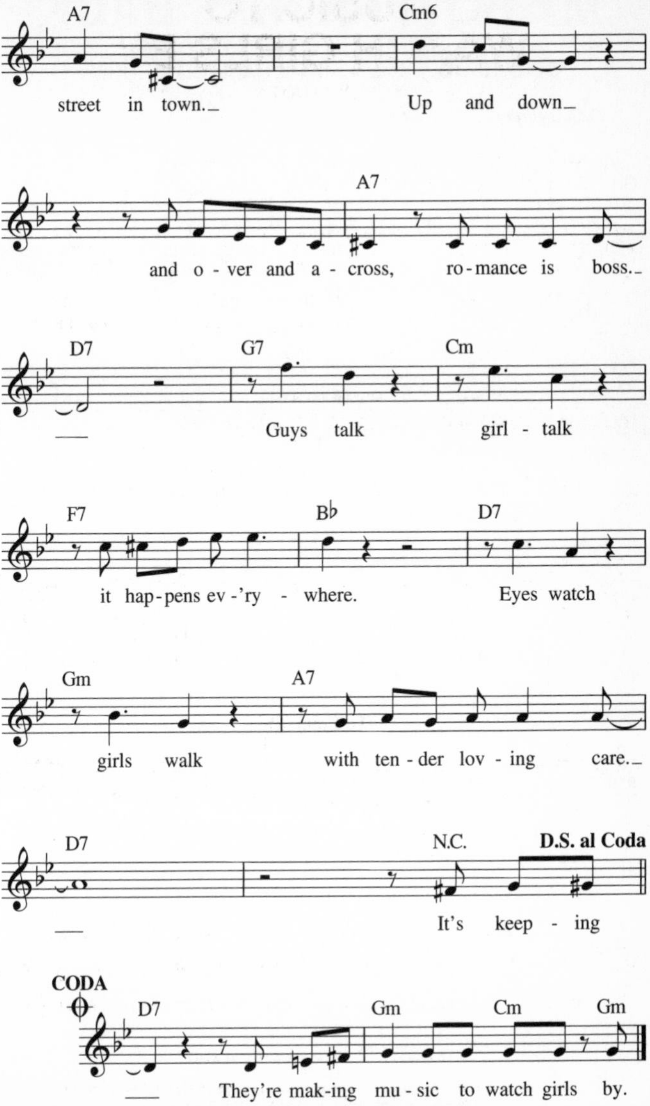
A7
Cm6
street in town.
Up and down
A7
and o - ver and a - cross, ro - mance is boss.
D7
G7
Cm
Guys talk girl - talk
F7
B♭
D7
it hap - pens ev - 'ry - where. Eyes watch
Gm
A7
girls walk with ten - der lov - ing care.
D7
N.C.
D.S. al Coda
It's keep - ing
CODA
D7
Gm
Cm
Gm
They're mak - ing mu - sic to watch girls by.

MY BOYFRIEND'S BACK

Words and Music by ROBERT FELDMAN,
GERALD GOLDSTEIN and RICHARD GOTTEHRER

Moderately
G
My boy-friend's back, and you're gon-na be in trou-ble.
He's been gone for such a long time.
C D7
(Hey, la - di - la, my boy-friend's back)
When you
G
see him com-in', bet-ter cut on the dou-ble.
Now he's back and things will be fine.
C D7
(Hey, la - di - la, my boy-friend's back)
You're
G
You've been spread-in' lies that I was un-true.
gon-na be sor-ry you ev-er were born.
C D7
(Hey, la - di - la, my boy-friend's back)
So
'Cause he's

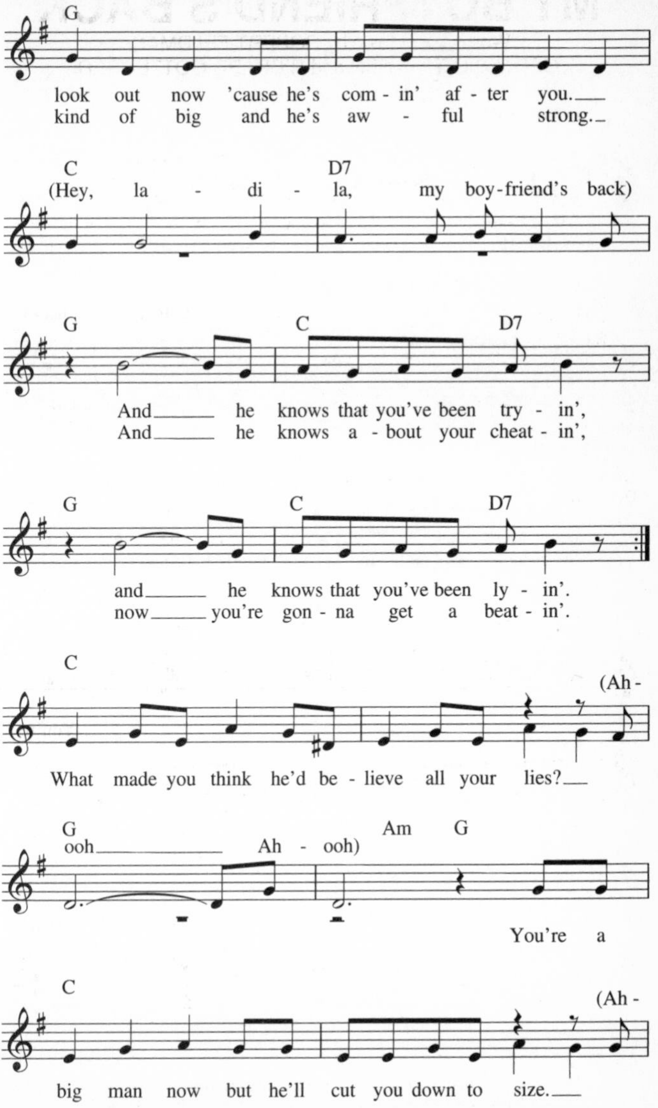
G
look out now 'cause he's com - in' af - ter you.
kind of big and he's aw - ful strong.
C D7
(Hey, la - di - la, my boy-friend's back)
G C D7
And he knows that you've been try - in',
And he knows a - bout your cheat - in',
G C D7
and he knows that you've been ly - in'.
now you're gon - na get a beat - in'.
C
(Ah -
What made you think he'd be - lieve all your lies?
G Am G
ooh Ah - ooh)
You're a
C
(Ah -
big man now but he'll cut you down to size.

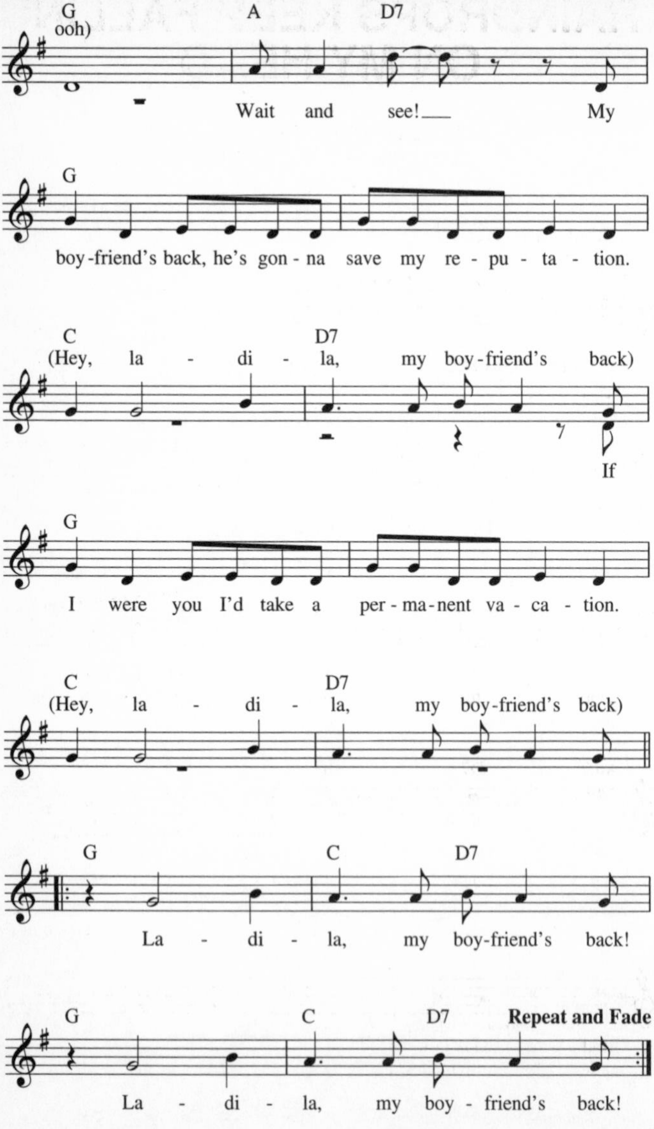
G A D7
ooh)
Wait and see! My
G
boy-friend's back, he's gon - na save my re - pu - ta - tion.
C D7
(Hey, la - di - la, my boy-friend's back)
If
G
I were you I'd take a per - ma - nent va - ca - tion.
C D7
(Hey, la - di - la, my boy-friend's back)
G C D7
La - di - la, my boy-friend's back!
G C D7
Repeat and Fade
La - di - la, my boy - friend's back!

RAINDROPS KEEP FALLIN' ON MY HEAD

Lyric by HAL DAVID
Music by BURT BACHARACH

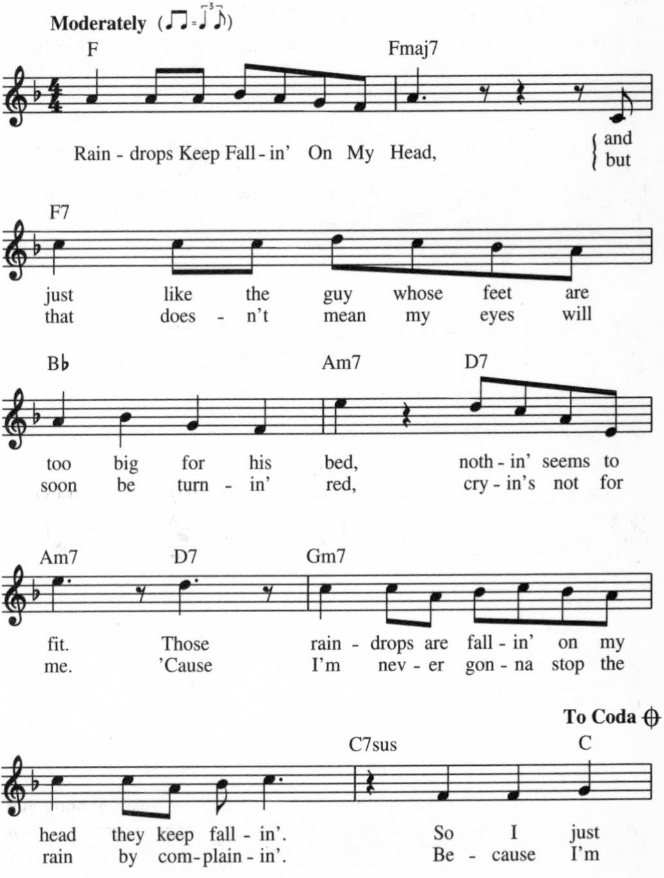
Moderately
F
Fmaj7
Rain - drops Keep Fall - in' On My Head,
and
but
F7
just like the guy whose feet are
that does - n't mean my eyes will
B♭
Am7
D7
too big for his bed, noth - in' seems to
soon be turn - in' red, cry - in's not for
Am7
D7
Gm7
fit. Those rain - drops are fall - in' on my
me. 'Cause I'm nev - er gon - na stop the
To Coda
C7sus
C
head they keep fall - in'. So I just
rain by com - plain - in'. Be - cause I'm

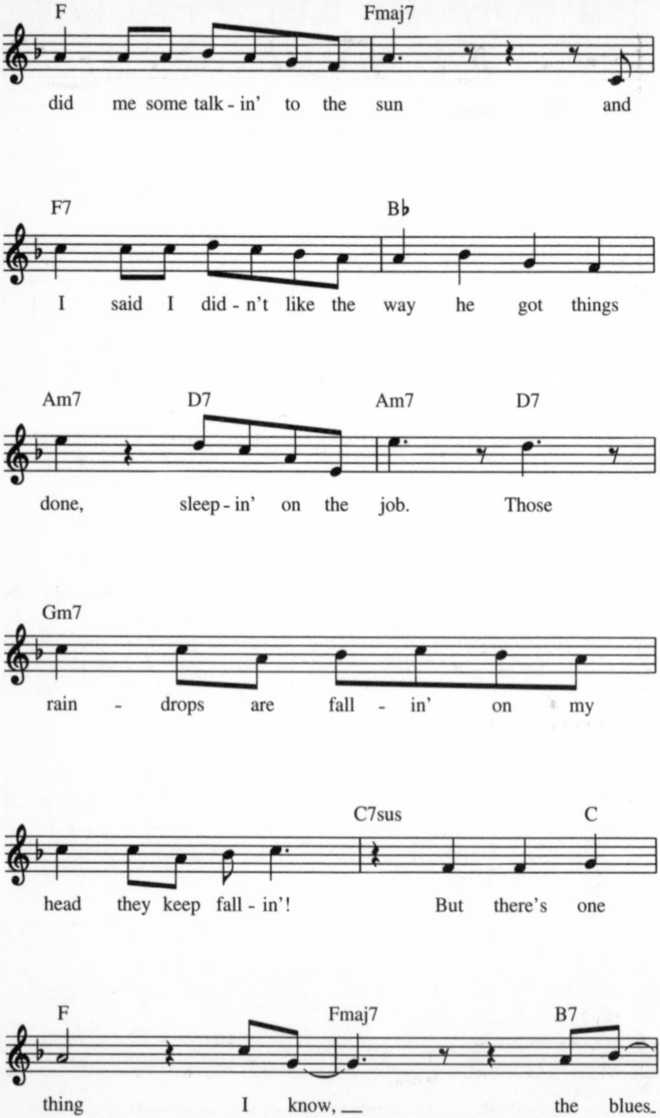
F Fmaj7
did me some talk - in' to the sun and
F7 B♭
I said I did - n't like the way he got things
Am7 D7 Am7 D7
done, sleep - in' on the job. Those
Gm7
rain - drops are fall - in' on my
C7sus C
head they keep fall - in'! But there's one
F Fmaj7 B7
thing I know, the blues

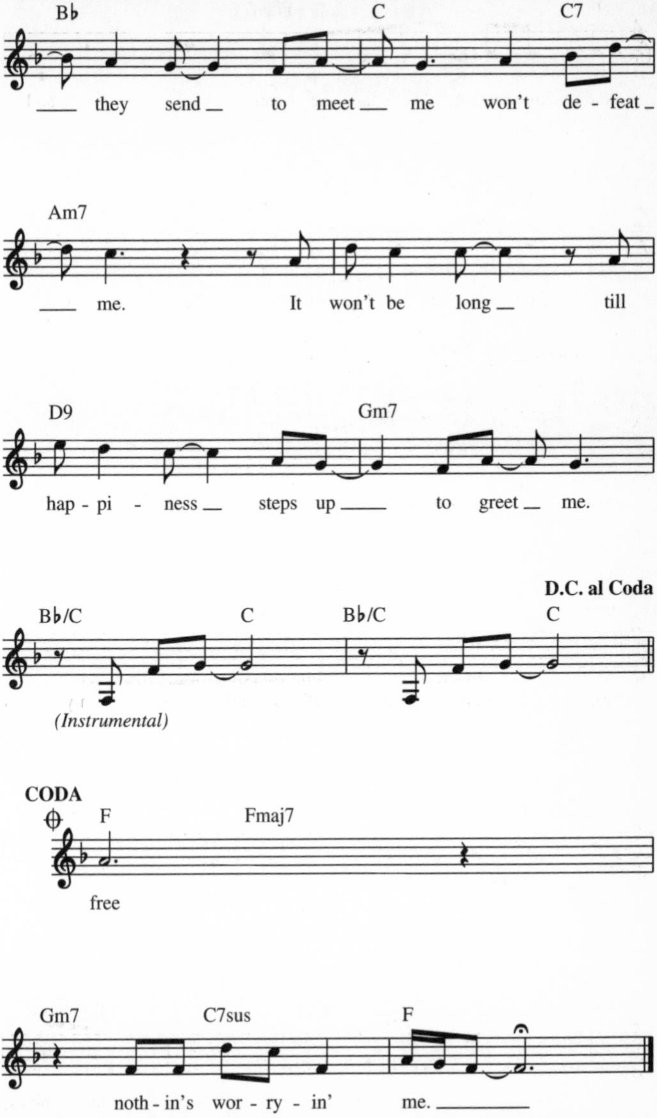
Bb C C7
they send to meet me won't de - feat
Am7
me. It won't be long till
D9 Gm7
hap - pi - ness steps up to greet me.
D.C. al Coda
Bb/C C Bb/C C
(Instrumental)
CODA
F Fmaj7
free
Gm7 C7sus F
noth - in's wor - ry - in' me.

MY GIRL

Words and Music by WILLIAM "SMOKEY" ROBINSON
and RONALD WHITE

Slowly
F
Bb
I've got sun - shine ____ on a cloud - y
F
Bb
F
day; When it's cold out - side,
Bb
F
Bb
I've got the month of May.
F
Gm
Bb
C
F
Gm
I guess you say, what can make me
Bb
C
F
feel this way? My girl, __________ talk-ing 'bout

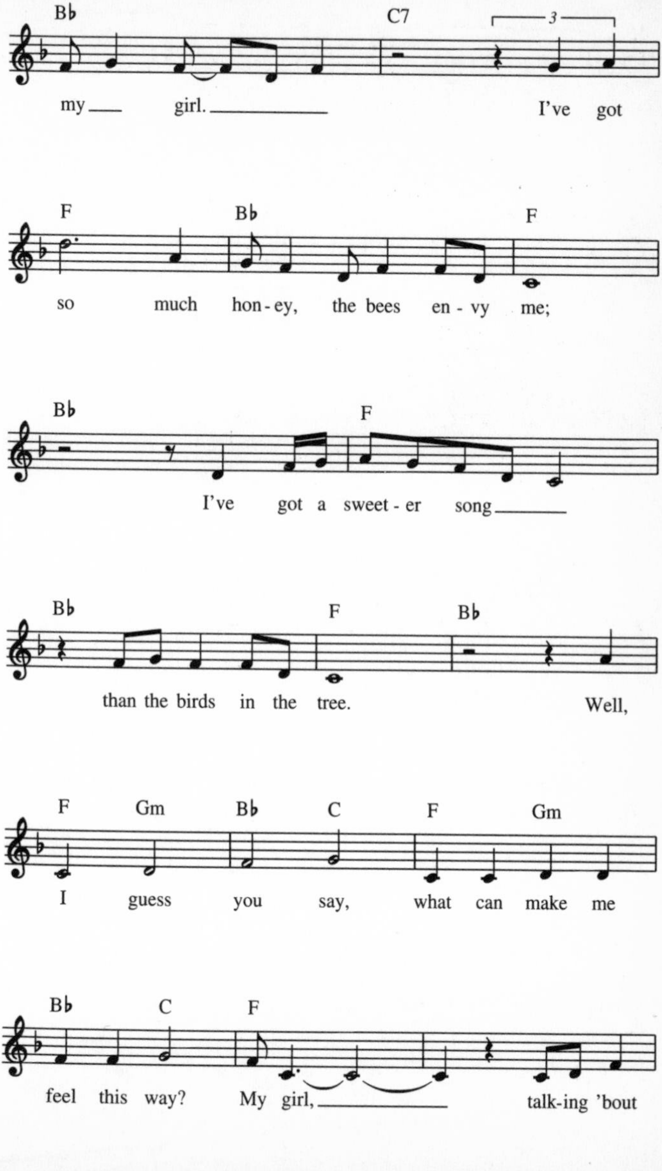

B♭ C7
my girl. I've got
F B♭ F
so much hon-ey, the bees en-vy me;
B♭ F
I've got a sweet-er song
B♭ F B♭
than the birds in the tree. Well,
F Gm B♭ C F Gm
I guess you say, what can make me
B♭ C F
feel this way? My girl, talk-ing 'bout

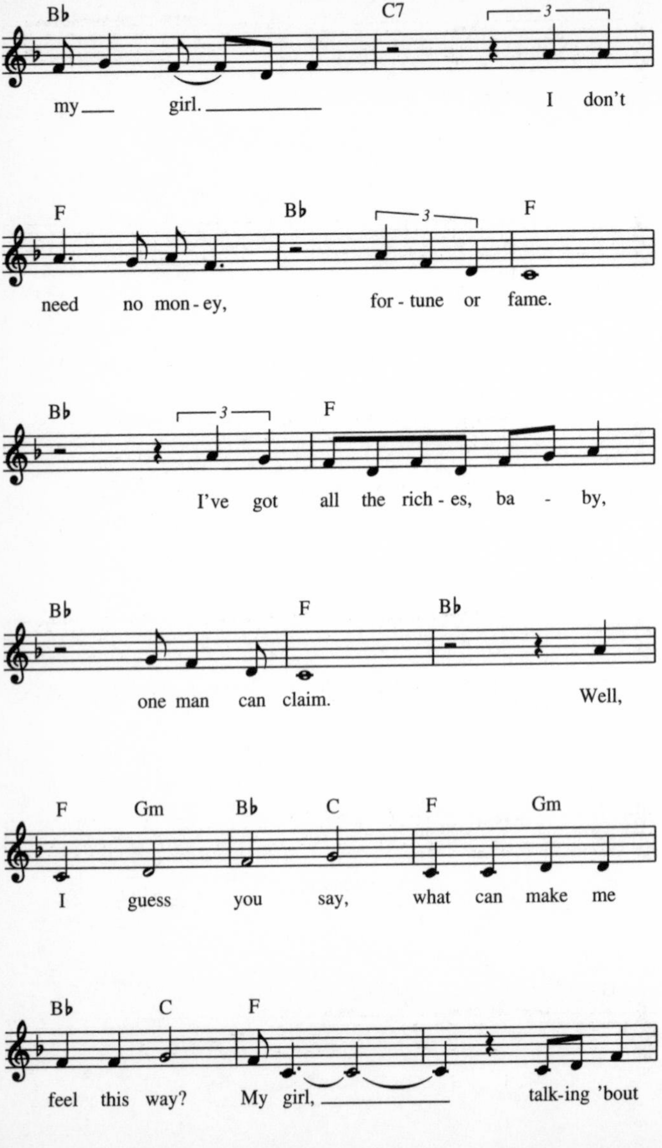
B♭
C7
3
my___ girl.___
I don't
F
B♭
3
F
need no mon-ey, for-tune or fame.
B♭
3
F
I've got all the rich-es, ba - by,
B♭
F
B♭
one man can claim.
Well,
F Gm B♭ C F Gm
I guess you say, what can make me
B♭ C F
feel this way? My girl,___
talk-ing 'bout

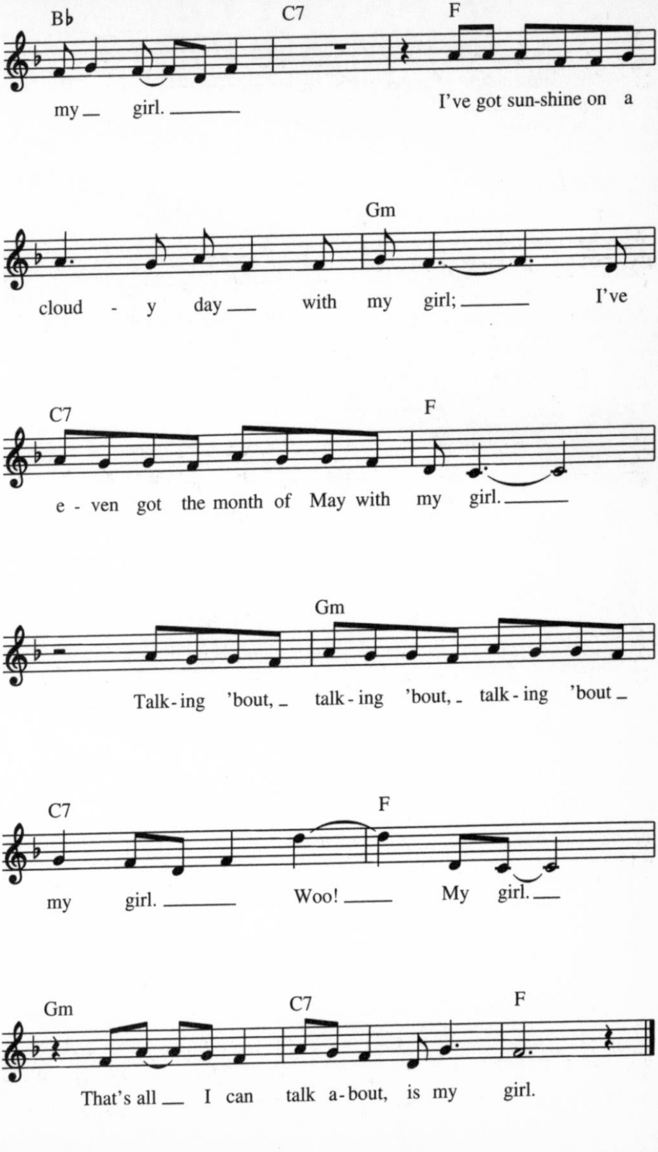
B♭ C7 F
my girl. I've got sun-shine on a
Gm
cloud - y day with my girl; I've
C7 F
e - ven got the month of May with my girl.
Gm
Talk-ing 'bout, talk-ing 'bout, talk-ing 'bout
C7 F
my girl. Woo! My girl.
Gm C7 F
That's all I can talk a-bout, is my girl.

NA NA HEY HEY KISS HIM GOODBYE

Words and Music by ARTHUR FRASHUER DALE,
PAUL ROGER LEKA and GARY CARLA

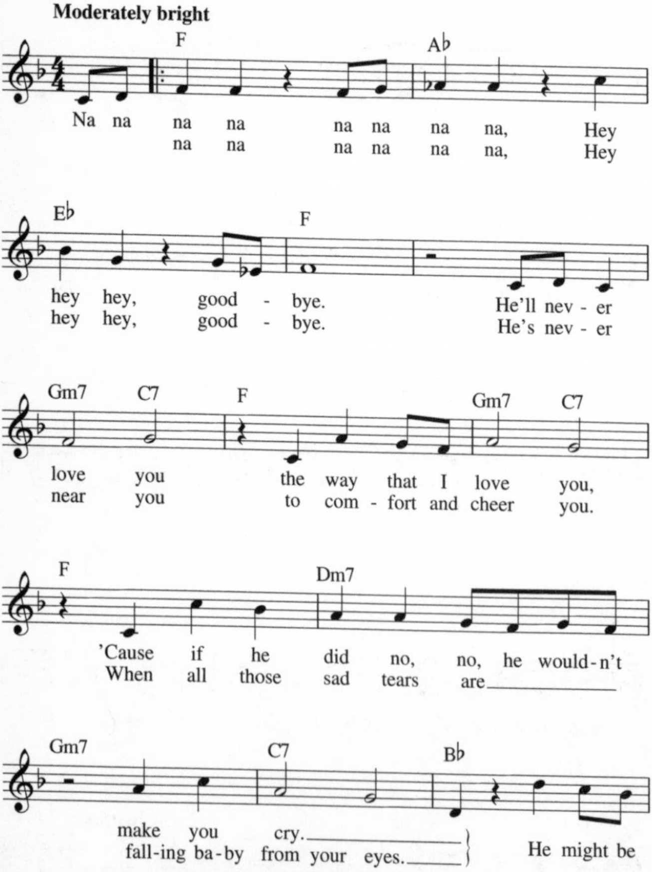
Moderately bright
F Ab
Na na na na na na na na, Hey
na na na na na na, Hey
Eb F
hey hey, good - bye. He'll nev - er
hey hey, good - bye. He's nev - er
Gm7 C7 F Gm7 C7
love you the way that I love you,
near you to com - fort and cheer you.
F Dm7
'Cause if he did no, no, he would - n't
When all those sad tears are
Gm7 C7 Bb
make you cry.
fall - ing ba - by from your eyes.
He might be

A7
Dm7
thrill - ing, ba - by, but, my love's so
G7
F
dog - gone will - ing so kiss him,
B♭
B♭m
Bmaj7
F
go on and kiss him good - bye Na na
A♭
1
E♭
F
na na Hey hey hey, good - bye. Na na
2
E♭
F
F
hey hey, good - bye. Na na na na na na
A♭
E♭
F
Repeat and Fade
na na, Hey hey hey, good - bye. Na na

NEVER MY LOVE

Words and Music by DON ADDRISI
and DICK ADDRISI

Moderately
C
(Instrumental) You ask me if
G/B Bb
there'll come a time when I grow tired
F/A C Am C
of you. Nev-er my love,
Fmaj7 C
nev - er my love. (Instrumental)
G/B
You won - der if this heart of mine
You say you fear I'll change my mind:
Bb F/A C
will lose its de - sire for you.
I won't re - quire you.

Am C Fmaj7
Never my love, never my love.
C E7sus E7 Am7 D9
What makes you think love will end when you know that my whole life depends on you?
How can you think love will end when I've asked you to spend your whole life with me?
Gmaj7 Cmaj9 Fmaj7 Dm7
To Coda
Em Am N.C. C
(Instrumental)
Da da da da da da da da
G/B Bb
da da da da
F/A C Am C
da. Never my love,
Fmaj7 C D.S. al Coda
never my love. (Instrumental)
CODA
Am9

ON BROADWAY

Words and Music by BARRY MANN,
CYNTHIA WEIL, MIKE STOLLER and JERRY LEIBER

Moderately
F Eb/F F Eb/F
They say the ne - on lights are bright
They say the wom - en treat you fine
They say that I won't last too long
on
F Eb/F F Eb/F F Eb/F
Broad - way;
They say there's al - ways
But look - in' at them
I'll catch a Grey - hound
F Eb/F F Eb/F
mag - ic in the air;
just gives me the blues;
bus for home, they say;
F Eb/F F Bb Ab/Bb
But when you're walk - in'
'Cause how ya gon - na
But they're dead wrong, I

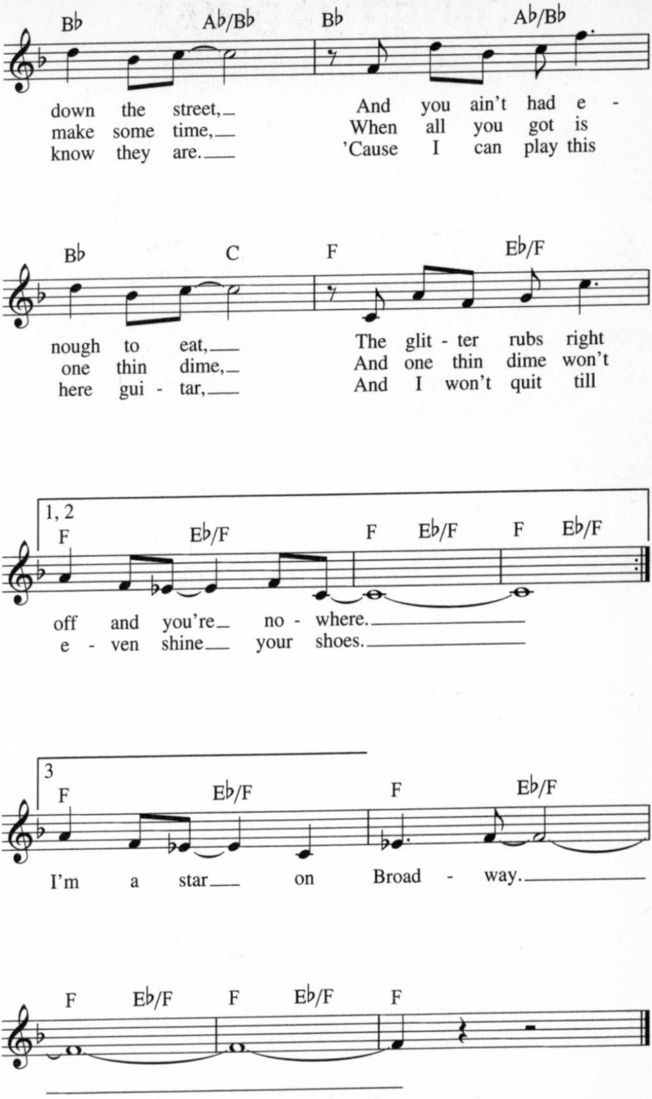
Bb Ab/Bb Bb Ab/Bb
down the street, And you ain't had e -
make some time, When all you got is
know they are. 'Cause I can play this
Bb C F Eb/F
nough to eat, The glit - ter rubs right
one thin dime, And one thin dime won't
here gui - tar, And I won't quit till
1, 2
F Eb/F F Eb/F F Eb/F
off and you're no - where.
e - ven shine your shoes.
3
F Eb/F F Eb/F
I'm a star on Broad - way.
F Eb/F F Eb/F F

ONE FINE DAY

Words and Music by GERRY GOFFIN
and CAROLE KING

Briskly
F
One fine day
The arms I long for
One fine day
C
you'll look at me,
will o - pen wide,
we'll meet once more,
Dm
and you will know our love was
and you'll be proud to have me
and then you'll want the love you
B♭
meant to be.
walk - ing by your side.
threw a - way be - fore.
F Dm11 Dm7 B♭
One fine day you're gon - na

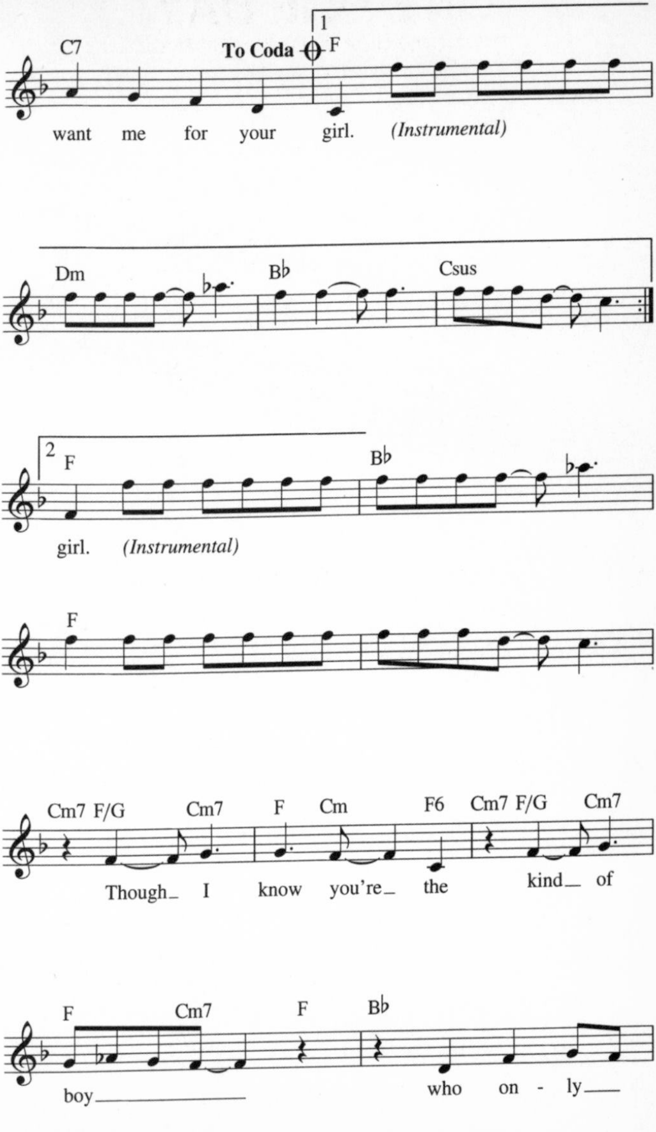
C7 To Coda 1 F
want me for your girl. (Instrumental)
Dm B♭ Csus
2 F B♭
girl. (Instrumental)
F
Cm7 F/G Cm7 F Cm F6 Cm7 F/G Cm7
Though I know you're the kind of
F Cm7 F B♭
boy who on - ly

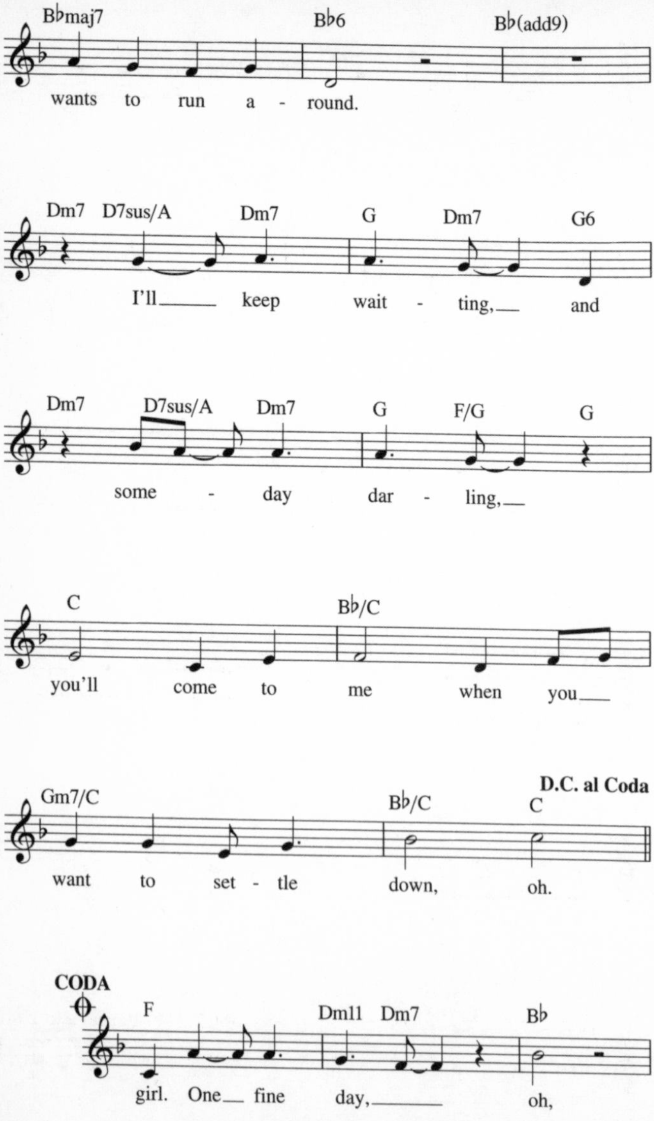
B♭maj7
B♭6
B♭(add9)
wants to run a - round.
Dm7
D7sus/A
Dm7
G
Dm7
G6
I'll keep wait - ting, and
Dm7
D7sus/A
Dm7
G
F/G
G
some - day dar - ling,
C
B♭/C
you'll come to me when you
Gm7/C
B♭/C
C
D.C. al Coda
want to set - tle down, oh.
CODA
F
Dm11
Dm7
B♭
girl. One fine day, oh,

C
F
oh, one fine
Dm11
Dm7
B♭
day you're gon - na
C
F
want me for your girl. Shoo - be - do - be - do - be -
Lead vocal 1st time only
Dm7
B♭
do - be - do wah, wah, shoo - be - do - be - do - be -
Gm7/C
F
do - be - do wah, wah.
(Instrumental ad lib. and fade)
Dm7
B♭
B♭/C
Repeat and Fade

RELEASE ME

Words and Music by ROBERT YOUNT,
EDDIE MILLER and DUB WILLIAMS

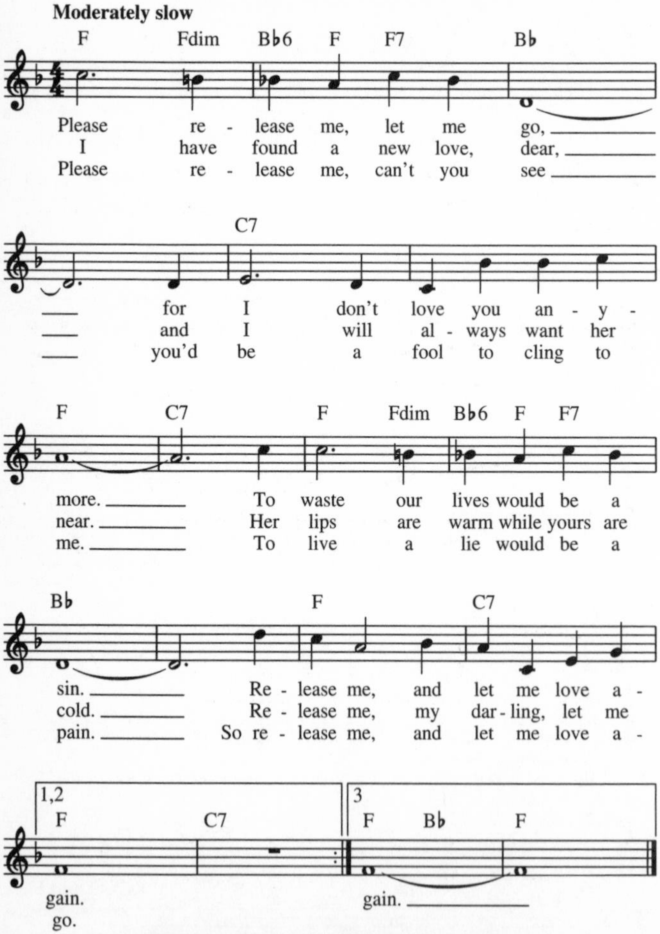
Moderately slow
F Fdim B♭6 F F7 B♭
Please re - lease me, let me go,
I have found a new love, dear,
Please re - lease me, can't you see
C7
for I don't love you an - y -
and I will al - ways want her
you'd be a fool to cling to
F C7 F Fdim B♭6 F F7
more. To waste our lives would be a
near. Her lips are warm while yours are
me. To live a lie would be a
B♭ F C7
sin. Re - lease me, and let me love a -
cold. Re - lease me, my dar - ling, let me
pain. So re - lease me, and let me love a -
1,2
F C7
gain.
go.
3
F B♭ F
gain.

RESPECT

Words and Music by
OTIS REDDING

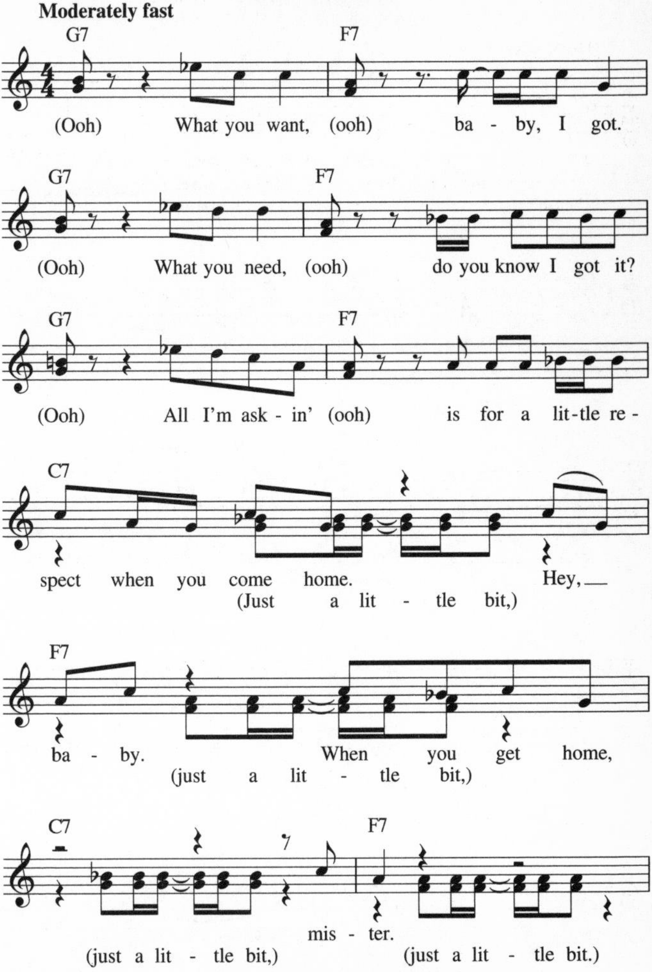
Moderately fast
G7
F7
(Ooh) What you want, (ooh) ba - by, I got.
G7
F7
(Ooh) What you need, (ooh) do you know I got it?
G7
F7
(Ooh) All I'm ask - in' (ooh) is for a lit-tle re -
C7
spect when you come home. Hey, __
(Just a lit - tle bit,)
F7
ba - by. When you get home,
(just a lit - tle bit,)
C7
F7
mis - ter.
(just a lit - tle bit,) (just a lit - tle bit.)

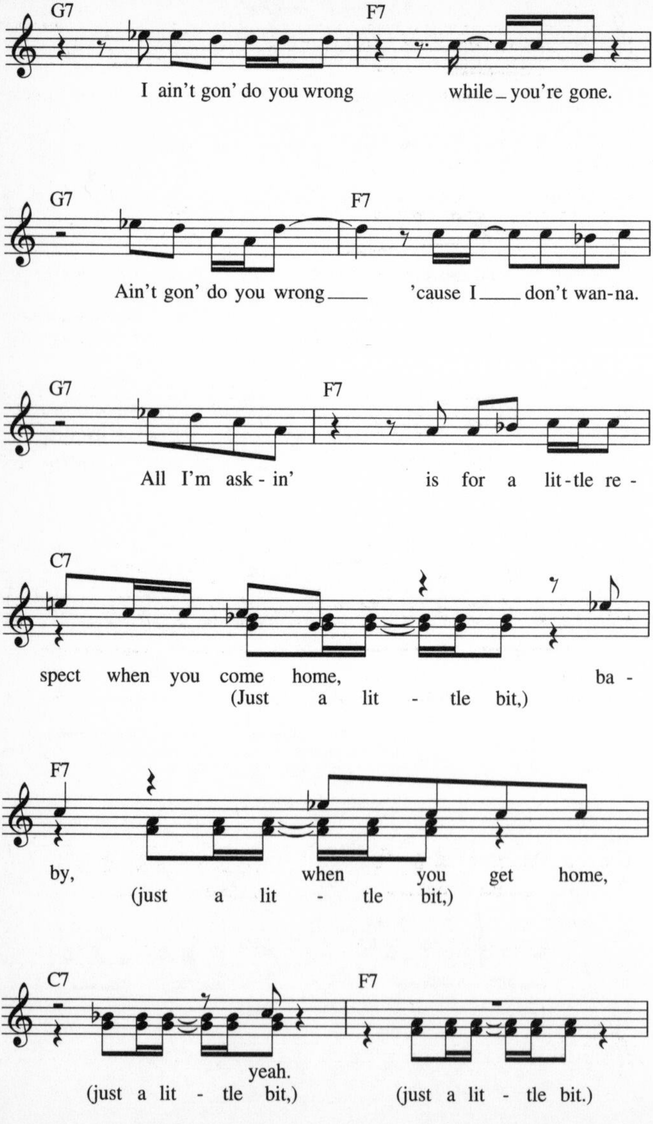
G7
F7
I ain't gon' do you wrong while _ you're gone.
G7
F7
Ain't gon' do you wrong ___ 'cause I ___ don't wan-na.
G7
F7
All I'm ask - in' is for a lit-tle re -
C7
spect when you come home, ba -
(Just a lit - tle bit,)
F7
by, when you get home,
(just a lit - tle bit,)
C7
F7
yeah.
(just a lit - tle bit,)
(just a lit - tle bit.)

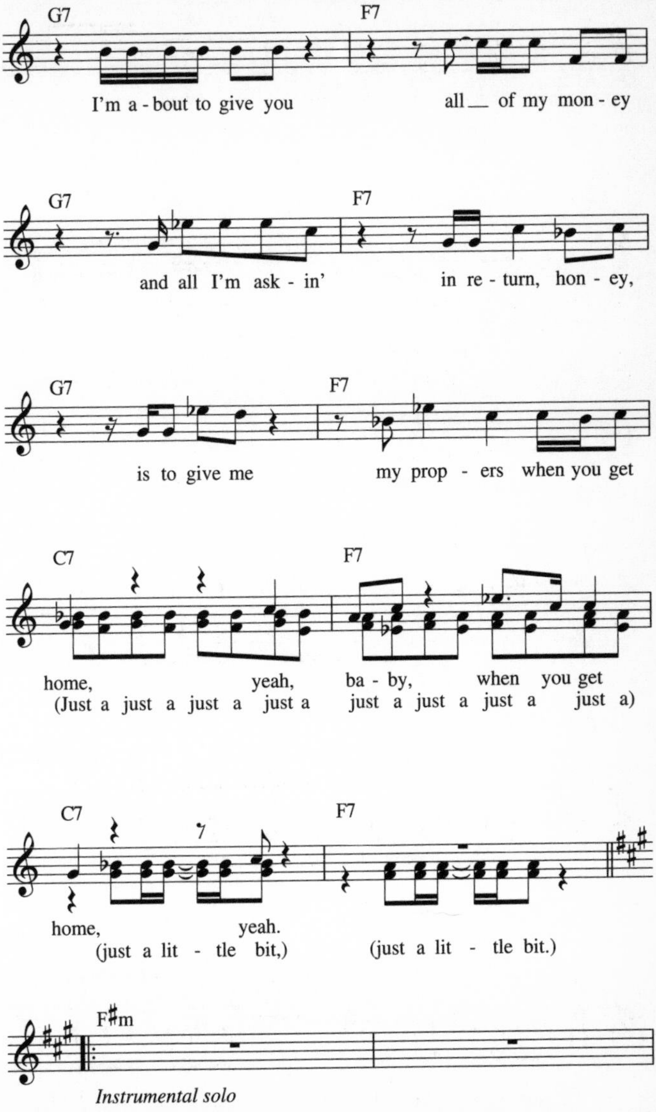
G7
F7
I'm a - bout to give you
all __ of my mon - ey
G7
F7
and all I'm ask - in'
in re - turn, hon - ey,
G7
F7
is to give me
my prop - ers when you get
C7
F7
home,
yeah,
ba - by,
when you get
(Just a just a just a just a
just a just a just a just a)
C7
F7
home,
yeah.
(just a lit - tle bit,)
(just a lit - tle bit.)
F♯m
Instrumental solo

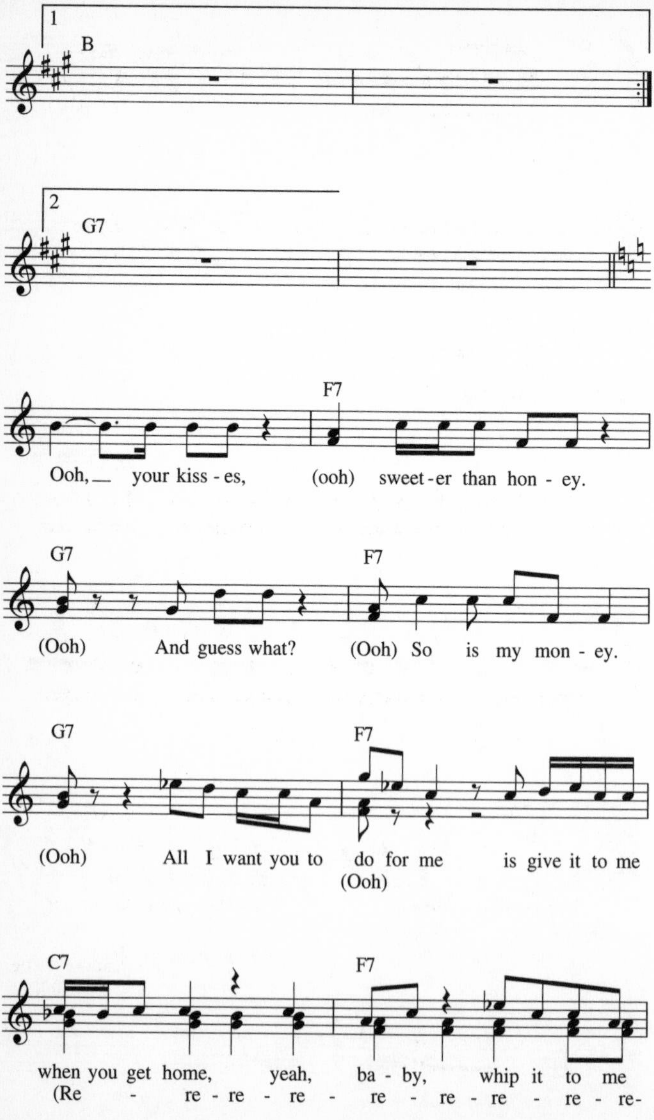
1
B
2
G7
F7
Ooh, your kiss - es, (ooh) sweet - er than hon - ey.
G7
F7
(Ooh) And guess what? (Ooh) So is my mon - ey.
G7
F7
(Ooh) All I want you to do for me is give it to me
(Ooh)
C7
F7
when you get home, yeah, ba - by, whip it to me
(Re - re - re - re - re - re - re - re - re-

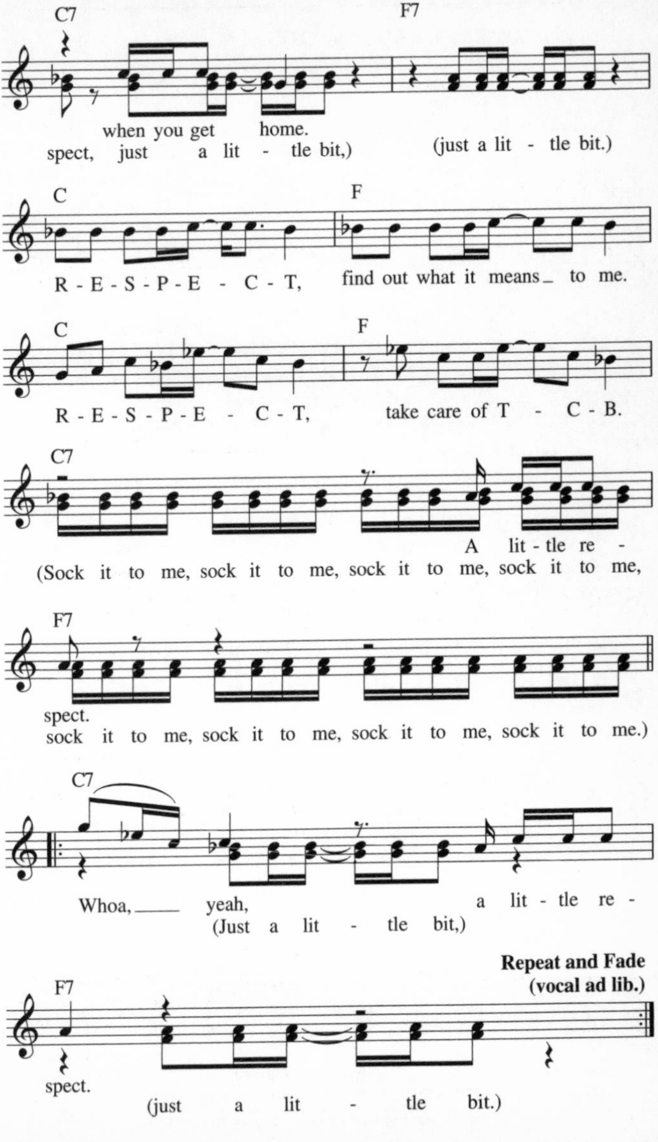
C7
F7
when you get home.
spect, just a lit - tle bit,)
(just a lit - tle bit.)
C
F
R - E - S - P - E - C - T,
find out what it means_ to me.
C
F
R - E - S - P - E - C - T,
take care of T - C - B.
C7
A lit - tle re -
(Sock it to me, sock it to me, sock it to me, sock it to me,
F7
spect.
sock it to me, sock it to me, sock it to me, sock it to me.)
C7
Whoa,___ yeah,
a lit - tle re -
(Just a lit - tle bit,)
Repeat and Fade
(vocal ad lib.)
F7
spect.
(just a lit - tle bit.)

RETURN TO SENDER

Words and Music by OTIS BLACKWELL
and WINFIELD SCOTT

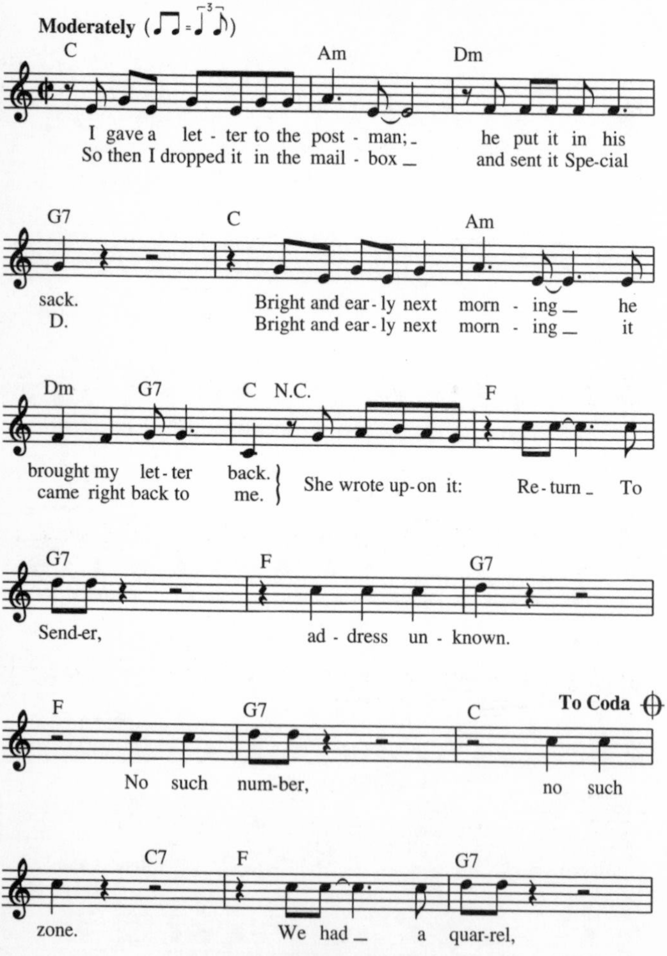
Moderately
C Am Dm
I gave a let - ter to the post - man; _ he put it in his
So then I dropped it in the mail - box _ and sent it Spe-cial
G7 C Am
sack. Bright and ear - ly next morn - ing _ he
D. Bright and ear - ly next morn - ing _ it
Dm G7 C N.C. F
brought my let - ter back.
came right back to me.
She wrote up-on it: Re - turn _ To
G7 F G7
Send-er, ad - dress un - known.
F G7 C To Coda
No such num-ber, no such
C7 F G7
zone. We had _ a quar-rel,

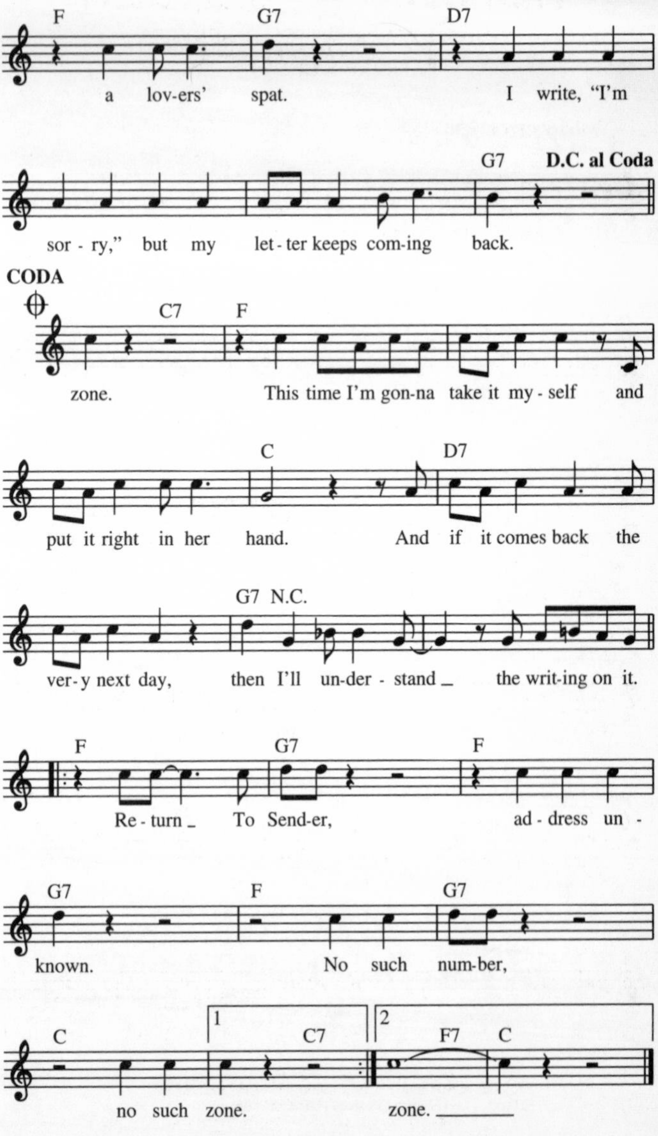
F G7 D7
a lov-ers' spat. I write, "I'm
G7 D.C. al Coda
sor - ry," but my let - ter keeps com-ing back.
CODA
C7 F
zone. This time I'm gon-na take it my - self and
C D7
put it right in her hand. And if it comes back the
G7 N.C.
ver- y next day, then I'll un-der - stand the writ-ing on it.
F G7 F
Re - turn To Send-er, ad - dress un -
G7 F G7
known. No such num-ber,
C 1 C7 2 F7 C
no such zone. zone.

RUNAWAY

Words and Music by DEL SHANNON
and MAX CROOK

Moderately bright
Fm Eb
As I walk a - long_ I won - der
Db
what went wrong_ with our love, a love that was_ so
C7 Fm
strong. And as I still walk on__ I
Eb Db
think of the things we've done_ to - geth - er
C7 F
while our hearts_ were young. I'm a - walk - in'
Dm
in the rain._ Tears are fall - in' and I

F
feel a pain, A - wish - in' you were
Dm
here by me To end this mis - er - y. And I
F Dm
won - der, wo - wo - wo - wo - won - der
F Dm
why, why-why-why-why-why she ran a-
F C7
way, And I won - der where she will stay,
C7sus F B♭
My lit - tle run - a - way, run - run - run - run -
1 F C7 2 F
run - a - way. run - a - way.

SAVE THE LAST DANCE FOR ME

Words and Music by DOC POMUS
and MORT SHUMAN

Moderately
E♭
You can dance ev - 'ry dance with the guy who
know that the mu - sic is fine, like
B♭7
gave you the eye; let him hold you tight.
spark - ling wine; go and have your fun.
You can smile ev - 'ry
Laugh and sing but while
smile for the man who held your hand 'neath the
we're a - part don't give your heart to
E♭
B♭7
E♭7
pale moon - light
an - y - one.
But don't for -
A♭
get who's tak - ing, you home and in whose arms you're

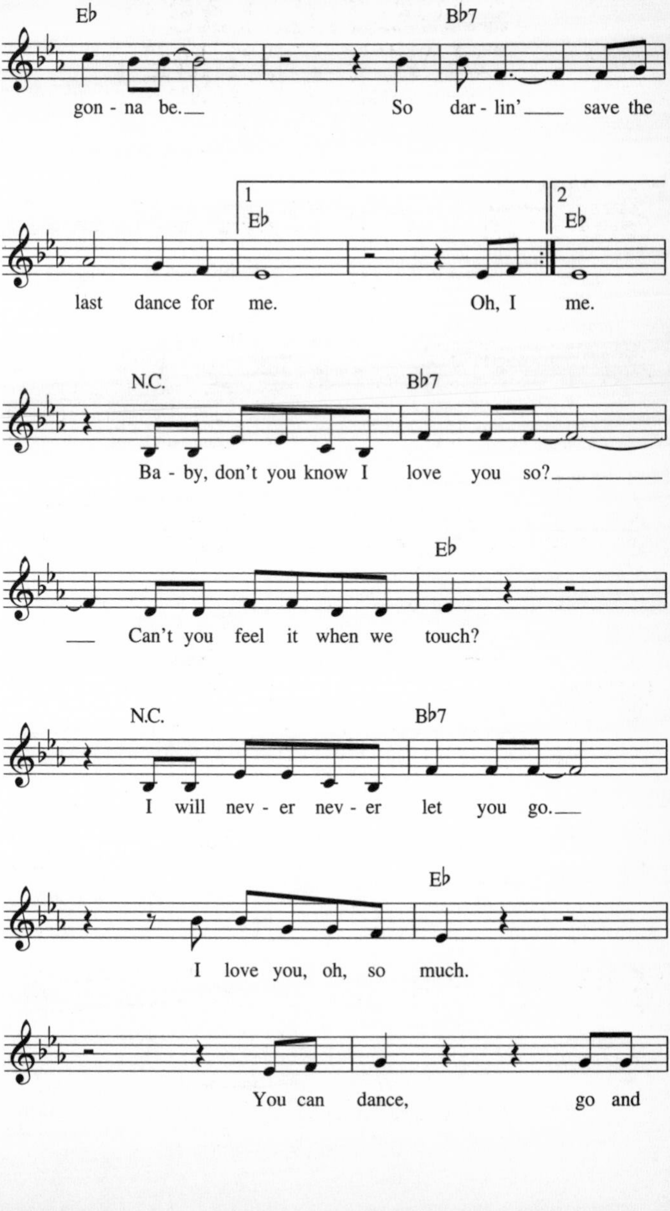

E♭
B♭7
gon - na be. So dar - lin' save the
1
E♭
2
E♭
last dance for me. Oh, I me.
N.C.
B♭7
Ba - by, don't you know I love you so?
E♭
Can't you feel it when we touch?
N.C.
B♭7
I will nev - er nev - er let you go.
E♭
I love you, oh, so much.
You can dance, go and

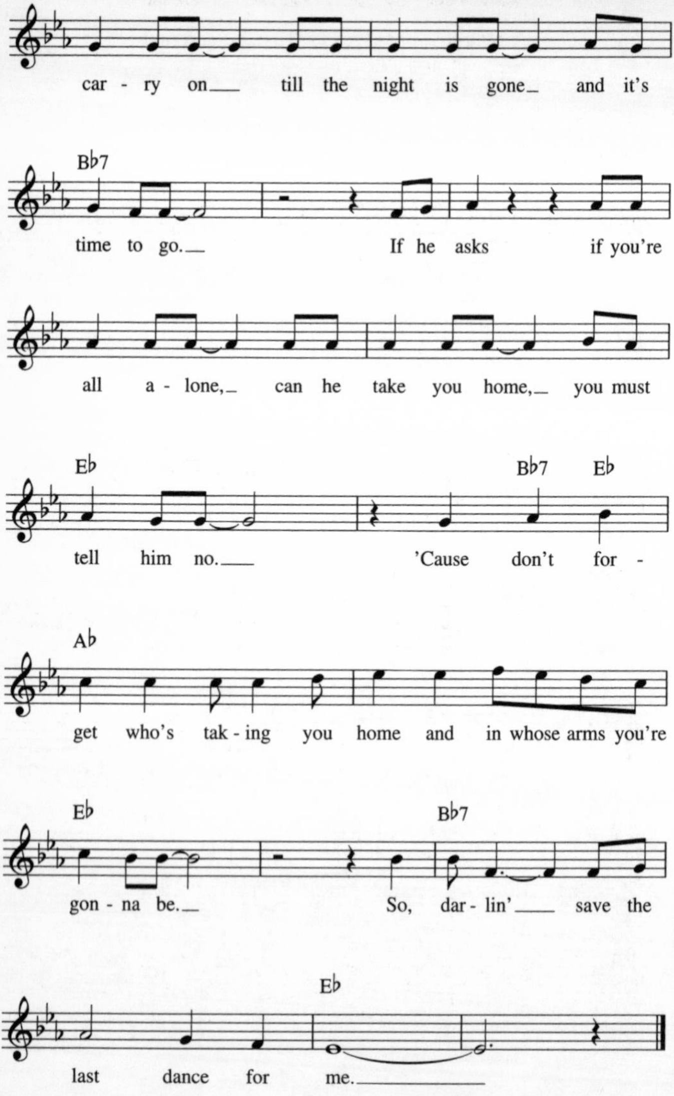
car - ry on till the night is gone and it's
B♭7
time to go. If he asks if you're
all a - lone, can he take you home, you must
E♭
tell him no. B♭7 'Cause don't E♭ for -
A♭
get who's tak - ing you home and in whose arms you're
E♭
gon - na be. B♭7 So, dar - lin' save the
E♭
last dance for me.

SHE LOVES YOU

Words and Music by JOHN LENNON
and PAUL McCARTNEY

Moderately
Em A7
She Loves You, yeah, yeah, yeah, She Loves You, yeah,
C G6
yeah, yeah, She Loves You, yeah, yeah, yeah, yeah.
G Em
You think you've lost your love? Well, I
Bm D G
saw her yes - ter - day. It's you she's think - ing of
Em Bm D
And she told me what to say: She says She
G6 Em
Loves You and you know that can't be bad.
Cm6
Yes, She Loves You and you know you should be glad.

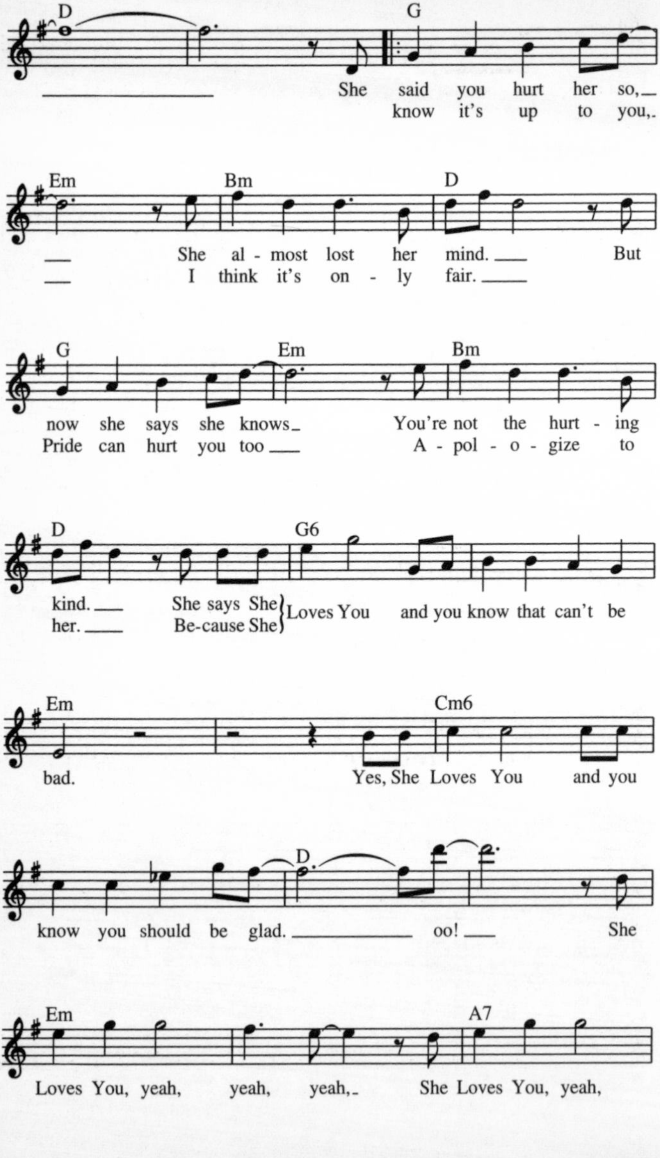
D G
She said you hurt her so,
know it's up to you,
Em Bm D
She al - most lost her mind. But
I think it's on - ly fair.
G Em Bm
now she says she knows You're not the hurt - ing
Pride can hurt you too A - pol - o - gize to
D G6
kind. She says She
her. Be-cause She
Loves You and you know that can't be
Em Cm6
bad. Yes, She Loves You and you
D
know you should be glad. oo! She
Em A7
Loves You, yeah, yeah, yeah, She Loves You, yeah,

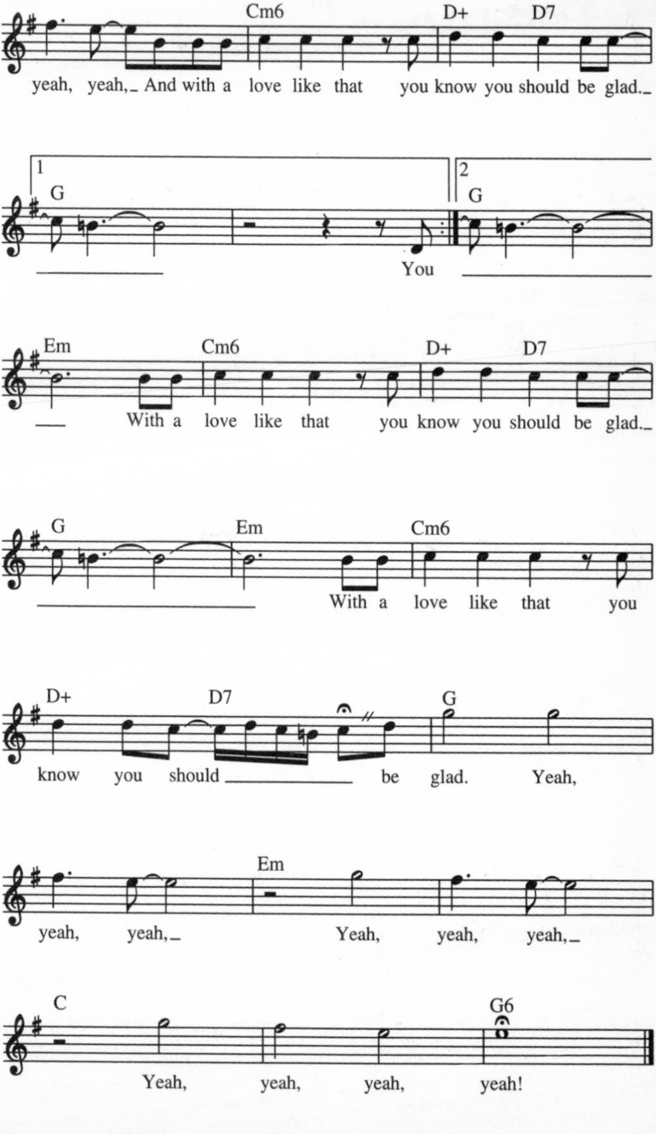
Cm6 D+ D7
yeah, yeah, And with a love like that you know you should be glad.
1 G
2 G
You
Em Cm6 D+ D7
With a love like that you know you should be glad.
G Em Cm6
With a love like that you
D+ D7 G
know you should be glad. Yeah,
Em
yeah, yeah, Yeah, yeah, yeah,
C G6
Yeah, yeah, yeah, yeah!

(Sittin' On)

THE DOCK OF THE BAY

Words and Music by STEVE CROPPER
and OTIS REDDING

Relaxed tempo
G B
Sit - tin' in the morn - ing sun, I'll be
left my home in Geor - gia,
Sit - tin' here rest-in' my bones, and this
C B B♭ A G B
sit-tin' when the eve - nin' come. Watch-in' the ships roll in,
head-ed for the Fris - co bay. I have noth - in' to live
lone-li-ness won't leave me a - lone. Two thou-sand miles I roam
C B B♭ A
then I watch 'em roll a - way a - gain.
for. Look like noth-in's gon - na come my way.
just to make this dock my home.
G Esus2
Yeah, I'm sit - tin' on the dock of the bay,
So I'm just gon-na sit on the dock of the bay,
Now I'm just gon-na sit at the dock of the bay,
E G Esus2
watch-in' the tide roll a - way.

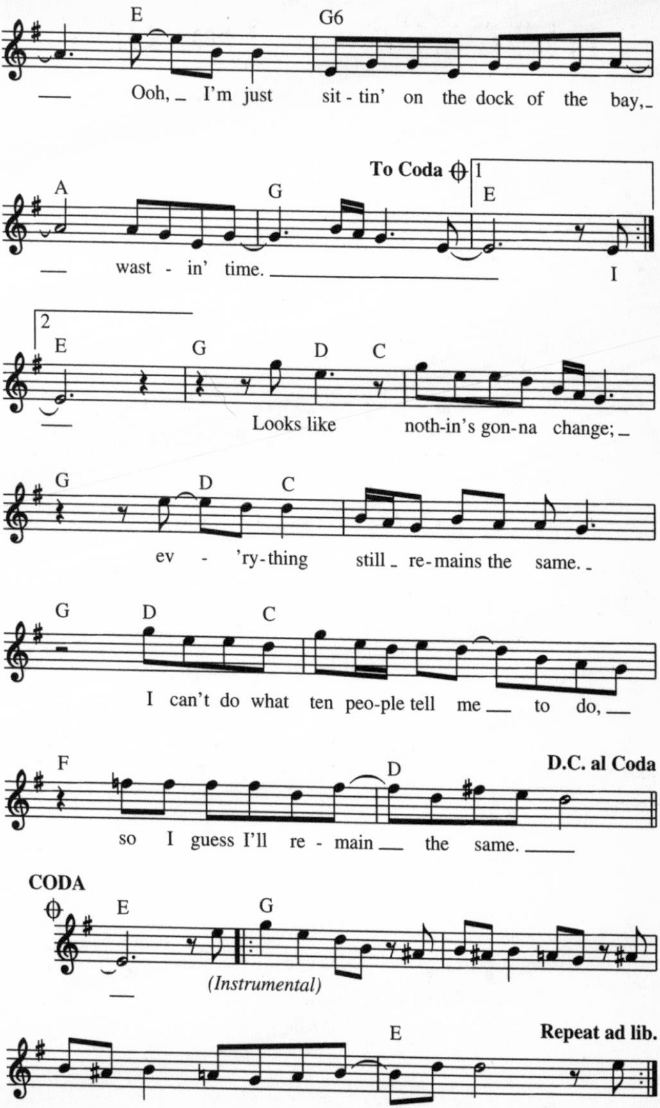
E
G6
Ooh, I'm just sit-tin' on the dock of the bay,
To Coda
1
A
G
E
wast-in' time.
I
2
E
G
D
C
Looks like noth-in's gon-na change;
G
D
C
ev-'ry-thing still re-mains the same.
G
D
C
I can't do what ten peo-ple tell me to do,
F
D
D.C. al Coda
so I guess I'll re-main the same.
CODA
E
G
(Instrumental)
E
Repeat ad lib.

SOLDIER BOY

Words and Music by LUTHER DIXON
and FLORENCE GREEN

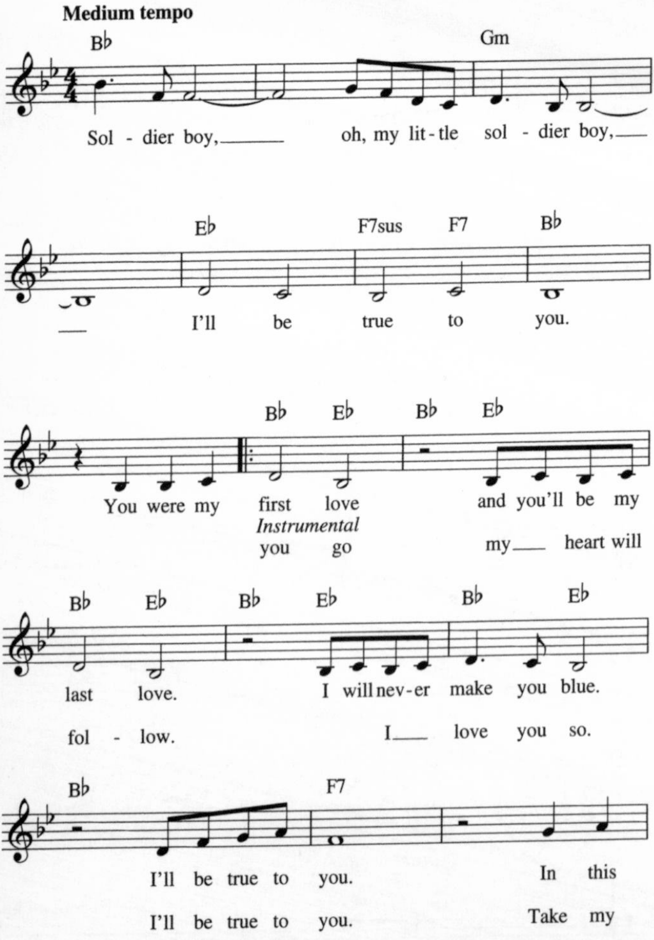
Medium tempo
Bb Gm
Sol - dier boy, oh, my lit - tle sol - dier boy,
Eb F7sus F7 Bb
I'll be true to you.
Bb Eb Bb Eb
You were my first love and you'll be my
Instrumental
you go my heart will
Bb Eb Bb Eb Bb Eb
last love. I will nev - er make you blue.
fol - low. I love you so.
Bb F7
I'll be true to you. In this
I'll be true to you. Take my

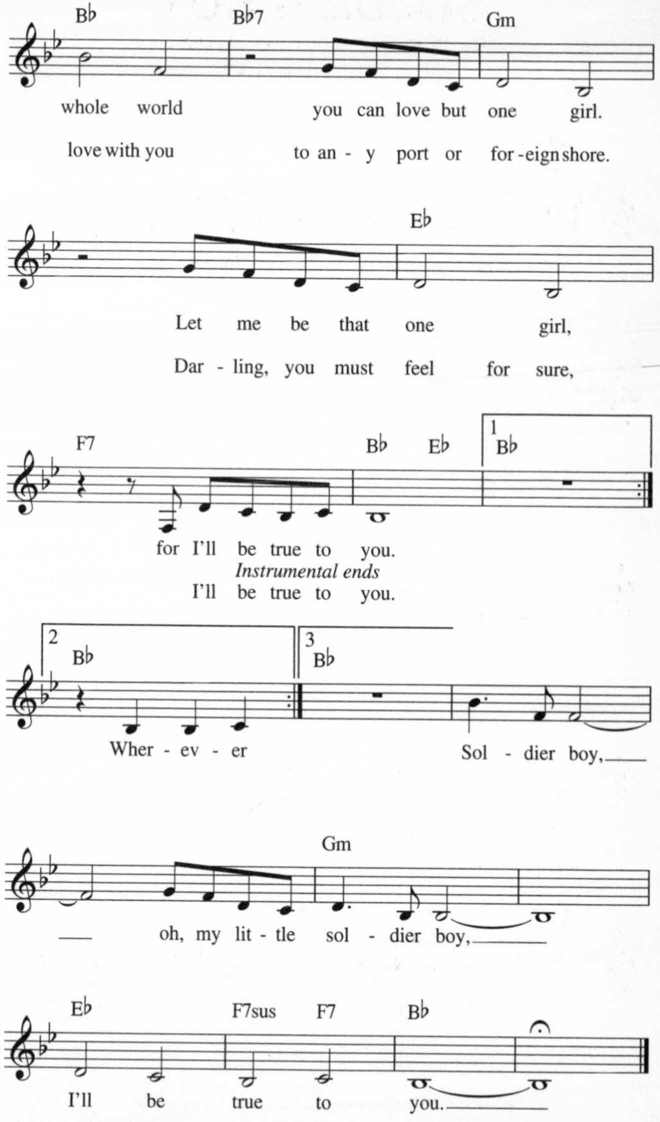
B♭ B♭7 Gm
whole world you can love but one girl.
love with you to an - y port or for - eign shore.
E♭
Let me be that one girl,
Dar - ling, you must feel for sure,
F7 B♭ E♭ 1 B♭
for I'll be true to you.
Instrumental ends
I'll be true to you.
2 B♭ 3 B♭
Wher - ev - er Sol - dier boy,
Gm
oh, my lit - tle sol - dier boy,
E♭ F7sus F7 B♭
I'll be true to you.

SOUL MAN

Words and Music by ISAAC HAYES
and DAVID PORTER

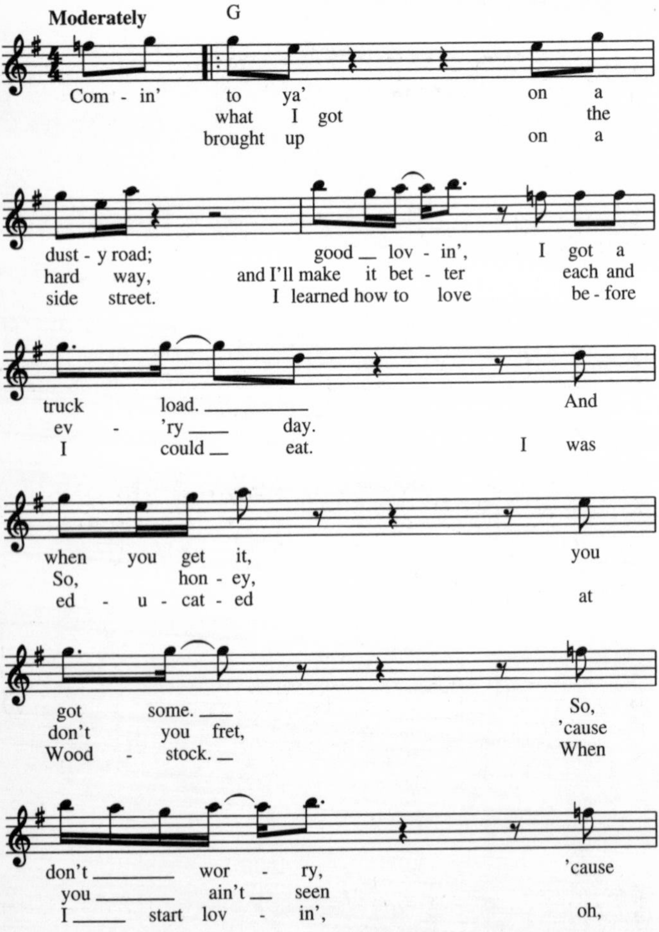
Moderately
G
Com - in' to ya' on a
what I got the
brought up on a
dust - y road; good __ lov - in', I got a
hard way, and I'll make it bet - ter each and
side street. I learned how to love be - fore
truck load. ___ And
ev - 'ry ___ day.
I could __ eat. I was
when you get it, you
So, hon - ey,
ed - u - cat - ed at
got some. ___ So,
don't you fret, 'cause
Wood - stock. __ When
don't ___ wor - ry, 'cause
you ___ ain't __ seen
I ___ start lov - in', oh,

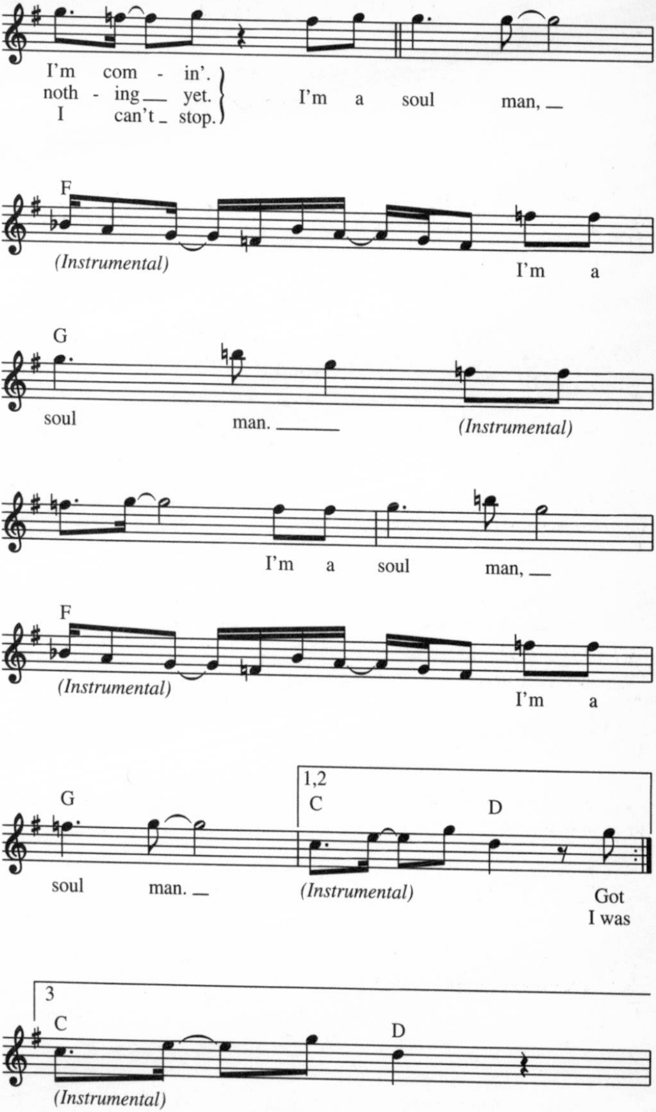
I'm com - in'.
noth - ing yet.
I can't stop.
I'm a soul man,
F
(Instrumental)
I'm a
G
soul man.
(Instrumental)
I'm a soul man,
F
(Instrumental)
I'm a
G
soul man.
1,2
C
D
(Instrumental)
Got
I was
3
C
D
(Instrumental)

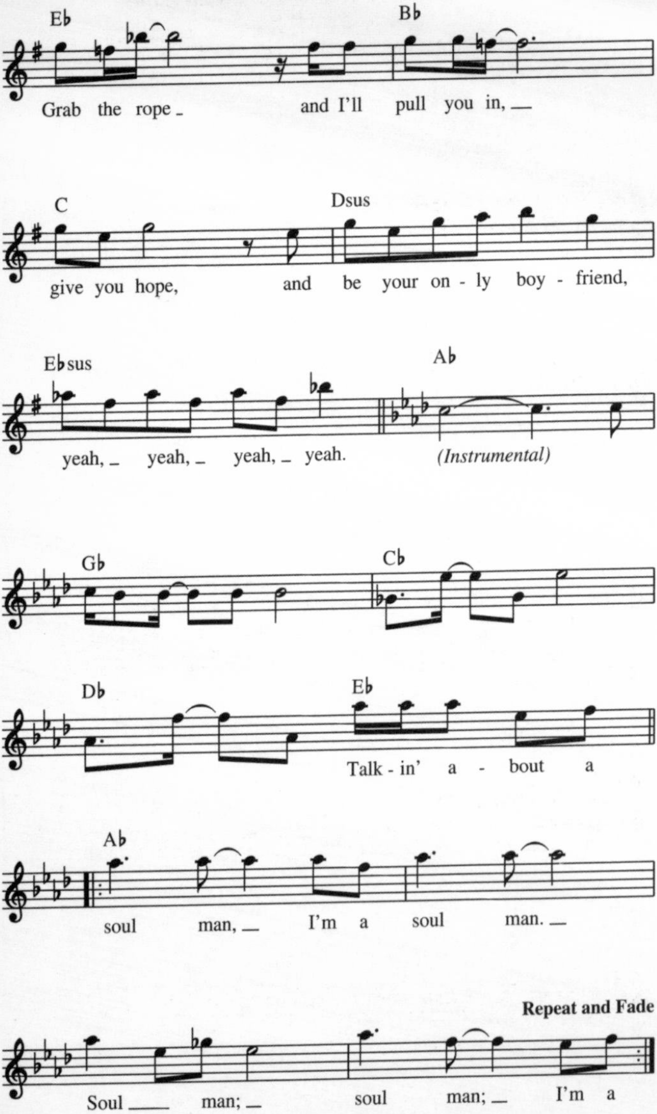
Eb
Bb
Grab the rope and I'll pull you in,
C
Dsus
give you hope, and be your on - ly boy - friend,
Ebsus
Ab
yeah, yeah, yeah, yeah.
(Instrumental)
Gb
Cb
Db
Eb
Talk - in' a - bout a
Ab
soul man, I'm a soul man.
Repeat and Fade
Soul man; soul man; I'm a

SPINNING WHEEL

Words and Music by
DAVID CLAYTON THOMAS

Funky, moderate Rock

E7#9 A7 D7#9 G
What goes _ up must come _ down,
E7#9 A7 D7#9 G
Spin-ning Wheel got to go 'round. _
E7#9 A7 D7#9 G
Talk-in' 'bout your trou-bles, it's a cry - in' sin, _
D7 N.C. D7#9
Ride a paint-ed po - ny, let the Spin-ning Wheel _ spin.
E7#9 A7 D7#9 G
You got no mon - ey, you got no home, _

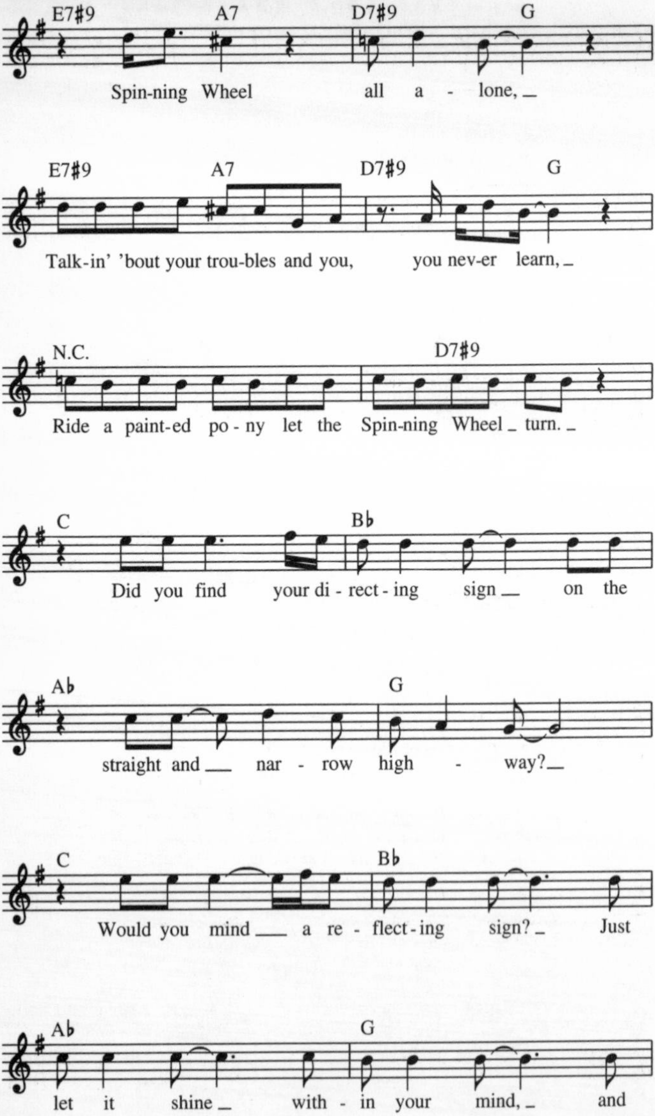
E7#9 A7 D7#9 G
Spin-ning Wheel all a - lone,
E7#9 A7 D7#9 G
Talk-in' 'bout your trou-bles and you, you nev-er learn,
N.C. D7#9
Ride a paint-ed po - ny let the Spin-ning Wheel turn.
C B♭
Did you find your di - rect - ing sign on the
A♭ G
straight and nar - row high - way?
C B♭
Would you mind a re - flect - ing sign? Just
A♭ G
let it shine with - in your mind, and

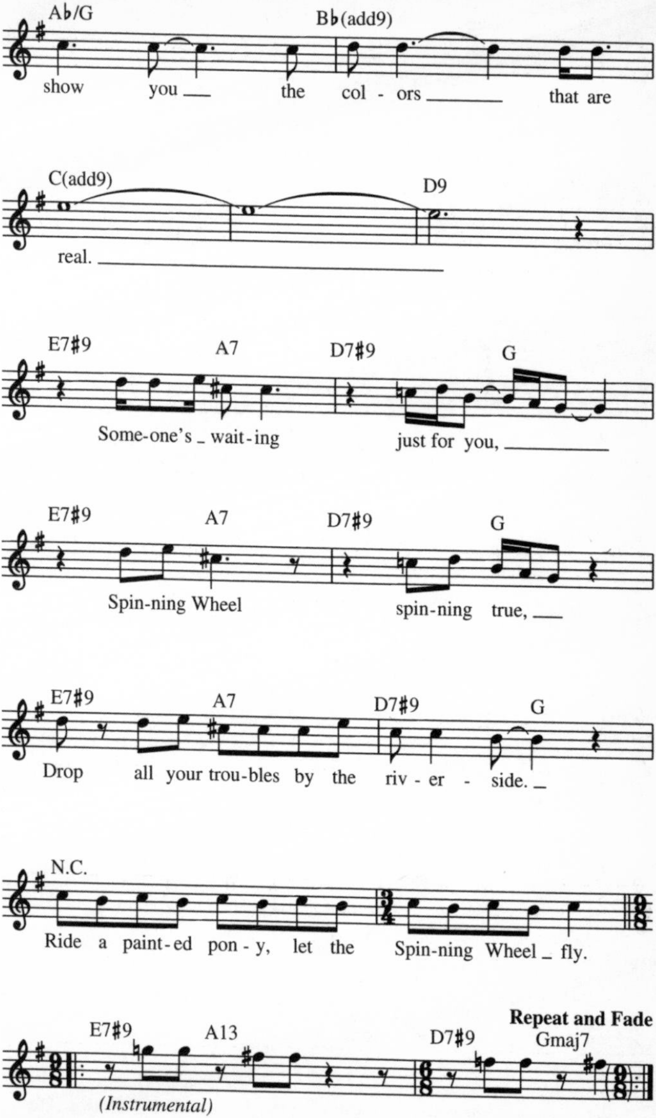
A♭/G
B♭(add9)
show you the col - ors that are
C(add9)
D9
real.
E7♯9
A7
D7♯9
G
Some-one's wait-ing just for you,
E7♯9
A7
D7♯9
G
Spin-ning Wheel spin-ning true,
E7♯9
A7
D7♯9
G
Drop all your trou-bles by the riv - er - side.
N.C.
Ride a paint-ed pon - y, let the Spin-ning Wheel fly.
Repeat and Fade
E7♯9
A13
D7♯9
Gmaj7
(Instrumental)

STAND BY ME

Words and Music by BEN E. KING,
JERRY LEIBER and MIKE STOLLER

Moderately, with a beat

F
When the night has come
sky that we look up-on
Dm C Dm
and the land is dark and the
should tum-ble and fall and the
B♭ C
moon is the on - ly light we
moun - tains should crum-ble in - to the
F
see, oh I won't be a - fraid
sea, I won't cry, I won't cry
Dm C
no I won't be a -
no I won't shed a
Dm B♭
fraid just as long as you
tear
C F
stand, stand by me. So

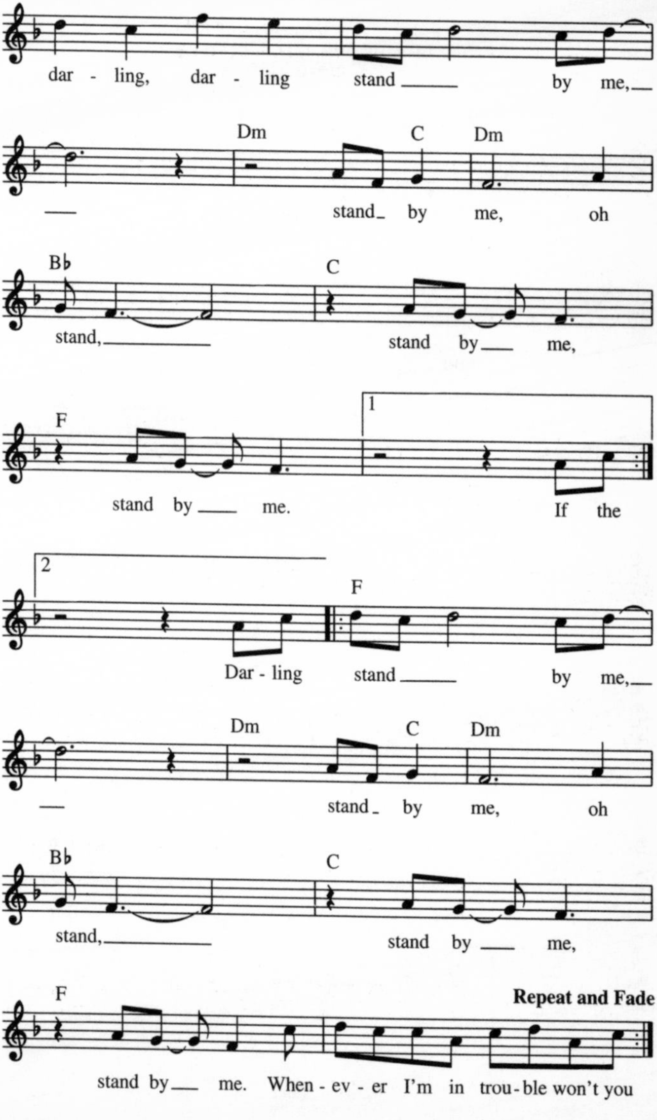
dar - ling, dar - ling stand by me,
Dm C Dm
stand by me, oh
B♭ C
stand, stand by me,
F
1
stand by me. If the
2
F
Dar - ling stand by me,
Dm C Dm
stand by me, oh
B♭ C
stand, stand by me,
F
Repeat and Fade
stand by me. When - ev - er I'm in trou - ble won't you

STAY

Words and Music by
MAURICE WILLIAMS

Moderately
B♭ Gm E♭ F7
Dance just a lit - tle bit
B♭ Gm E♭ F7
long - er,
B♭ Gm E♭ F7
Please, please, please, please tell me that you're
B♭ Gm E♭ F7
go - in' to. Now your
B♭ Gm E♭ F7
dad - dy don't mind, and your
B♭ Gm E♭ F7
mom - my don't mind, could we
B♭ Gm E♭ F7
have an - oth - er dance, dear. Just a - one more,

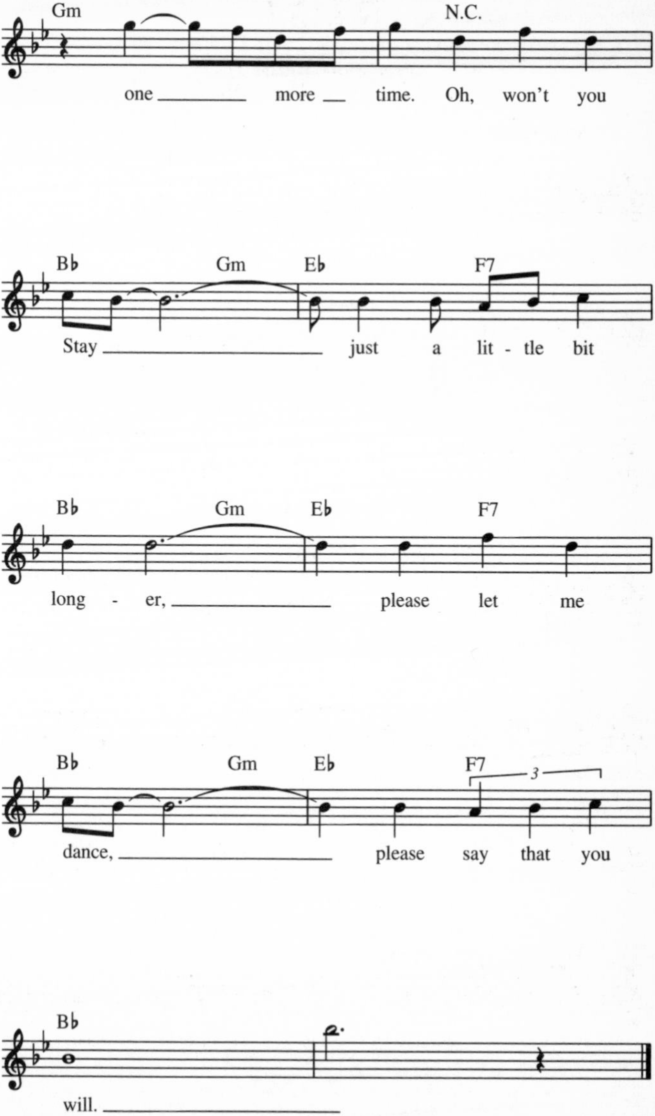
Gm
N.C.
one more time. Oh, won't you
B♭ Gm E♭ F7
Stay just a lit - tle bit
B♭ Gm E♭ F7
long - er, please let me
B♭ Gm E♭ F7
3
dance, please say that you
B♭
will.

SUGAR, SUGAR

Words and Music by ANDY KIM
and JEFF BARRY

Moderately
C F C
Sug - ar, ah, hon - ey, hon - ey,
F C F
you are my can - dy girl
G C F G
and you've got me want - ing you.
C F C
Hon - ey, ah, sug - ar, sug - ar,
F C F
you are my can - dy girl

G
C
and you've got me want-ing you.
F
C
I just can't be-lieve the love-li-ness of lov-ing you.
When I kissed you, girl, I knew how sweet a kiss could be. (I
F
C
(I just can't be-lieve it's true.)
know how sweet a kiss can be.)
F
C
I just can't be-lieve the one to love this feel-ing to.
Like the sum-mer sun-shine, pour your sweet-ness o-ver me.
1
F
G
G7
(I just can't be-lieve it's true.) Ah,

2
F G
Oh,
(Pour your sweet-ness o - ver me.)
C F
Pour a lit-tle sug - ar on it, hon - ey.
Sug - ar,
C F
Pour a lit - tle sug - ar on it, ba - by.
C F G7
I'm gon-na make your life so sweet, yeah, yeah, yeah.
1
C F G7
Pour a lit - tle sug - ar on it, yeah, yeah, yeah.
2
C
Pour a lit-tle sug - ar on it, hon - ey. Ah!

SURFIN' U.S.A.

Words and Music by
CHUCK BERRY

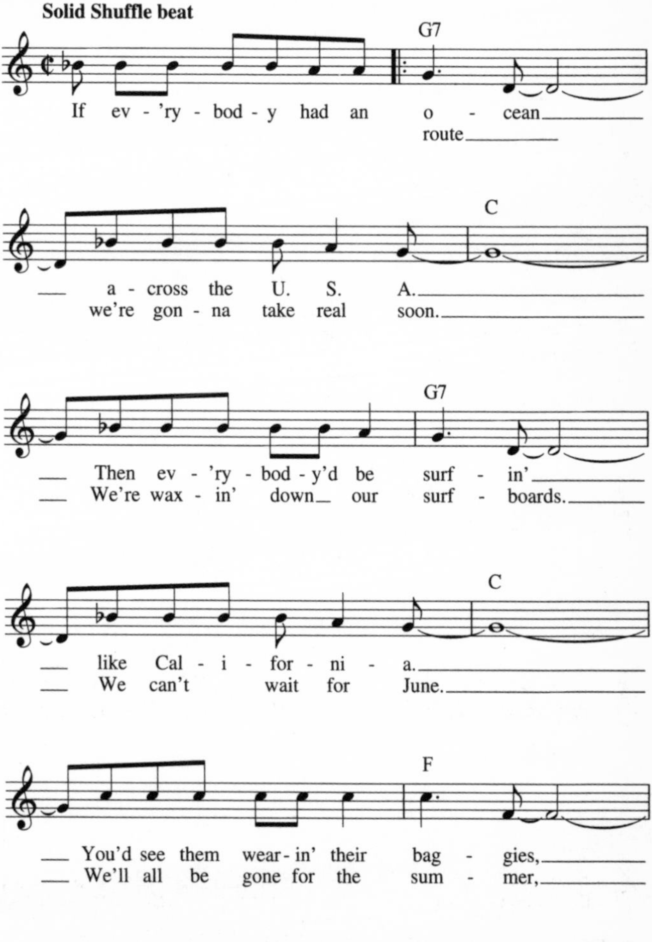
Solid Shuffle beat
G7
If ev - 'ry - bod - y had an o - cean
route
C
a - cross the U. S. A.
we're gon - na take real soon.
G7
Then ev - 'ry - bod - y'd be surf - in'
We're wax - in' down our surf - boards.
C
like Cal - i - for - ni - a.
We can't wait for June.
F
You'd see them wear - in' their bag - gies,
We'll all be gone for the sum - mer,

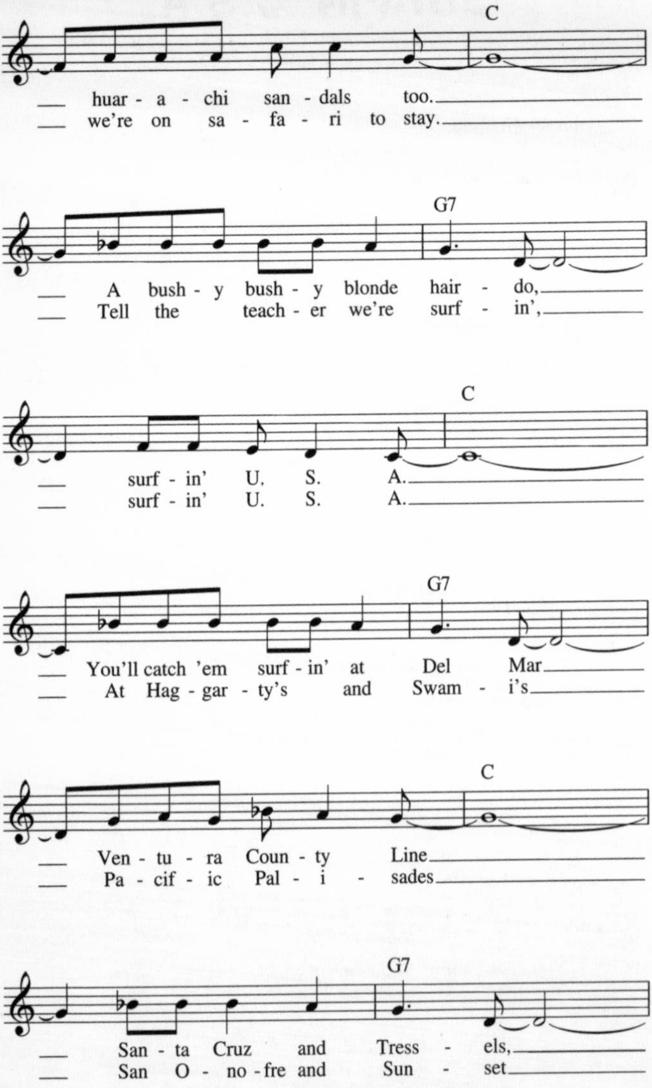
C
huar - a - chi san - dals too.
we're on sa - fa - ri to stay.
G7
A bush - y bush - y blonde hair - do,
Tell the teach - er we're surf - in',
C
surf - in' U. S. A.
surf - in' U. S. A.
G7
You'll catch 'em surf - in' at Del Mar
At Hag - gar - ty's and Swam - i's
C
Ven - tu - ra Coun - ty Line
Pa - cif - ic Pal - i - sades
G7
San - ta Cruz and Tress - els,
San O - no - fre and Sun - set

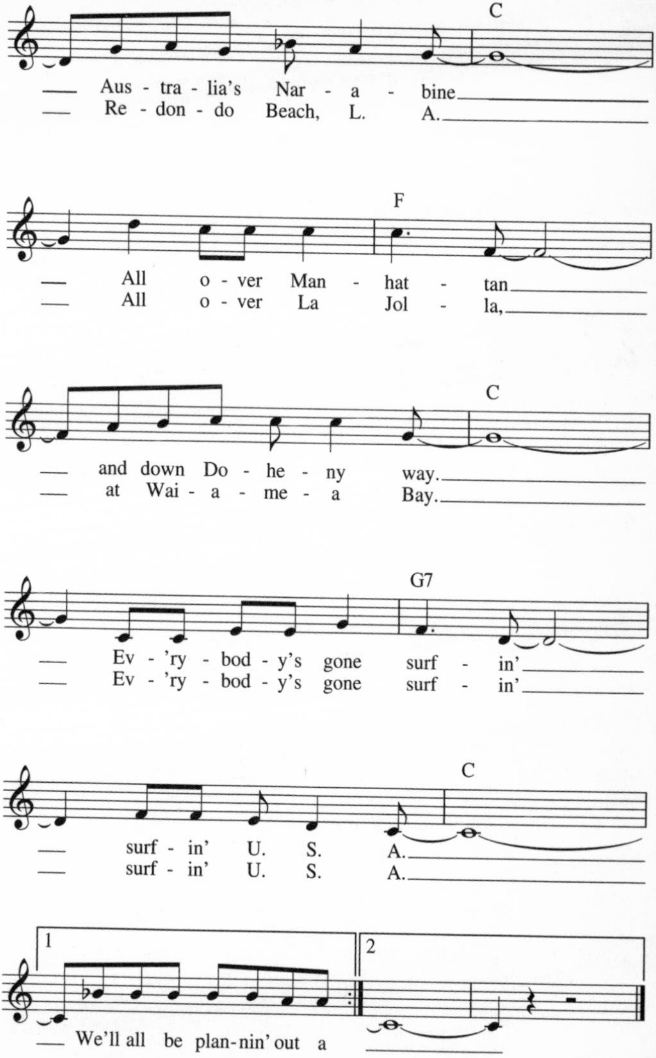
C
Aus - tra - lia's Nar - a - bine
Re - don - do Beach, L. A.
F
All o - ver Man - hat - tan
All o - ver La Jol - la,
C
and down Do - he - ny way.
at Wai - a - me - a Bay.
G7
Ev - 'ry - bod - y's gone surf - in'
Ev - 'ry - bod - y's gone surf - in'
C
surf - in' U. S. A.
surf - in' U. S. A.
1
We'll all be plan-nin' out a
2

SO NICE
(Summer Samba)

Original Words and Music by MARCOS VALLE and
PAULO SERGIO VALLE
English Words by NORMAN GIMBEL

Moderately
F
Some-one to hold me tight, that would be ver - y nice
Bm7 E7
some-one to love me right that would be ver - y nice.
B♭maj7 B♭6
Some-one to un-der-stand each lit-tle dream in me,
E♭9
some-one to take my hand, to be a team with me.
Am7 D7♭9 Gm7
So nice, life would be so nice
Em7♭5 A7♯5 Dm Dm7 G13
if one day I'd find some-one who would

Gm7
D7♭9
C9
take my hand and sam - ba thru life___ with me.
F
Some-one to cling to me, stay with me right_ or wrong,
Bm7
E7
some-one to sing to me some lit - tle sam - ba song.
B♭maj7
B♭6
Some-one to take my heart, then give his heart_ to me.
E♭9
Some-one who's read - y to give love a start_ with me.
Am7
D7♭9
Gm7
Oh, yes,___ that would be so nice.___
C7♭9
F
B♭9
— Should it be you and me, I could see it would be
1
F
Gm7
C7♭9
2
F6
nice.
nice.___

TEEN ANGEL

Words and Music by
JEAN SURREY

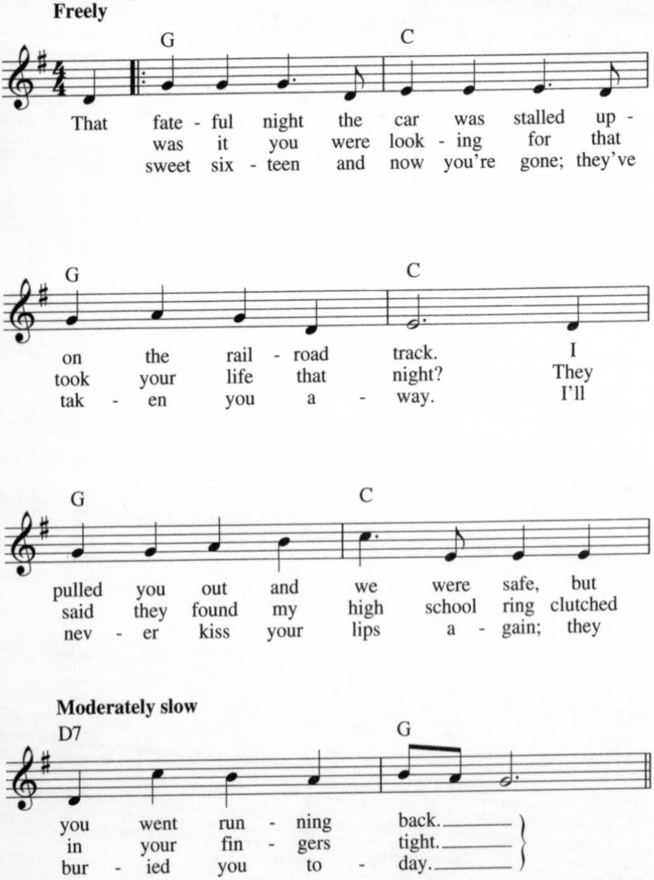
Freely
G
C
That fate - ful night the car was stalled up -
was it you were look - ing for that
sweet six - teen and now you're gone; they've
G
C
on the rail - road track. I
took your life that night? They
tak - en you a - way. I'll
G
C
pulled you out and we were safe, but
said they found my high school ring clutched
nev - er kiss your lips a - gain; they
Moderately slow
D7
G
you went run - ning back.
in your fin - gers tight.
bur - ied you to - day.

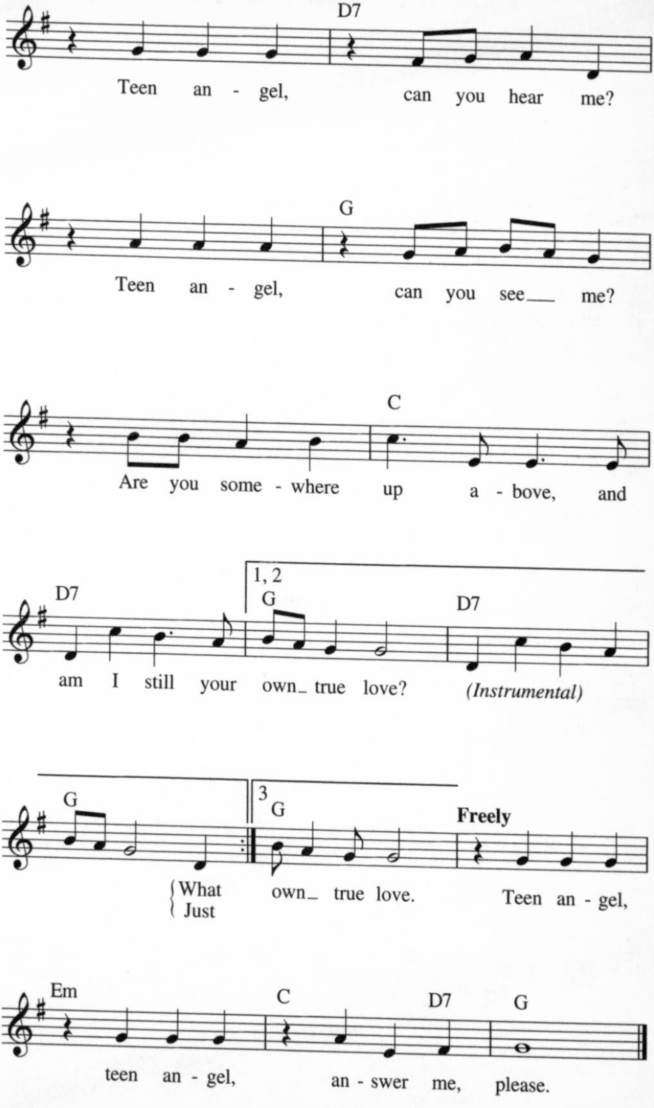
D7
Teen an - gel, can you hear me?
G
Teen an - gel, can you see me?
C
Are you some - where up a - bove, and
D7
1, 2
G
D7
am I still your own true love?
(Instrumental)
G
3
G
Freely
What
Just
own true love.
Teen an - gel,
Em
C
D7
G
teen an - gel, an - swer me, please.

TELL IT LIKE IT IS

Words and Music by GEORGE DAVIS
and LEE DIAMOND

Slow 4
Gm
If you want some-thing to
C7 F Fmaj7
play with go and find your-self a toy.
F6 D7 Gm
Ba-by my time is too ex-pen-sive,
C7 F Fmaj7
and I'm not a lit-tle boy.
F6 F Am Dm
If you are se-ri-ous,
Am Dm
don't play with my heart it makes me fu-ri-ous.
Am B♭
But if you want me to love you ba-by I

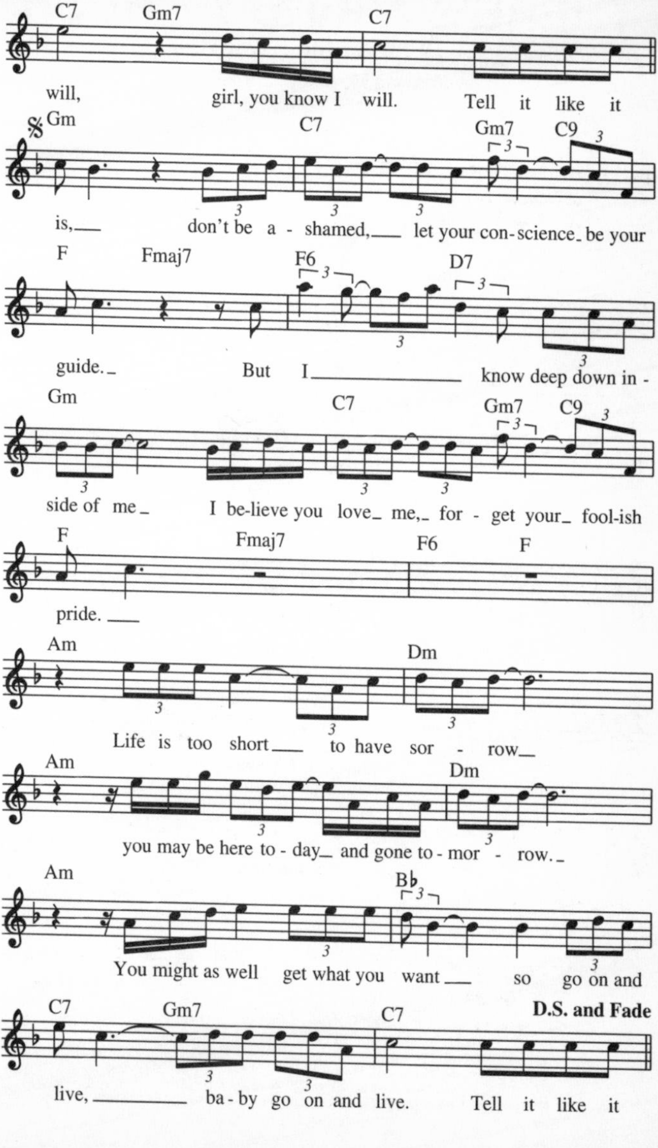
C7 Gm7 C7
will, girl, you know I will. Tell it like it
Gm C7 Gm7 C9
is,__ don't be a - shamed,__ let your con-science_ be your
F Fmaj7 F6 D7
guide._ But I__________ know deep down in -
Gm C7 Gm7 C9
side of me_ I be-lieve you love_ me,_ for - get your_ fool-ish
F Fmaj7 F6 F
pride.___
Am Dm
Life is too short___ to have sor - row_
Am Dm
you may be here to - day_ and gone to - mor - row._
Am B♭
You might as well get what you want___ so go on and
C7 Gm7 C7
D.S. and Fade
live,__________ ba - by go on and live. Tell it like it

THERE'S A KIND OF HUSH

(All Over the World)

Words and Music by LES REED
and GEOFF STEPHENS

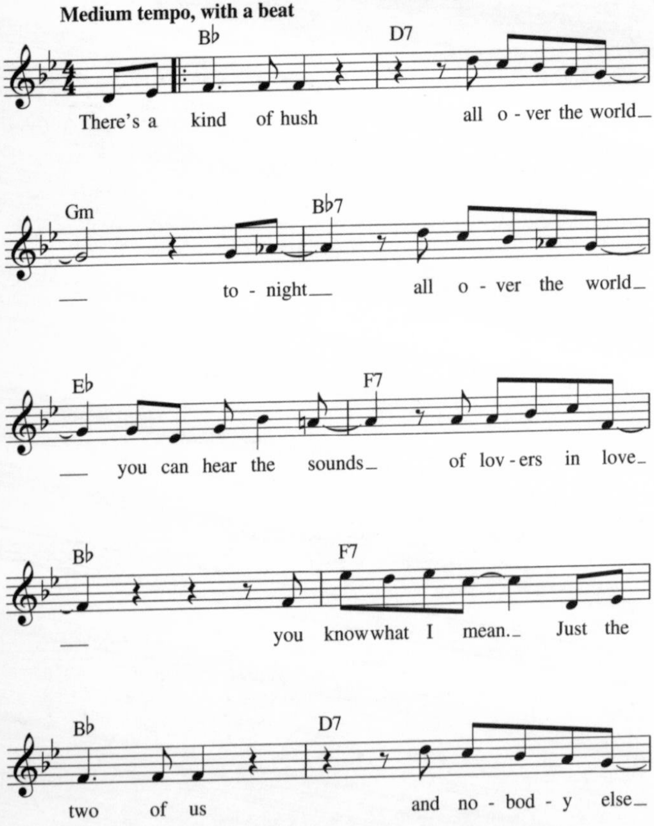
Medium tempo, with a beat
B♭ D7
There's a kind of hush all o - ver the world
Gm B♭7
to - night all o - ver the world
E♭ F7
you can hear the sounds of lov - ers in love
B♭ F7
you know what I mean. Just the
B♭ D7
two of us and no - bod - y else

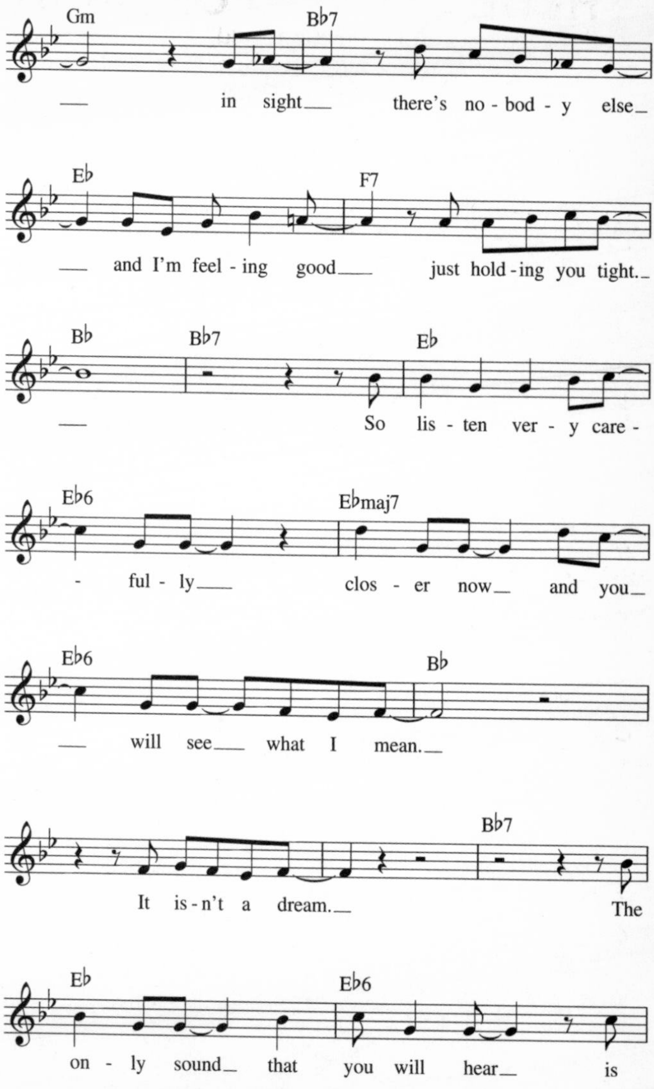
Gm
Bb7
— in sight__ there's no - bod - y else_
Eb
F7
— and I'm feel - ing good___ just hold - ing you tight._
Bb
Bb7
Eb
— So lis - ten ver - y care -
Eb6
Ebmaj7
- ful - ly__ clos - er now_ and you_
Eb6
Bb
— will see__ what I mean._
Bb7
It is - n't a dream._ The
Eb
Eb6
on - ly sound_ that you will hear_ is

Ebmaj7
Eb6
when I whis - per in your ear, I love you
F7
for - ev - er and ev - er.
Bb
D7
There's a kind of hush all o - ver the world
Gm
Bb7
to - night all o - ver the world
Eb
F7
you can hear the sounds of lov - ers in love.
1
Bb
F7
There's a
2
Bb Cm7/F Bb6

THINGS

Words and Music by
BOBBY DARIN

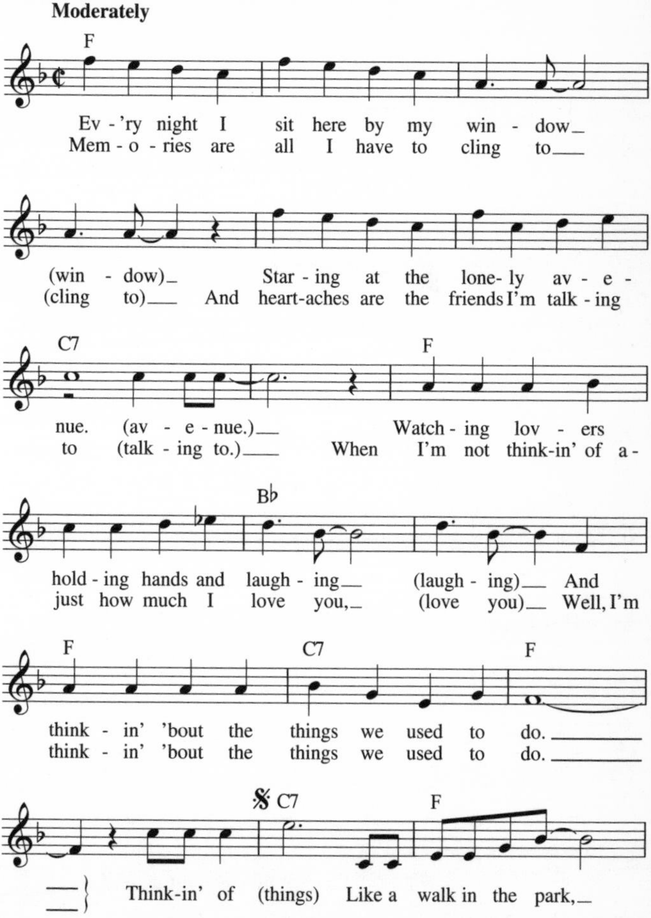
Moderately
F
Ev - 'ry night I sit here by my win - dow_
Mem - o - ries are all I have to cling to___
(win - dow)_ Star - ing at the lone- ly av - e -
(cling to)___ And heart-aches are the friends I'm talk - ing
C7
F
nue. (av - e - nue.)___ Watch - ing lov - ers
to (talk - ing to.)___ When I'm not think-in' of a -
B♭
hold - ing hands and laugh - ing__ (laugh - ing)___ And
just how much I love you,_ (love you)__ Well, I'm
F
C7
F
think - in' 'bout the things we used to do. ________
think - in' 'bout the things we used to do. ________
C7
F
Think-in' of (things) Like a walk in the park,_

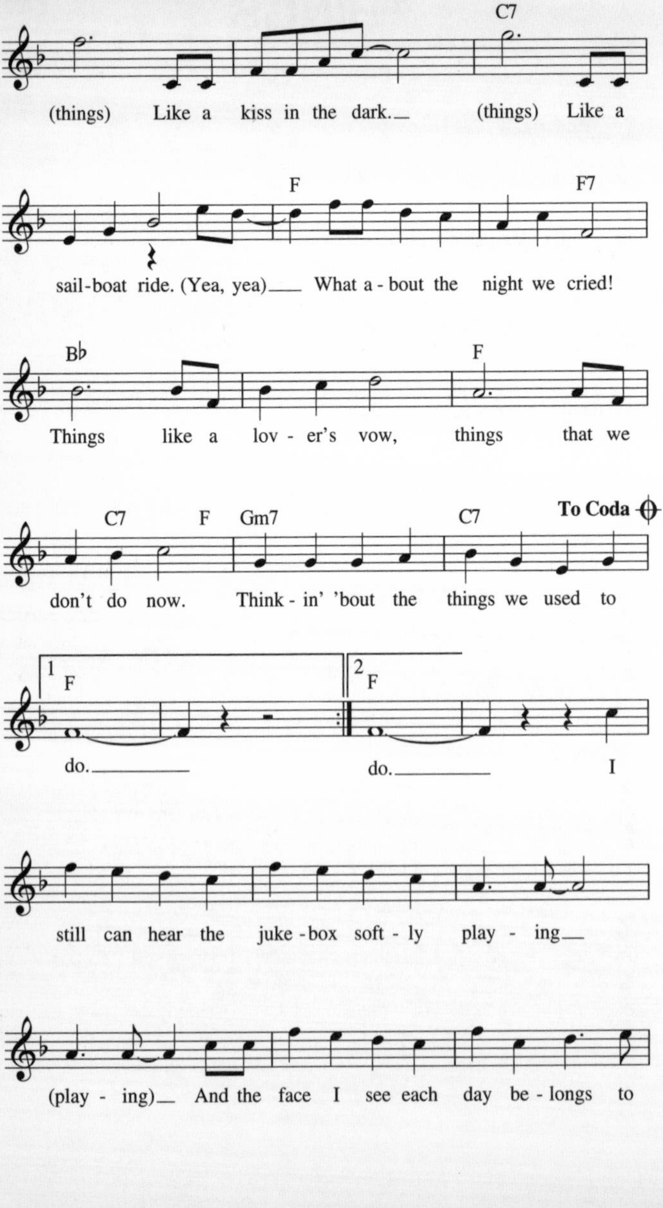
C7
(things) Like a kiss in the dark.
(things) Like a
F
F7
sail-boat ride. (Yea, yea)
What a-bout the night we cried!
B♭
F
Things like a lov-er's vow, things that we
C7
F
Gm7
C7
To Coda
don't do now. Think-in' 'bout the things we used to
1
F
2
F
do.
do.
I
still can hear the juke-box soft-ly play-ing
(play-ing)
And the face I see each day be-longs to

C7
F
you. (Be - longs to you.)___ Though there's not a sin - gle
B♭
sound and there's no - bod - y else a - round, Well, there's a -
F
C7
F
just me think - in' 'bout the things we used to do.___
D.S. al Coda
___ (Think-in' of
CODA
F
do.___ And the
Gm7
C7
F
heart - aches are the friends I'm talk - ing to.___
think - in' 'bout the things we used to do.___
Star - in' at the lone - ly av - e - nue.___
1
2
3
___ You got me ___ ___

THOSE WERE THE DAYS

Words and Music by
GENE RASKIN

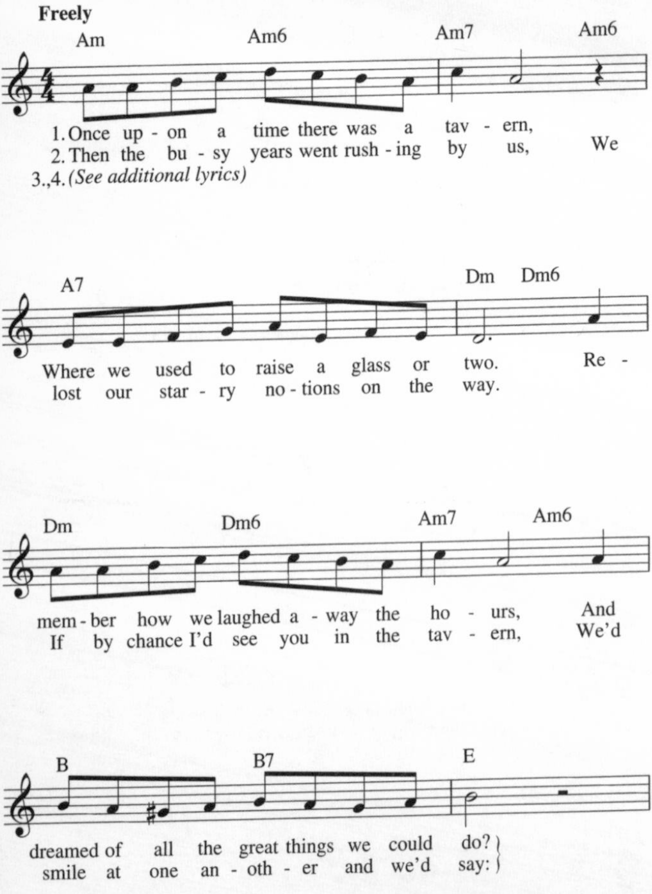
Freely
Am
Am6
Am7
Am6
1. Once up - on a time there was a tav - ern,
2. Then the bu - sy years went rush - ing by us, We
3.,4. (See additional lyrics)
A7
Dm
Dm6
Where we used to raise a glass or two. Re -
lost our star - ry no - tions on the way.
Dm
Dm6
Am7
Am6
mem - ber how we laughed a - way the ho - urs, And
If by chance I'd see you in the tav - ern, We'd
B
B7
E
dreamed of all the great things we could do?
smile at one an - oth - er and we'd say:

CHORUS

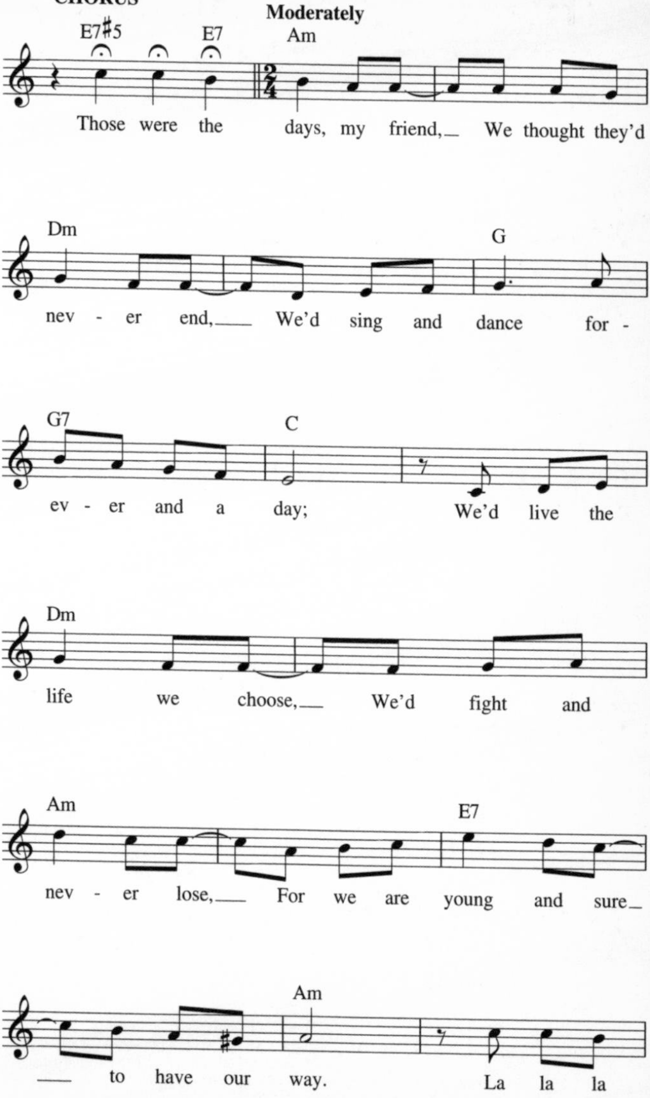
Moderately
E7♯5 E7 Am
Those were the days, my friend,_ We thought they'd
Dm G
nev - er end,___ We'd sing and dance for -
G7 C
ev - er and a day; We'd live the
Dm
life we choose,__ We'd fight and
Am E7
nev - er lose,___ For we are young and sure_
Am
___ to have our way. La la la

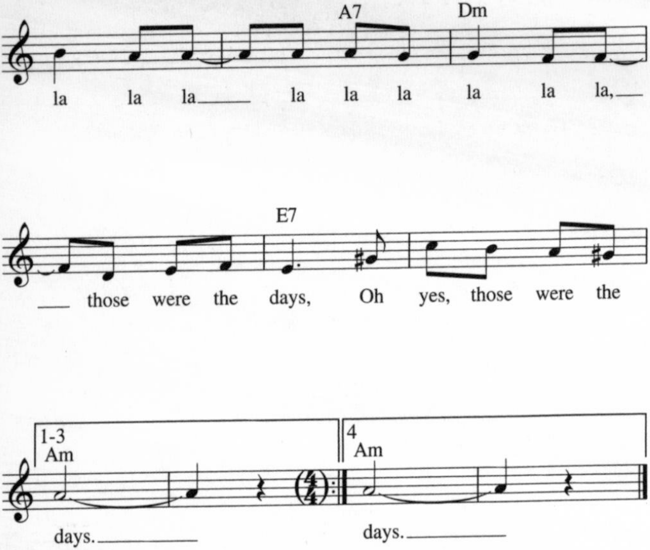
A7
Dm
la la la___ la la la la la la,___
E7
___ those were the days, Oh yes, those were the
1-3
Am
days.______
4
Am
days.______

Additional Lyrics

3. Just tonight I stood before the tavern,
   Nothing seemed the way it used to be.
   In the glass I saw a strange reflection.
   Was that lonely fellow really me?
   Chorus

4. Through the door there came familiar laughter,
   I saw your face and heard you call my name.
   Oh, my friend, we're older but no wiser,
   For in our hearts the dreams are still the same.
   Chorus

A TIME FOR US

(Love Theme)

from the Paramount Picture ROMEO AND JULIET

Words by LARRY KUSIK and EDDIE SNYDER
Music by NINO ROTA

Slowly and expressively
Dm/F
A Time For Us some - day there'll
Eb Bb/D
be when chains are torn by cour - age
Cm Gm
born of a love that's free. A time when
Dm/F Eb
dreams so long de - nied can
Cm Dm
flour - ish as
Gm Dm
we un - veil the love we now must

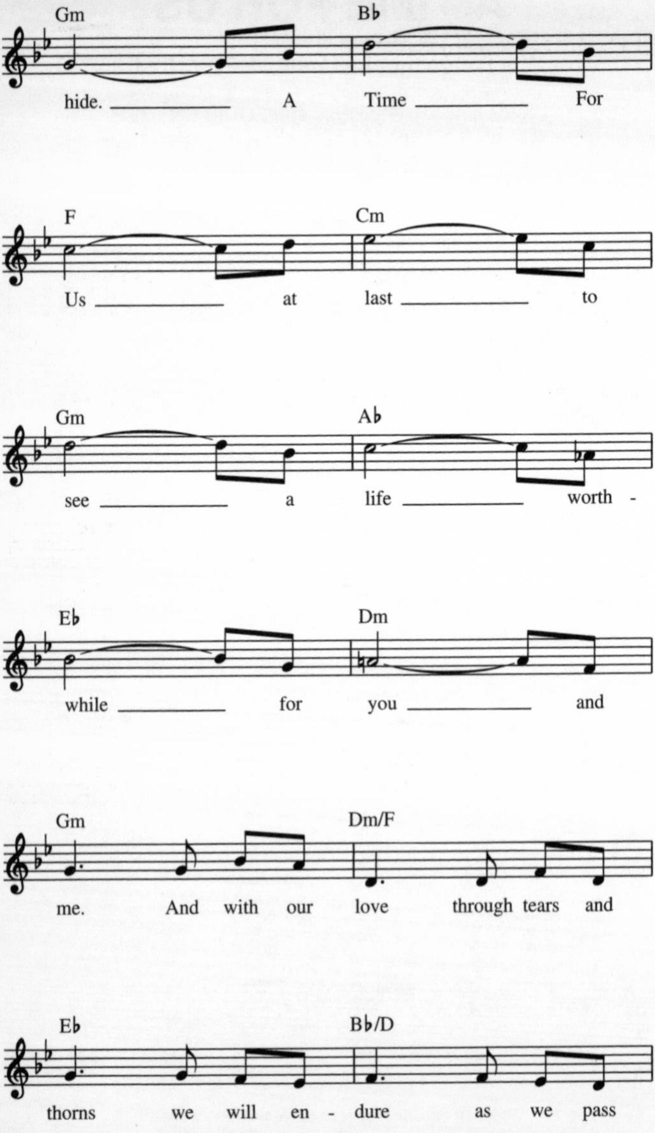
Gm
B♭
hide. A Time For
F
Cm
Us at last to
Gm
A♭
see a life worth -
E♭
Dm
while for you and
Gm
Dm/F
me. And with our love through tears and
E♭
B♭/D
thorns we will en - dure as we pass

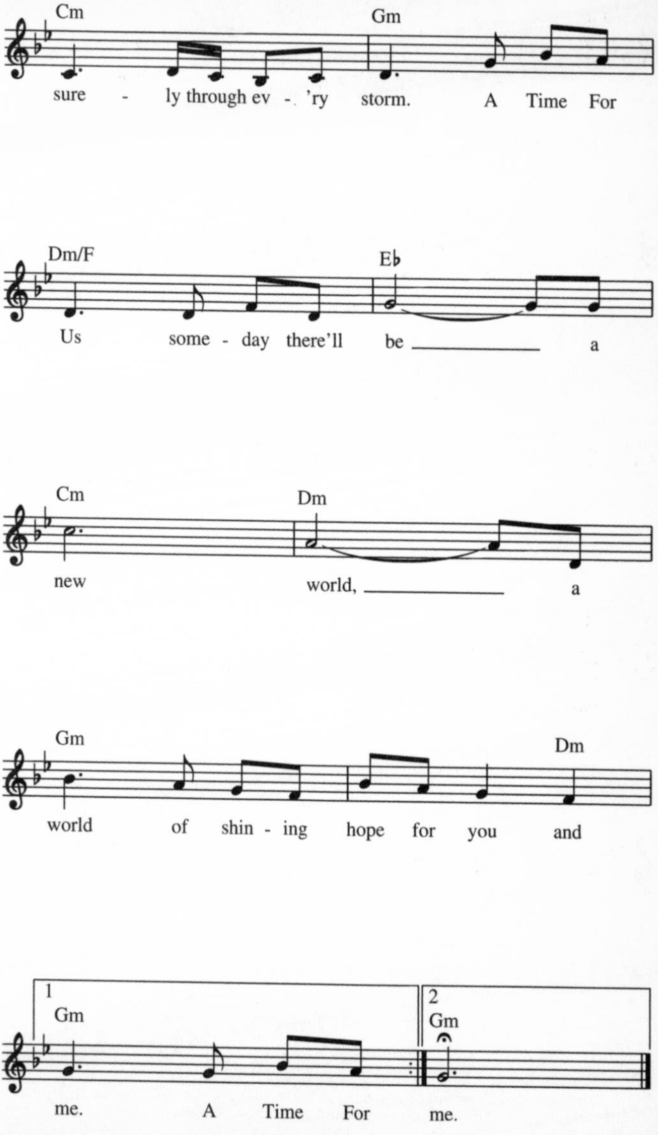
Cm
Gm
sure - ly through ev - 'ry storm. A Time For
Dm/F
E♭
Us some - day there'll be a
Cm
Dm
new world, a
Gm
Dm
world of shin - ing hope for you and
1
Gm
2
Gm
me. A Time For me.

TRAVELIN' MAN

Words and Music by
JERRY FULLER

Moderate Rock

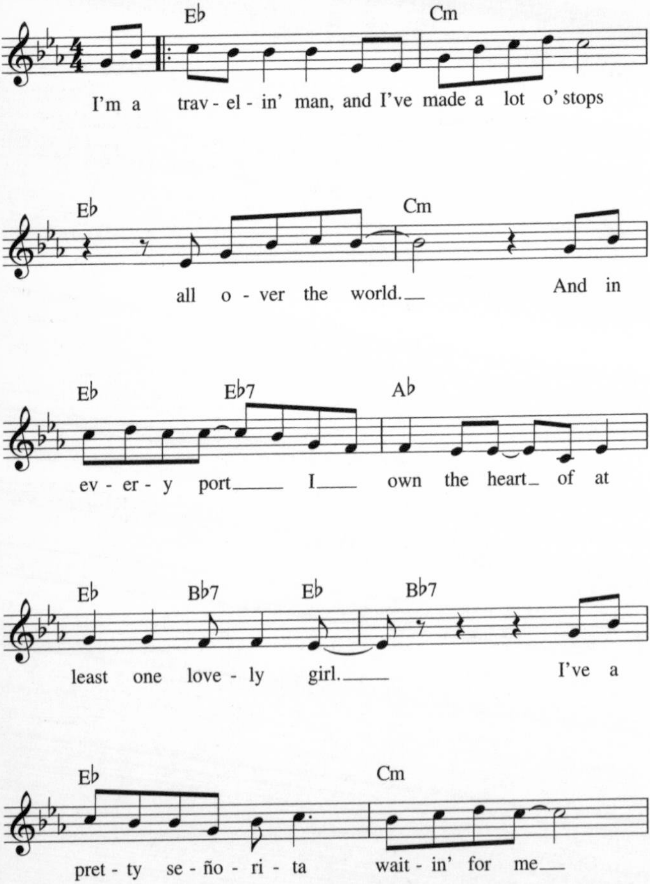
Eb Cm
I'm a trav - el - in' man, and I've made a lot o' stops
Eb Cm
all o - ver the world.__ And in
Eb Eb7 Ab
ev - er - y port____ I____ own the heart_ of at
Eb Bb7 Eb Bb7
least one love - ly girl.____ I've a
Eb Cm
pret - ty se - ño - ri - ta wait - in' for me___

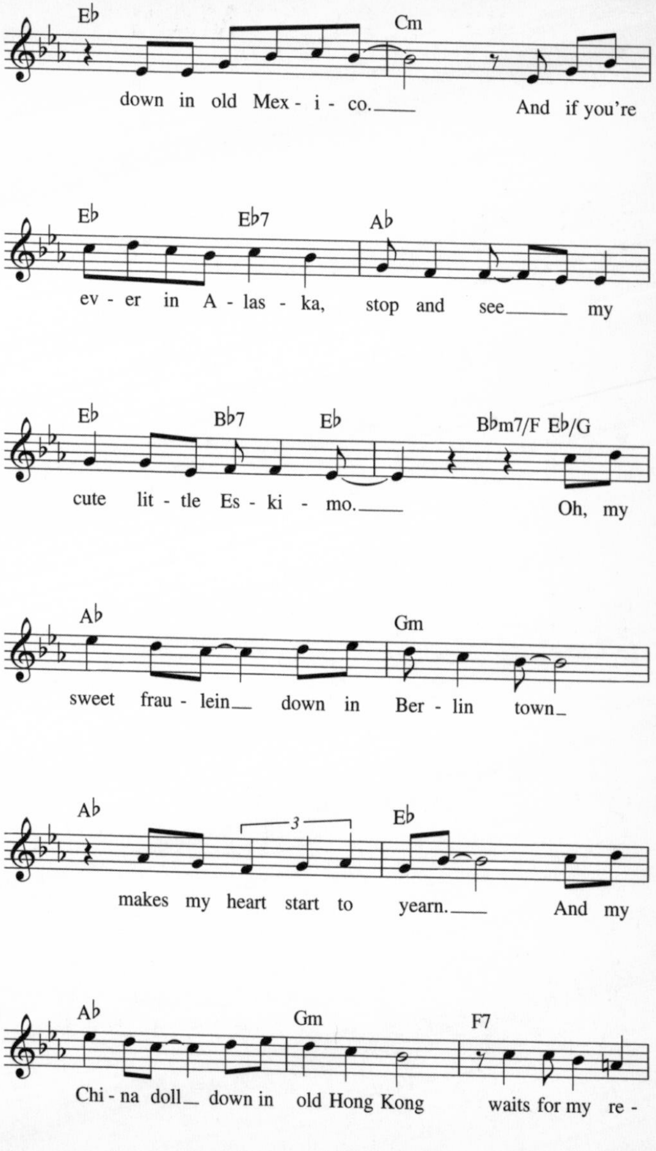
E♭ Cm
down in old Mex - i - co. And if you're
E♭ E♭7 A♭
ev - er in A - las - ka, stop and see my
E♭ B♭7 E♭ B♭m7/F E♭/G
cute lit - tle Es - ki - mo. Oh, my
A♭ Gm
sweet frau - lein down in Ber - lin town
A♭ 3 E♭
makes my heart start to yearn. And my
A♭ Gm F7
Chi - na doll down in old Hong Kong waits for my re -

Bb7
Eb
turn. Pret - ty Pol - y - ne - sian ba - by
Cm
Eb
o - ver the sea,_ I re - mem - ber the night_
Cm
Eb
Eb7
_ when we walked on the sands of
Ab
Eb
Bb7
Eb
Wai - ki - ki_ and I held you oh, so tight._
1
Bb7
2
Bb7
_ I'm a _
Eb
Cm
Repeat and Fade
Oh,_
Yes,_
I'm a trav - el - in' man._

TWIST AND SHOUT

Words and Music by BERT RUSSELL
and PHIL MEDLEY

Moderately, with a beat
D
G
Well, shake it up, ba - by, now.
(Shake it up, ba -
A7
D
G
- by) Twist And Shout.
(Twist And Shout)
A7
D
G
Come on, come on, come on, come on, ba - by now,
(Come on, ba -
A7
D
G
Come on and work it on out.
- by)
(Work it on out)
A7
D
G
1. Well, work it on out,
(Work it on out)
2.,3. You know you twist, lit - tle girl,
(Twist lit - tle girl)

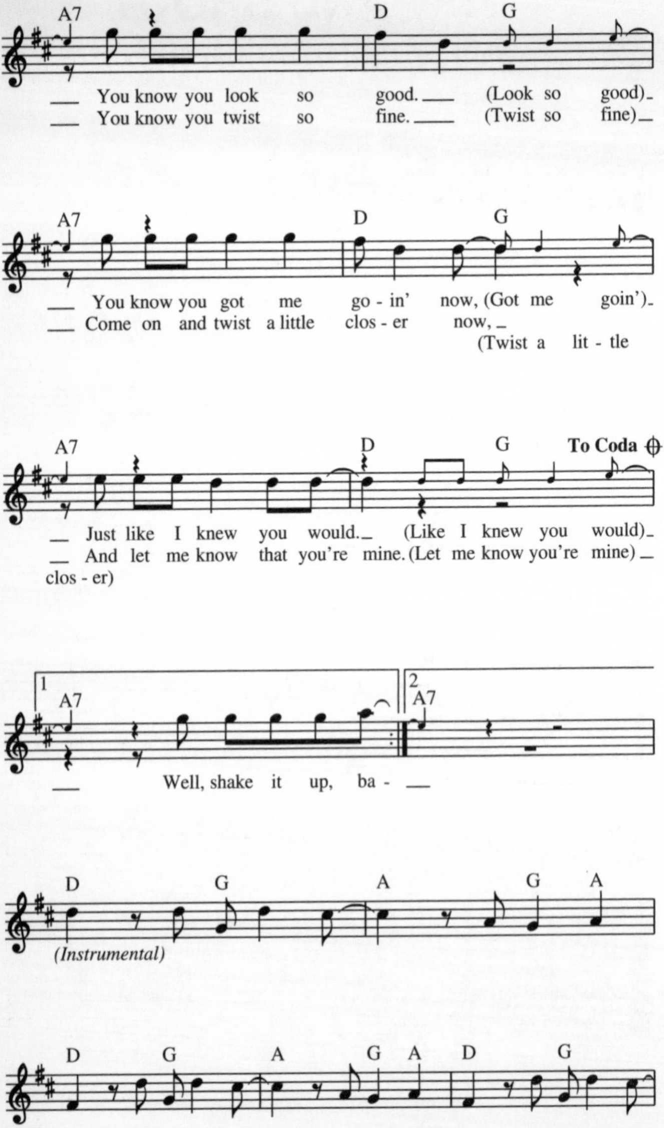
A7
D
G
— You know you look so good. — (Look so good) —
— You know you twist so fine. — (Twist so fine) —
A7
D
G
— You know you got me go - in' now, (Got me goin') —
— Come on and twist a little clos - er now, —
(Twist a lit - tle
A7
D
G
To Coda
— Just like I knew you would. — (Like I knew you would) —
— And let me know that you're mine. (Let me know you're mine) —
clos - er)
1
A7
— Well, shake it up, ba - —
2
A7
D
G
A
G
A
(Instrumental)
D
G
A
G
A
D
G

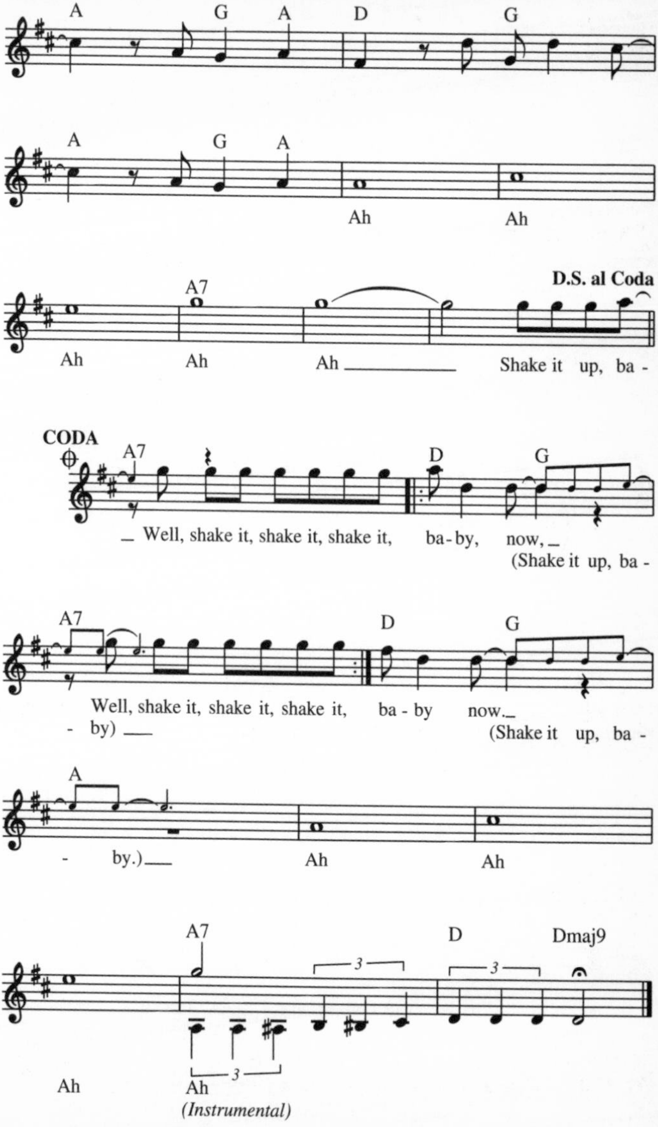
A G A D G
A G A
Ah Ah
D.S. al Coda
A7
Ah Ah Ah Shake it up, ba -
CODA
A7 D G
Well, shake it, shake it, shake it, ba-by, now,
(Shake it up, ba -
A7 D G
Well, shake it, shake it, shake it, ba - by now.
- by)
(Shake it up, ba -
A
- by.) Ah Ah
A7 D Dmaj9
3
Ah Ah
(Instrumental)

THE TWIST

Words and Music by
HANK BALLARD

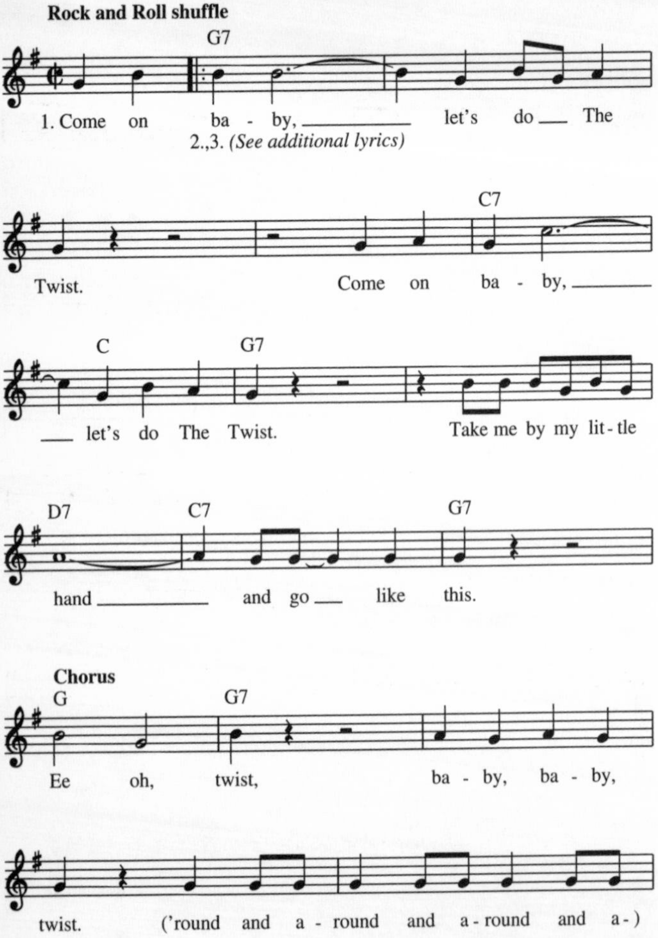
Rock and Roll shuffle
G7
1. Come on ba - by, let's do The
2.,3. (See additional lyrics)
C7
Twist. Come on ba - by,
C
G7
let's do The Twist. Take me by my lit - tle
D7
C7
G7
hand and go like this.
Chorus
G
G7
Ee oh, twist, ba - by, ba - by,
twist. ('round and a - round and a - round and a -)

C7 C
Just, just like
G7
this. ('round and a - round) Come on lit - tle
D7 C7
miss, and do The
1,2
G7
Twist. ('round and a - round) While dad - dy is
3
G7 C E♭7 D G9
Twist.

Additional Lyrics

2. While daddy is sleeping and mama ain't around.
   While daddy is sleeping and mama ain't around.
   We're gonna twisty, twisty, twisty until we tear the house down.
   Chorus

3. You should see my little sis.
   You should see my little sis.
   She knows how to rock and she knows how to twist.
   Chorus

UNDER THE BOARDWALK

Words and Music by ARTIE RESNICK
and KENNY YOUNG

Moderately, with a beat
G
Oh, when the sun beats down and burns the
park you hear the hap - py
Instrumental
D7
tar up - on the roof,
sound of a car - ou - sel,
and your
you can
shoes get so hot you wish your tired feet were fire -
al - most taste the hot - dogs and french fries
G
- proof.
they sell.
End instrumental
Un - der the board -
C
- walk,
down by the sea,
G
yeah,
on a

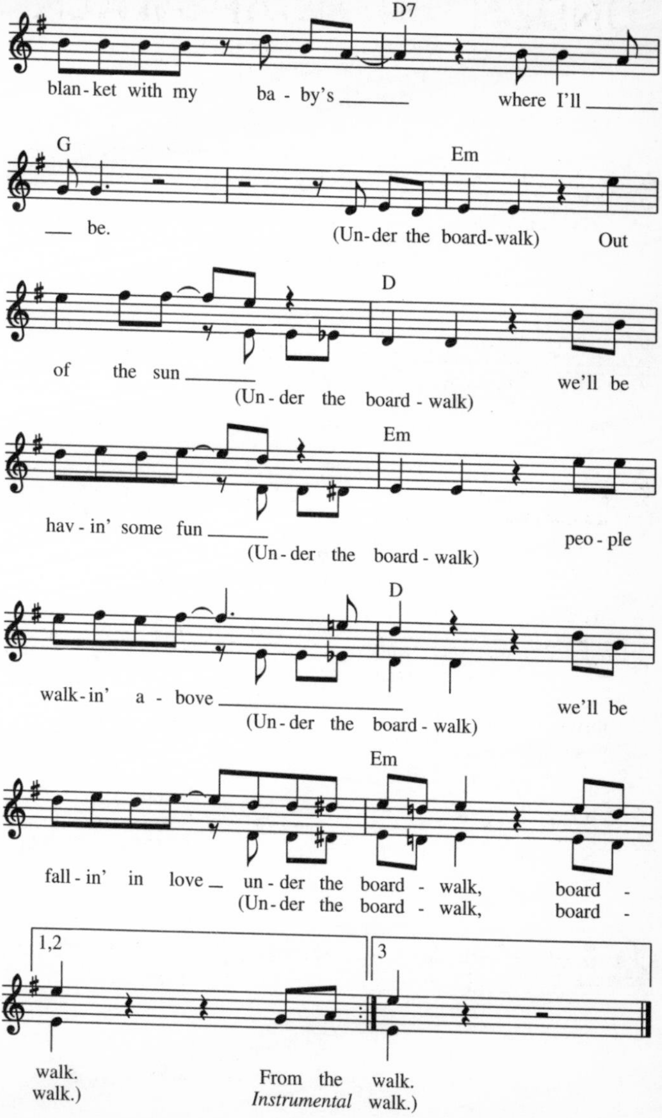
D7
blan-ket with my ba - by's ___ where I'll ___
G
___ be.
Em
(Un-der the board-walk) Out
of the sun ___
(Un - der the board - walk)
D
we'll be
hav - in' some fun ___
(Un - der the board - walk)
Em
peo - ple
walk-in' a - bove ___
(Un - der the board - walk)
D
we'll be
Em
fall - in' in love _ un - der the board - walk, board -
(Un - der the board - walk, board -
1,2
walk.
walk.)
From the
3
walk.
Instrumental
walk.)

UP, UP AND AWAY

Words and Music by
JIMMY WEBB

With a beat
G
Would you like to ride in my
world's a nic - er place in my
Love is wait - ing there in my
F
beau - ti - ful bal - loon?
beau - ti - ful bal - loon. It
beau - ti - ful bal - loon.
B♭
Would you like to glide in my
wears a nic - er face in my
Way up in the air in my
A♭
beau - ti - ful bal - loon? We could float
beau - ti - ful bal - loon. We can sing
beau - ti - ful bal - loon. If you'll hold
D♭ D♭maj7 D♭7
a - mong the stars to - geth - er
a song and sail a - long the
my hand we'll chase your dream a -

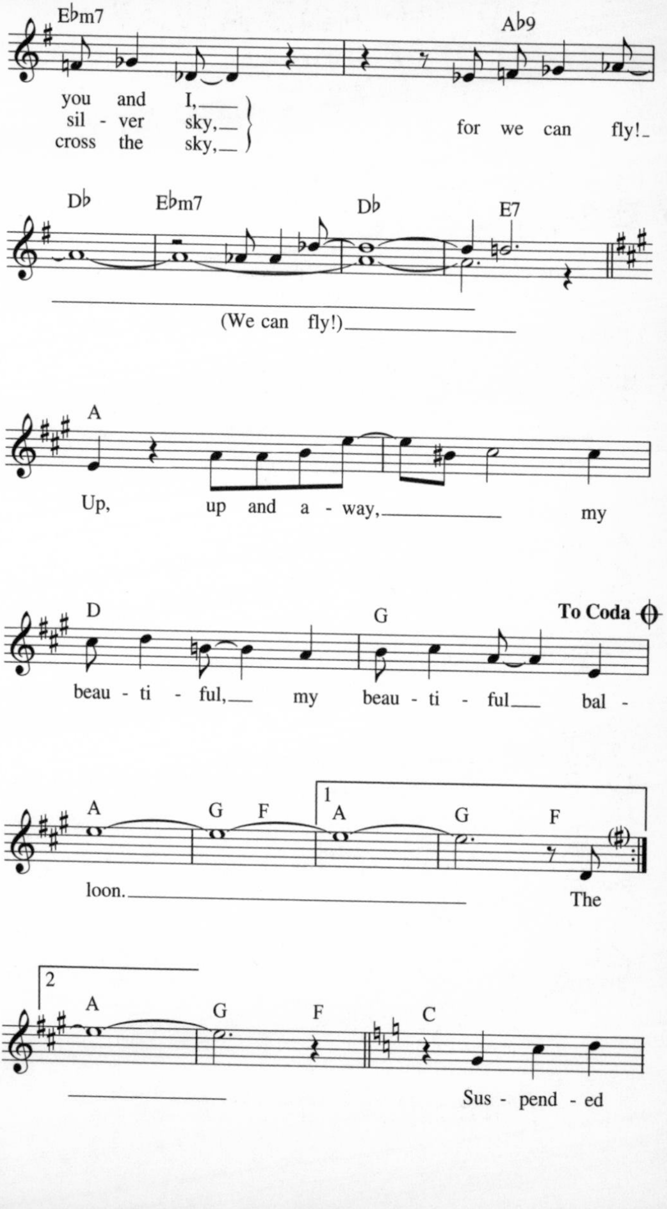
E♭m7
A♭9
you and I,
sil - ver sky,
cross the sky,
for we can fly!
D♭
E♭m7
D♭
E7
(We can fly!)
A
Up, up and a - way, my
D
G
To Coda
beau - ti - ful, my beau - ti - ful bal -
A
G
F
1
A
G
F
loon. The
2
A
G
F
C
Sus - pend - ed

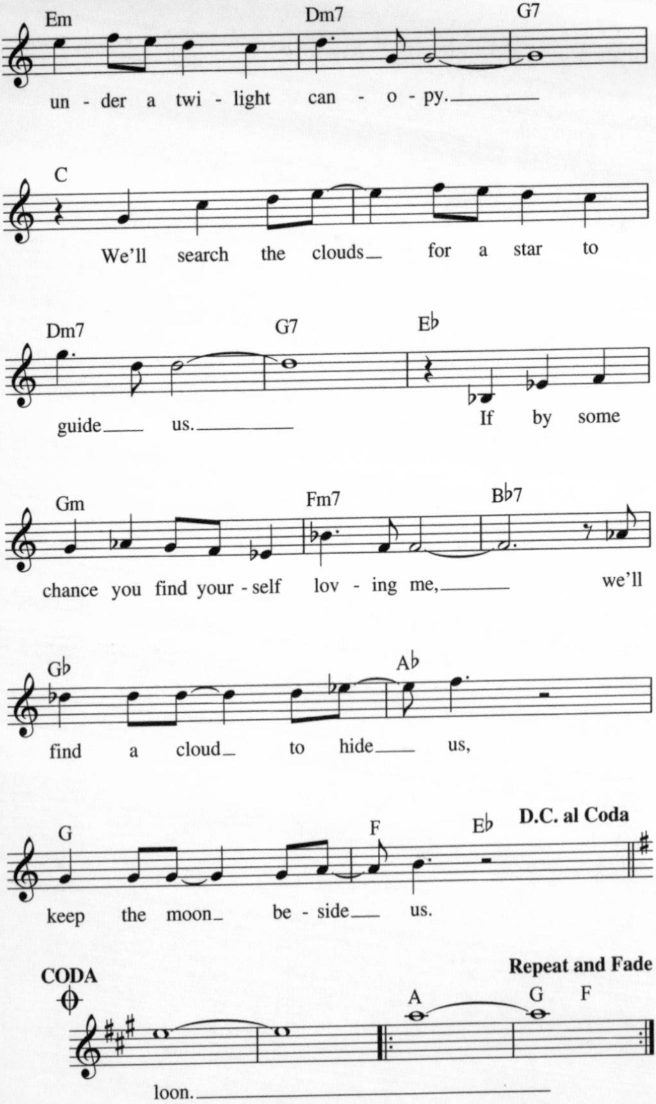
Em
Dm7
G7
un - der a twi - light can - o - py.
C
We'll search the clouds for a star to
Dm7
G7
E♭
guide us. If by some
Gm
Fm7
B♭7
chance you find your - self lov - ing me, we'll
G♭
A♭
find a cloud to hide us,
G
F
E♭
D.C. al Coda
keep the moon be - side us.
CODA
Repeat and Fade
A
G
F
loon.

WEDDING BELL BLUES

Words and Music by
LAURA NYRO

Moderately, with a beat

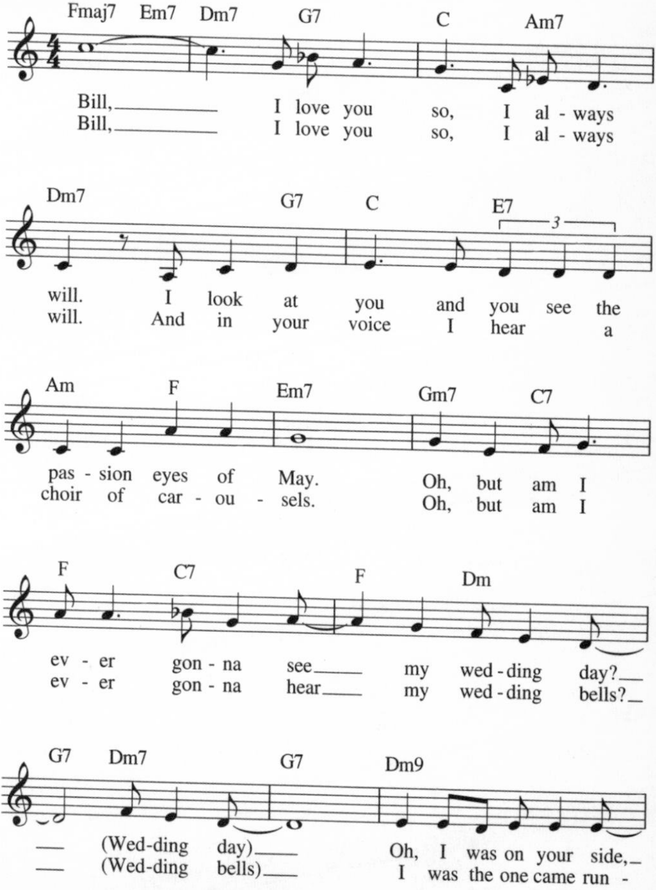
Fmaj7 Em7 Dm7 G7 C Am7
Bill, I love you so, I al - ways
Bill, I love you so, I al - ways
Dm7 G7 C E7
3
will. I look at you and you see the
will. And in your voice I hear a
Am F Em7 Gm7 C7
pas - sion eyes of May. Oh, but am I
choir of car - ou - sels. Oh, but am I
F C7 F Dm
ev - er gon - na see my wed - ding day?
ev - er gon - na hear my wed - ding bells?
G7 Dm7 G7 Dm9
(Wed-ding day) Oh, I was on your side,
(Wed-ding bells) I was the one came run -

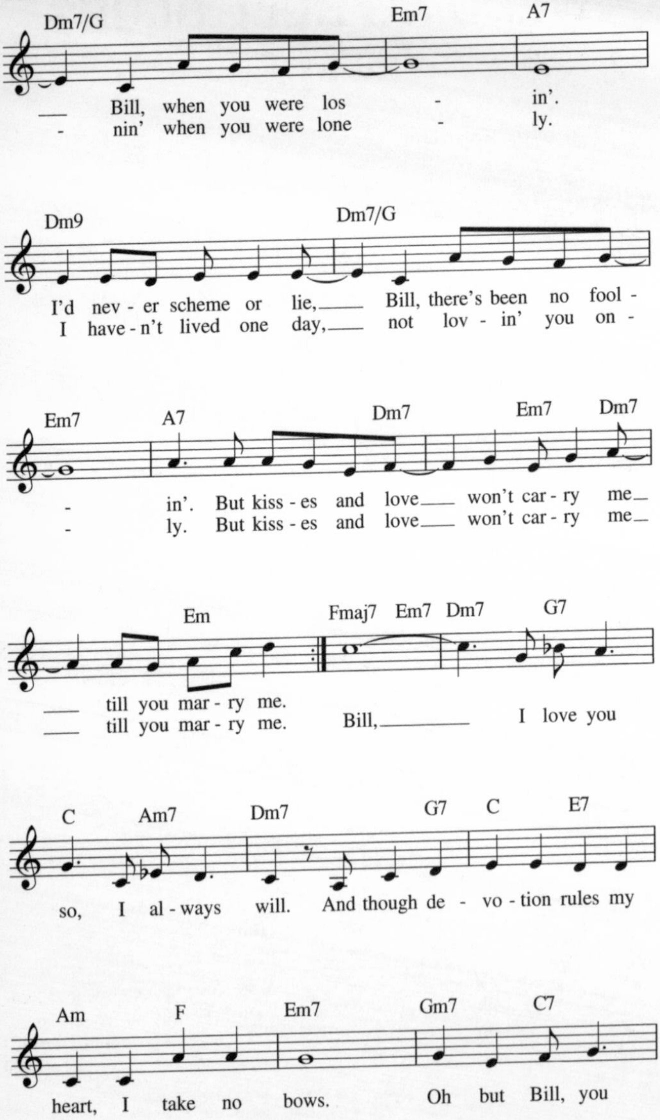
Dm7/G
Em7
A7
Bill, when you were los - in'.
- nin' when you were lone - ly.
Dm9
Dm7/G
I'd nev - er scheme or lie, Bill, there's been no fool -
I have - n't lived one day, not lov - in' you on -
Em7
A7
Dm7
Em7
Dm7
- in'. But kiss - es and love won't car - ry me
- ly. But kiss - es and love won't car - ry me
Em
Fmaj7
Em7
Dm7
G7
till you mar - ry me.
till you mar - ry me. Bill, I love you
C
Am7
Dm7
G7
C
E7
so, I al - ways will. And though de - vo - tion rules my
Am
F
Em7
Gm7
C7
heart, I take no bows. Oh but Bill, you

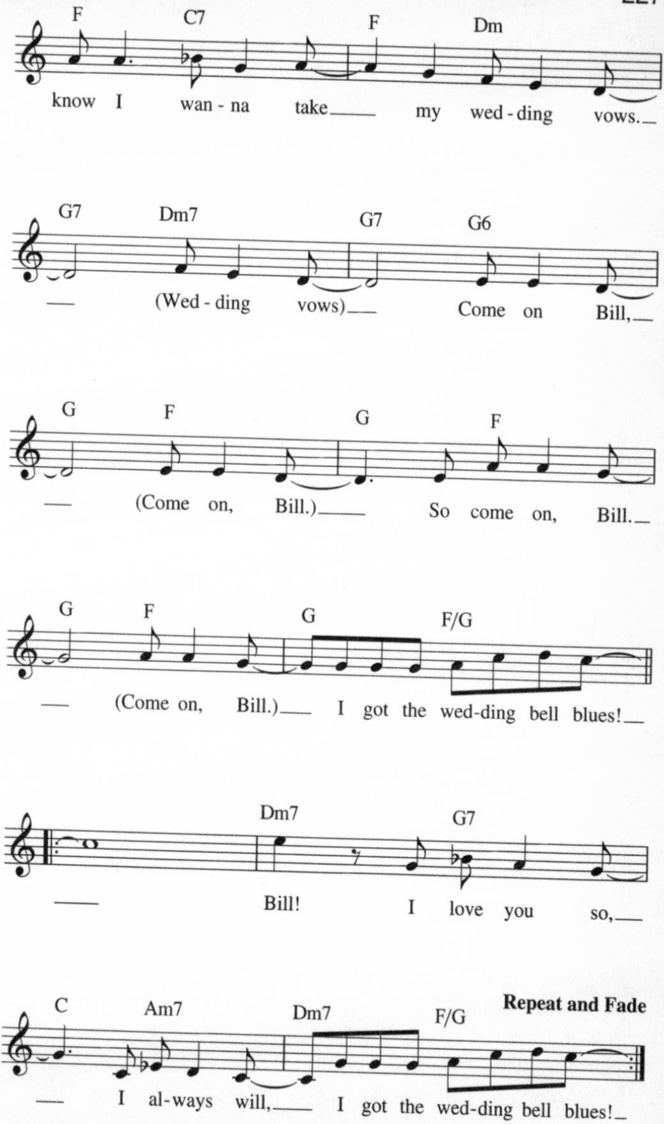
F C7 F Dm
know I wan - na take my wed - ding vows.
G7 Dm7 G7 G6
(Wed - ding vows) Come on Bill,
G F G F
(Come on, Bill.) So come on, Bill.
G F G F/G
(Come on, Bill.) I got the wed-ding bell blues!
Dm7 G7
Bill! I love you so,
C Am7 Dm7 F/G
Repeat and Fade
I al-ways will, I got the wed-ding bell blues!

WALK LIKE A MAN

Words and Music by BOB CREWE
and BOB GAUDIO

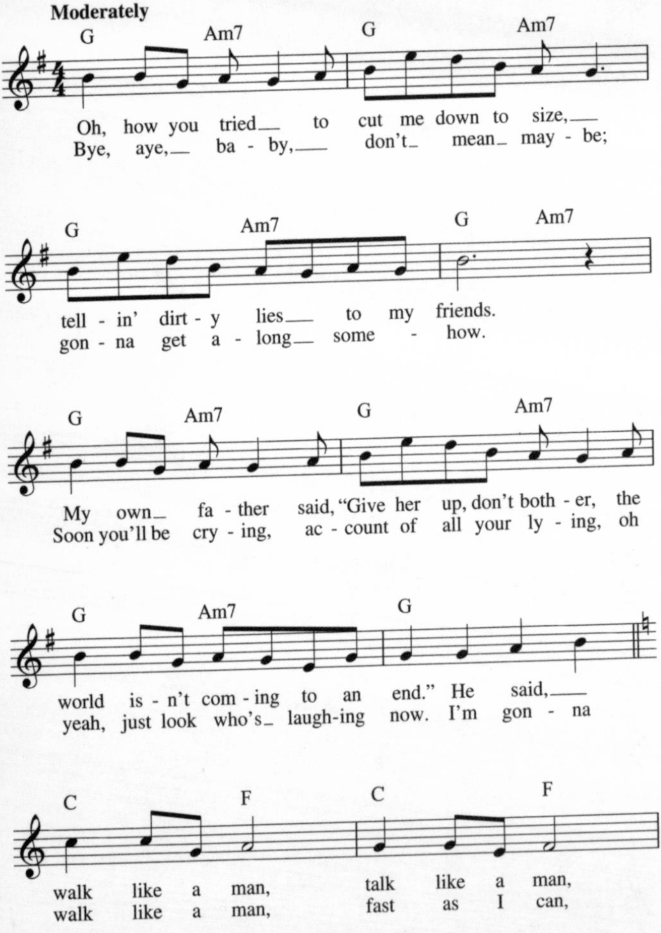
Moderately
G Am7 G Am7
Oh, how you tried to cut me down to size,
Bye, aye, ba - by, don't mean may - be;
G Am7 G Am7
tell - in' dirt - y lies to my friends.
gon - na get a - long some - how.
G Am7 G Am7
My own fa - ther said, "Give her up, don't both - er, the
Soon you'll be cry - ing, ac - count of all your ly - ing, oh
G Am7 G
world is - n't com - ing to an end." He said,
yeah, just look who's laugh-ing now. I'm gon - na
C F C F
walk like a man, talk like a man,
walk like a man, fast as I can,

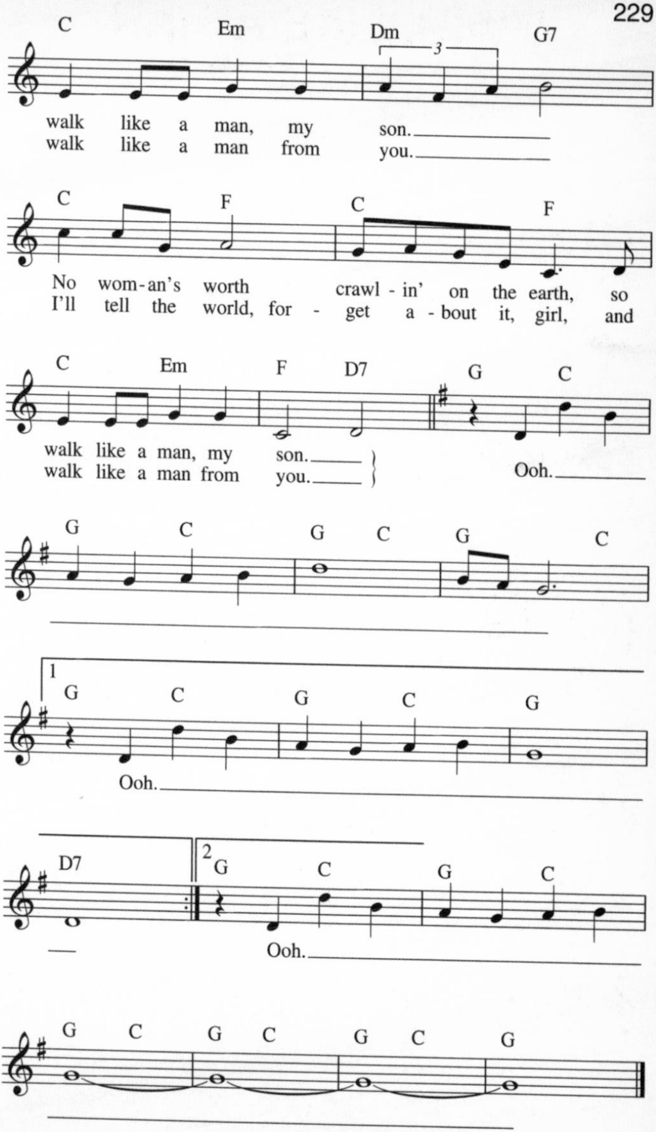
C Em Dm G7
3
walk like a man, my son.
walk like a man from you.
C F C F
No wom-an's worth crawl - in' on the earth, so
I'll tell the world, for - get a - bout it, girl, and
C Em F D7 G C
walk like a man, my son.
walk like a man from you.
Ooh.
G C G C G C
1
G C G C G
Ooh.
D7
2
G C G C
Ooh.
G C G C G C G

WALK RIGHT IN

Words and Music by GUS CANNON
and H. WOODS

Moderately
G
E7
Walk right in, set right down,
Walk right in, set right down,
A7
D7
G
dad - dy, let your mind roll on.
ba - by, let your hair hang down.
E7
Walk right in, set right down,
Walk right in, set right down,
A7
D7
dad - dy, let your mind roll on.
ba - by, let your hair hang down.

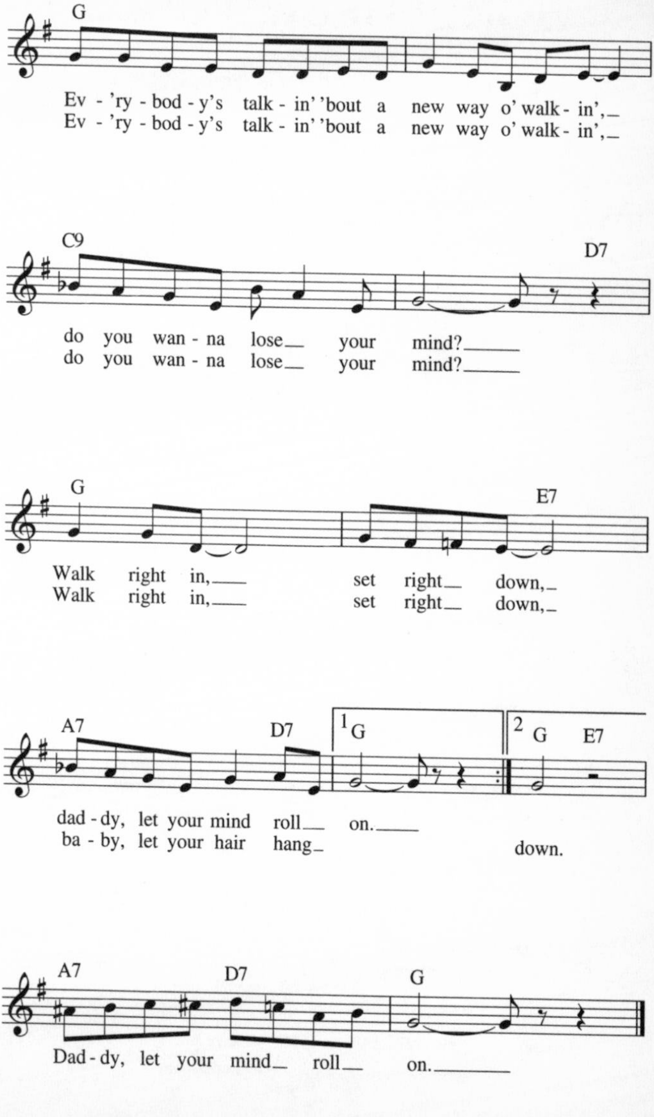
G
Ev - 'ry - bod - y's talk - in' 'bout a new way o' walk - in',
Ev - 'ry - bod - y's talk - in' 'bout a new way o' walk - in',
C9
D7
do you wan - na lose your mind?
do you wan - na lose your mind?
G
E7
Walk right in, set right down,
Walk right in, set right down,
A7
D7
1 G
2 G E7
dad - dy, let your mind roll on.
ba - by, let your hair hang down.
A7
D7
G
Dad - dy, let your mind roll on.

WHAT A WONDERFUL WORLD

Words and Music by GEORGE DAVID WEISS
and BOB THIELE

Slowly
F Am B♭ Am Gm7 F
I see trees of green, red ros-es too, I see them bloom
A7 Dm D♭
for me and you, and I think to my-self
C11 C7 F F+ B♭maj7 C7
What A Won-der-ful World. I see
F Am B♭ Am Gm7 F
skies of blue and clouds of white, the bright bless-ed day, the
A7 Dm D♭
dark sa-cred night, and I think to my-self
C11 C7 F B♭ F
What A Won-der-ful World. The

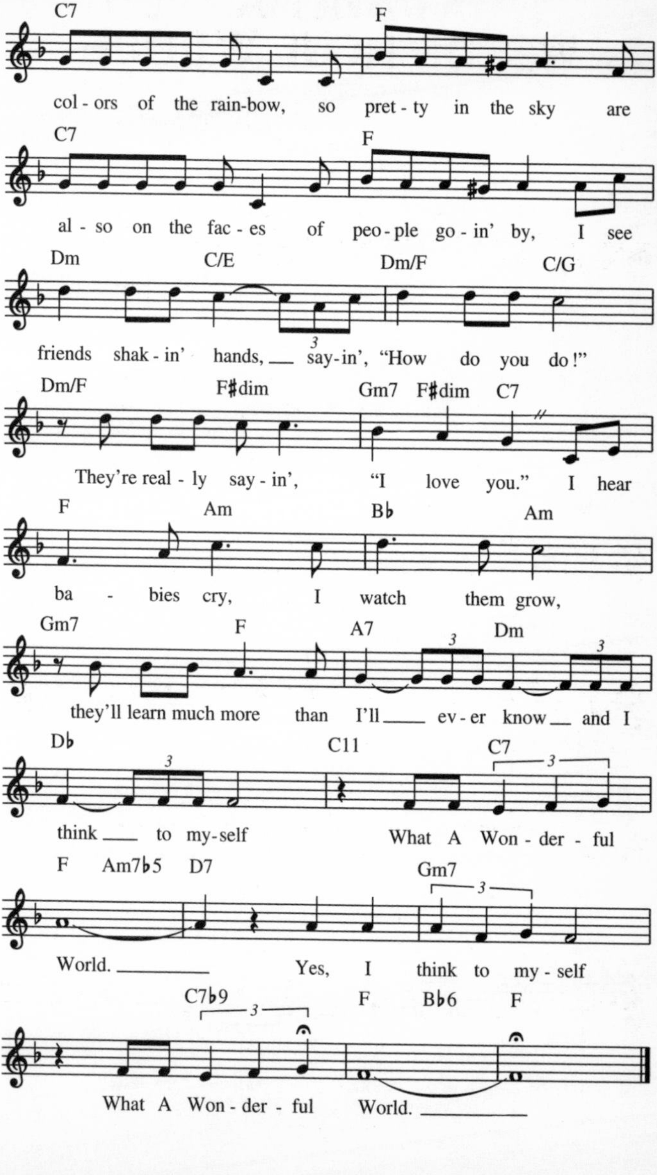
C7 F
col - ors of the rain-bow, so pret - ty in the sky are
C7 F
al - so on the fac - es of peo - ple go - in' by, I see
Dm C/E Dm/F C/G
friends shak - in' hands, ___ say-in', "How do you do!"
Dm/F F♯dim Gm7 F♯dim C7
They're real - ly say - in', "I love you." I hear
F Am B♭ Am
ba - bies cry, I watch them grow,
Gm7 F A7 Dm
they'll learn much more than I'll ___ ev - er know ___ and I
D♭ C11 C7
think ___ to my-self What A Won - der - ful
F Am7♭5 D7 Gm7
World. ___ Yes, I think to my - self
C7♭9 F B♭6 F
What A Won - der - ful World. ___

WHAT THE WORLD NEEDS NOW IS LOVE

Lyric by HAL DAVID
Music by BURT BACHARACH

Moderate Jazz Waltz
Bm7 Em7
What the world needs now is
Bm7 Em7 C6
love, sweet love. It's the on - ly thing
C D6 D7
that there's just too lit - tle of. What the
Bm7 Em7 Bm7
world needs now is love, sweet
Em7 C6
love. No, not just for some,

To Coda
B
B7
— but for ev - 'ry - one.
Em9
Lord, we don't need an - oth - er
Lord, we don't need an - oth - er
Dm9
moun - tain, there are moun - tains and
mead - ow, there are corn - fields and
G6/9
Cmaj7
3
hill - sides e - nough to climb;
wheat - fields e - nough to grow;
C6
Dm9
— There are o - ceans and
— There are sun - beams and

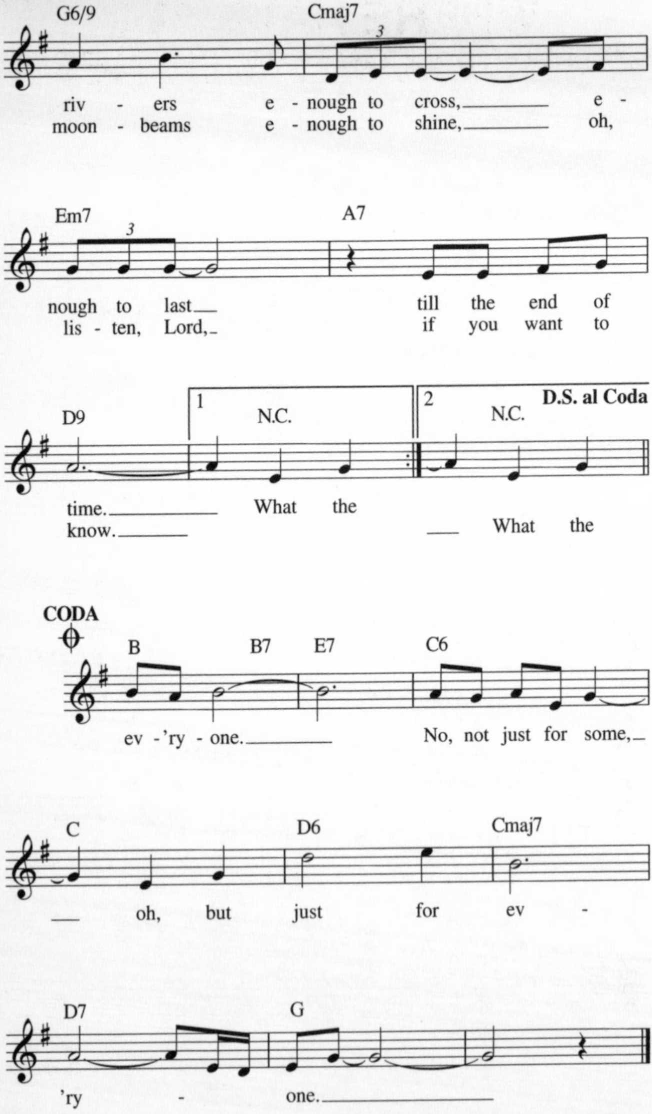
G6/9
Cmaj7
riv - ers e - nough to cross, e -
moon - beams e - nough to shine, oh,
Em7
A7
nough to last till the end of
lis - ten, Lord, if you want to
D9
1
N.C.
2
D.S. al Coda
N.C.
time. What the
know. What the
CODA
B
B7
E7
C6
ev - 'ry - one. No, not just for some,
C
D6
Cmaj7
oh, but just for ev -
D7
G
'ry - one.

WHERE HAVE ALL THE FLOWERS GONE?

Words and Music by
PETE SEEGER

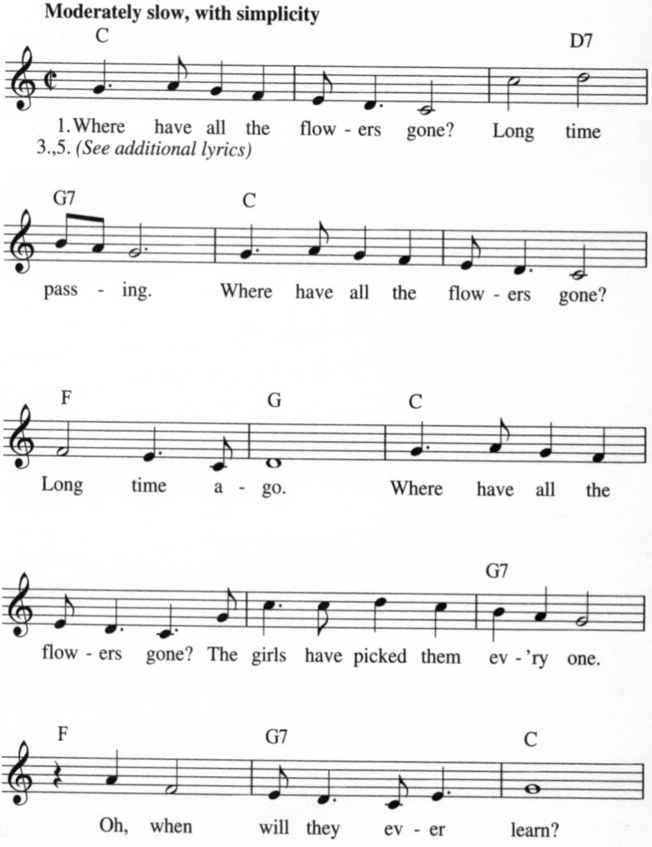
Moderately slow, with simplicity
C
D7
1. Where have all the flow - ers gone? Long time
3.,5. (See additional lyrics)
G7
C
pass - ing. Where have all the flow - ers gone?
F
G
C
Long time a - go. Where have all the
G7
flow - ers gone? The girls have picked them ev - 'ry one.
F
G7
C
Oh, when will they ev - er learn?

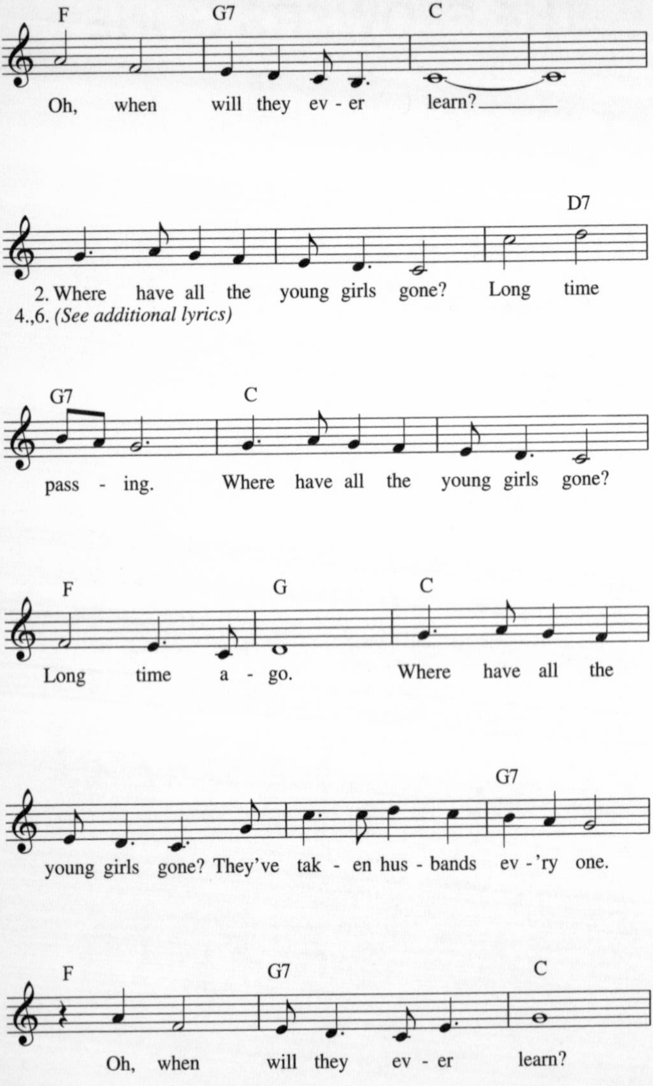
F G7 C
Oh, when will they ev - er learn?
D7
2. Where have all the young girls gone? Long time
4.,6. (See additional lyrics)
G7 C
pass - ing. Where have all the young girls gone?
F G C
Long time a - go. Where have all the
G7
young girls gone? They've tak - en hus - bands ev - 'ry one.
F G7 C
Oh, when will they ev - er learn?

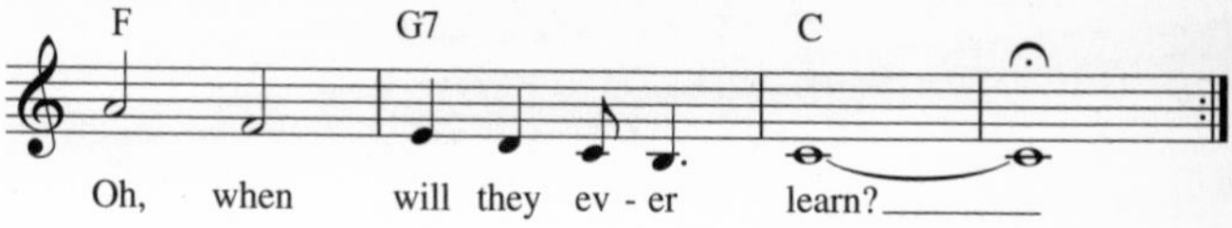
F
G7
C
Oh, when will they ev - er learn?

Additional Lyrics

3. Where have all the young men gone? Long time passing.
   Where have all the young men gone? Long time ago.
   Where have all the young men gone?
   They're all in uniform.
   Oh, when will they ever learn?
   Oh, when will they ever learn?

4. Where have all the soldiers gone? Long time passing.
   Where have all the soldiers gone? Long time ago.
   Where have all the soldiers gone?
   They've gone to graveyards, every one.
   Oh, when will they ever learn?
   Oh, when will they ever learn?

5. Where have all the graveyards gone? Long time passing.
   Where have all the graveyards gone? Long time ago.
   Where have all the graveyards gone?
   They're covered with flowers, every one.
   Oh, when will they ever learn?
   Oh, when will they ever learn?

6. Where have all the flowers gone? Long time passing.
   Where have all the flowers gone? Long time ago.
   Where have all the flowers gone?
   Young girls have picked them, every one.
   Oh, when will they ever learn?
   Oh, when will they ever learn?

A WHITER SHADE OF PALE

Words and Music by KEITH REID
and GARY BROOKER

In a slow 4
C C/B C/A C/G F F/E Dm Dm/C
(Instrumental)
G G/F Em G7 C F G F G7
C C/B Am Am/G
We skipped the light _ fan - dan - go. ___
She said, "I'm home _ on shore leave." ___
F F/E Dm7
Turned cart - wheels _ 'cross the floor, _
Though in truth we ___ were at sea, _
G G/F Em G7
I was feel - ing kind of sea - sick
So I took her by the looking glass
C C/B Am Em
The crowd called _ out for more The
And forced her ___ to ___ a - gree

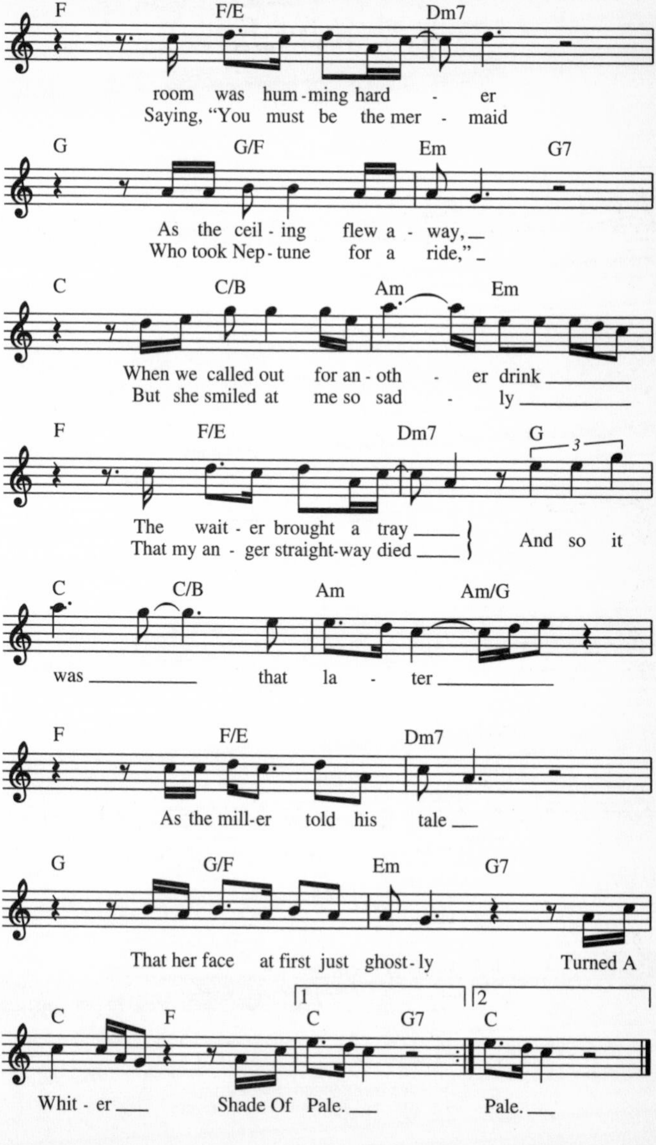
F F/E Dm7
room was hum-ming hard - er
Saying, "You must be the mer - maid
G G/F Em G7
As the ceil-ing flew a - way,
Who took Nep-tune for a ride,"
C C/B Am Em
When we called out for an-oth - er drink
But she smiled at me so sad - ly
F F/E Dm7 G
3
The wait - er brought a tray
That my an - ger straight-way died
And so it
C C/B Am Am/G
was that la - ter
F F/E Dm7
As the mill-er told his tale
G G/F Em G7
That her face at first just ghost-ly
Turned A
1
2
C F C G7 C
Whit - er Shade Of Pale. Pale.

WHO PUT THE BOMP

(In the Bomp Ba Bomp Ba Bomp)

Words and Music by BARRY MANN
and GERRY GOFFIN

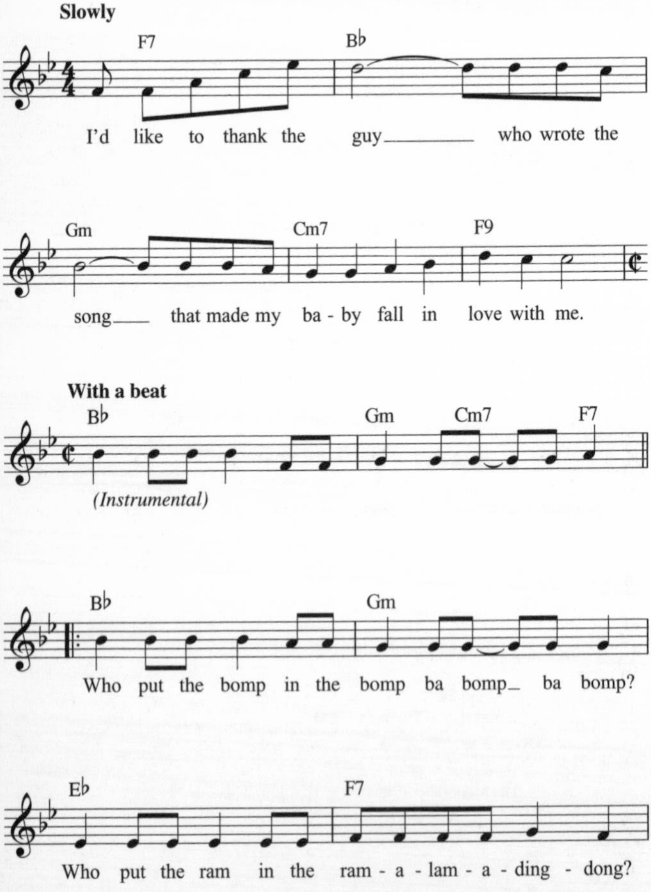
Slowly
F7
Bb
I'd like to thank the guy ___ who wrote the
Gm
Cm7
F9
song ___ that made my ba - by fall in love with me.
With a beat
Bb
Gm
Cm7
F7
(Instrumental)
Bb
Gm
Who put the bomp in the bomp ba bomp _ ba bomp?
Eb
F7
Who put the ram in the ram - a - lam - a - ding - dong?

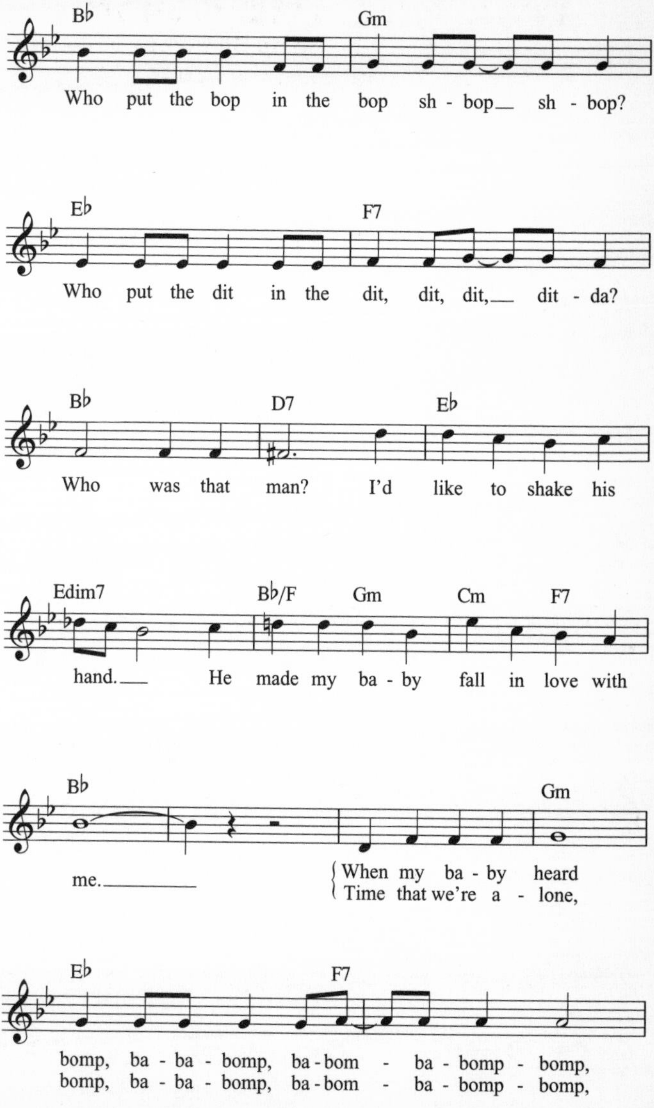

B♭ Gm
Who put the bop in the bop sh - bop__ sh - bop?
E♭ F7
Who put the dit in the dit, dit, dit,__ dit - da?
B♭ D7 E♭
Who was that man? I'd like to shake his
Edim7 B♭/F Gm Cm F7
hand.__ He made my ba - by fall in love with
B♭ Gm
me.________
When my ba - by heard
Time that we're a - lone,
E♭ F7
bomp, ba - ba - bomp, ba - bom - ba - bomp - bomp,
bomp, ba - ba - bomp, ba - bom - ba - bomp - bomp,

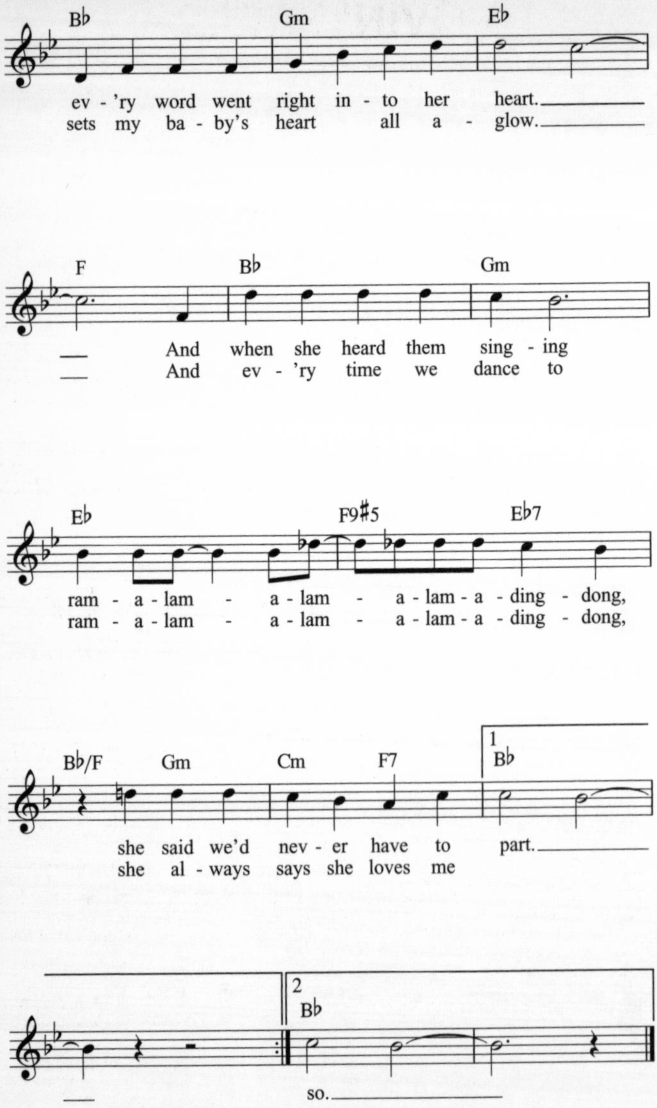
B♭ Gm E♭
ev - 'ry word went right in - to her heart.
sets my ba - by's heart all a - glow.
F B♭ Gm
And when she heard them sing - ing
And ev - 'ry time we dance to
E♭ F9♯5 E♭7
ram - a - lam - a - lam - a - lam - a - ding - dong,
ram - a - lam - a - lam - a - lam - a - ding - dong,
B♭/F Gm Cm F7 1 B♭
she said we'd nev - er have to part.
she al - ways says she loves me
2 B♭
so.

YOU'VE LOST THAT LOVIN' FEELIN'

Words and Music by BARRY MANN,
CYNTHIA WEIL and PHIL SPECTOR

Slowly
Bb/C
You nev - er close your eyes __ an - y -
wel - come look __ in your
more when I kiss your lips. __ And there's no
eyes when I reach for you. __ And, girl, you're
C
Bb/C
ten - der - ness __ like be - fore in your fin - ger - tips. __
start - ing to __ crit - i - cize lit - tle things _ I do. __
C
Dm7
You're try - ing hard not to show it, __
It makes me just feel like cry - ing, __
Em7
Fmaj7
F/G
G
but, ba - by, __ ba - by, I know _ it. __
'cause ba - by, __ some-thing beau - ti - ful's dy - ing. _
C
Dm/C
G7
You've Lost _ That Lov - in' Feel - in', woh oh, that lov -
C
Dm/C
- in' feel - in'. You've Lost That Lov - in' Feel - in'! Now it's

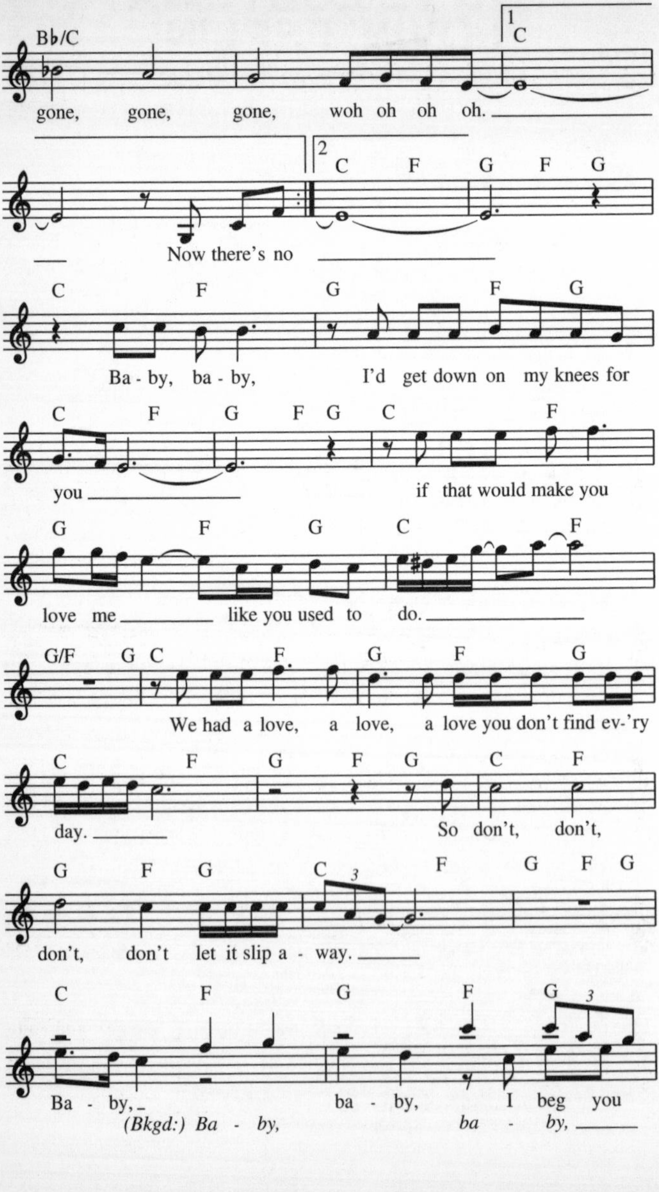
Bb/C
1
C
gone, gone, gone, woh oh oh oh.
2
C F G F G
Now there's no
C F G F G
Ba - by, ba - by, I'd get down on my knees for
C F G F G C F
you if that would make you
G F G C F
love me like you used to do.
G/F G C F G F G
We had a love, a love, a love you don't find ev-'ry
C F G F G C F
day. So don't, don't,
G F G C 3 F G F G
don't, don't let it slip a - way.
C F G F G 3
Ba - by, ba - by, I beg you
(Bkgd:) Ba - by, ba - by,

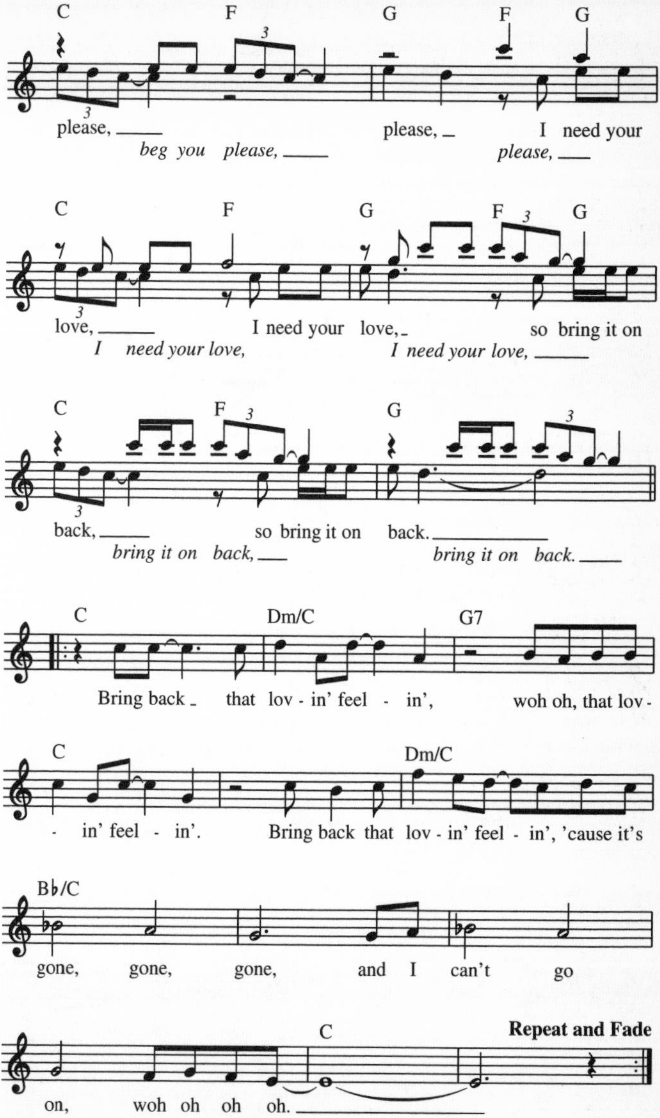
C F G F G
please, please, I need your
beg you please, please,
C F G F G
love, I need your love, so bring it on
I need your love, I need your love,
C F G
back, so bring it on back.
bring it on back, bring it on back.
C Dm/C G7
Bring back that lov - in' feel - in', woh oh, that lov -
C Dm/C
- in' feel - in'. Bring back that lov - in' feel - in', 'cause it's
B♭/C
gone, gone, gone, and I can't go
C
Repeat and Fade
on, woh oh oh oh.

WINDY

Words and Music by
RUTHANN FRIEDMAN

Moderately
F Eb Bb F
Who's peek - in' out from un - der a stair - way,
Who's trip - pin' down the streets of the cit - y,
Instrumental solo
Eb Bb C
call - ing a name that's light - er than air?
smil - in' at ev - 'ry - bod - y she sees?
F Eb Bb F/C
Who's bend - in' down to give me a rain - bow?
Who's reach-ing out to cap - ture a mo - ment?
F Eb Bb6 F N.C./C
Ev - 'ry - one knows it's Wind - y.
End solo
Gm7 C7 F
And Wind - y has storm - y eyes
N.C. Gm7 C N.C.
that flash at the sound of lies. And Wind - y has

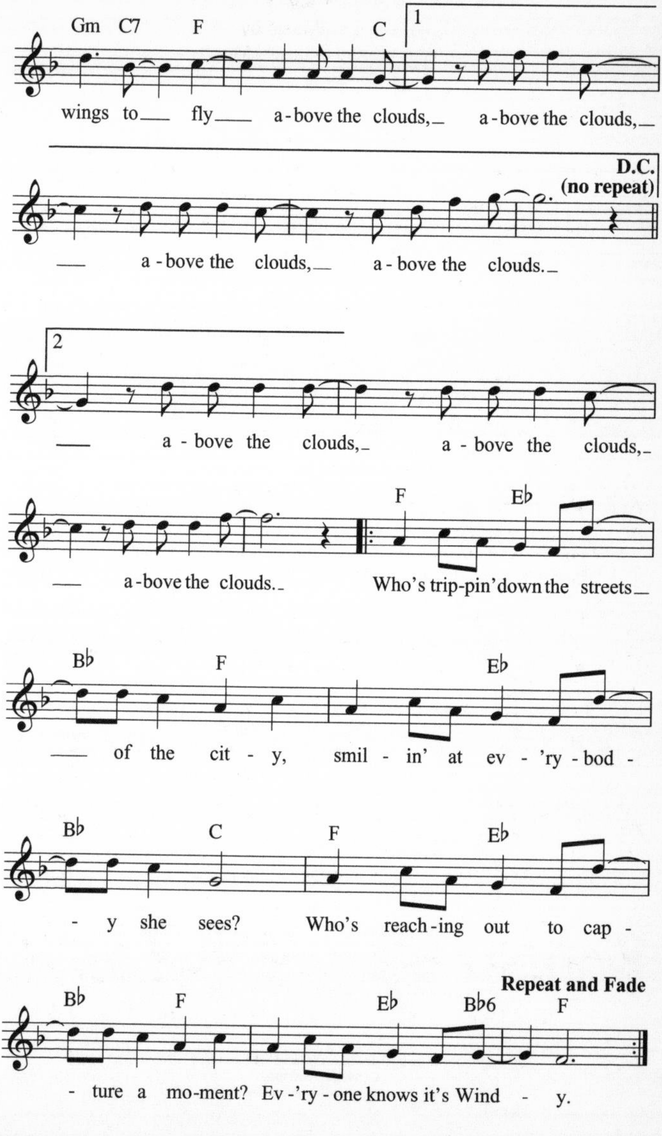
Gm C7 F C
1
wings to___ fly___ a-bove the clouds,_ a-bove the clouds,_
D.C.
(no repeat)
— a-bove the clouds,_ a-bove the clouds._
2
— a - bove the clouds,_ a - bove the clouds,_
F Eb
— a-bove the clouds._ Who's trip-pin' down the streets_
Bb F Eb
— of the cit - y, smil - in' at ev - 'ry - bod -
Bb C F Eb
- y she sees? Who's reach-ing out to cap -
Repeat and Fade
Bb F Eb Bb6 F
- ture a mo-ment? Ev - 'ry - one knows it's Wind - y.

WOOLY BULLY

Words and Music by
DOMINGO SAMUDIO

Moderately
Eb
1. Mat - ty told Hat - ty a - bout a
2., 3. (See additional lyrics)
thing she saw. Had
two big horns and a
Ab7
wool - ly jaw. Wool - y Bul - ly,
Eb7
Wool - y Bul - ly,

Bb7
Wool - y Bul - ly, Wool - y
Ab7
Eb7
Bul - ly, Wool - y Bul - ly.
1, 2
Bb7
3
Bb7
Eb7
(Instrumental)

Additional Lyrics

2. Hatty told Matty
   Let's don't take no chance
   Let's not be L 7
   Come and learn to dance
   Wooly Bully, Wooly Bully,
   Wooly Bully, Wooly Bully, Wooly Bully.

3. Matty told Hatty
   That's the thing to do,
   Get yo' someone really
   To pull the wool with you -
   Wooly Bully, Wooly Bully,
   Wooly Bully, Wooly Bully, Wooly Bully.

GUITAR CHORD FRAMES

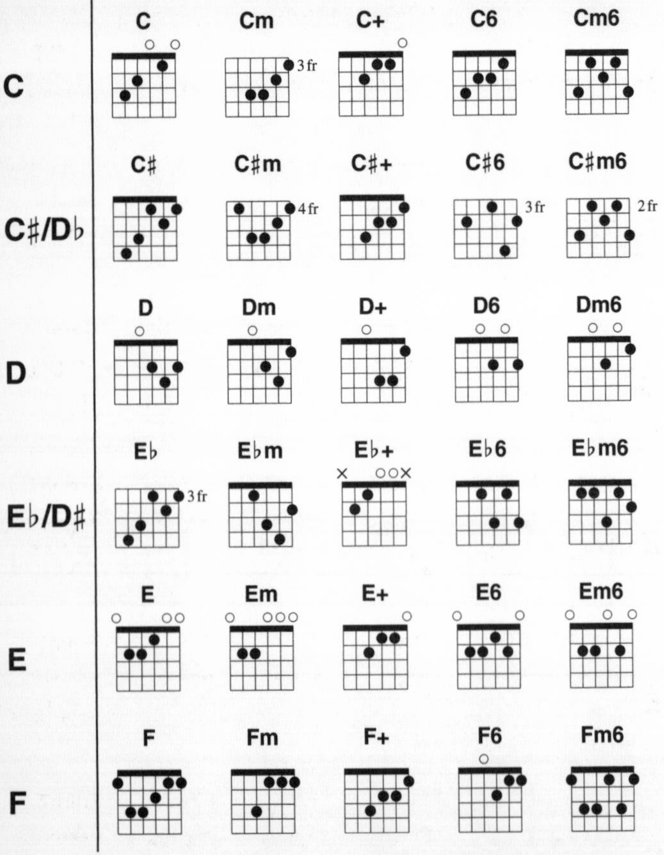
C
C
Cm
C+
C6
Cm6
3 fr
C♯/D♭
C♯
C♯m
C♯+
C♯6
C♯m6
4 fr
3 fr
2 fr
D
D
Dm
D+
D6
Dm6
E♭/D♯
E♭
E♭m
E♭+
E♭6
E♭m6
3 fr
E
E
Em
E+
E6
Em6
F
F
Fm
F+
F6
Fm6

This guitar chord reference includes 120 commonly used chords. For a more complete guide to guitar chords, see "THE PAPERBACK CHORD BOOK" (HL00702009).

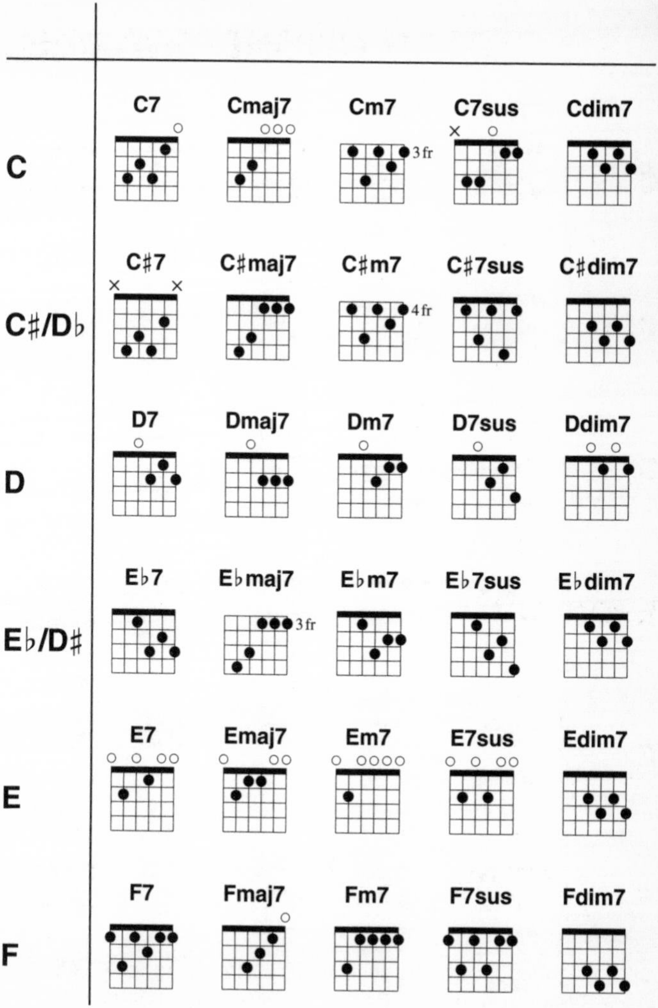
C
C7
Cmaj7
Cm7
3 fr
C7sus
Cdim7
C♯/D♭
C♯7
C♯maj7
C♯m7
4 fr
C♯7sus
C♯dim7
D
D7
Dmaj7
Dm7
D7sus
Ddim7
E♭/D♯
E♭7
E♭maj7
3 fr
E♭m7
E♭7sus
E♭dim7
E
E7
Emaj7
Em7
E7sus
Edim7
F
F7
Fmaj7
Fm7
F7sus
Fdim7

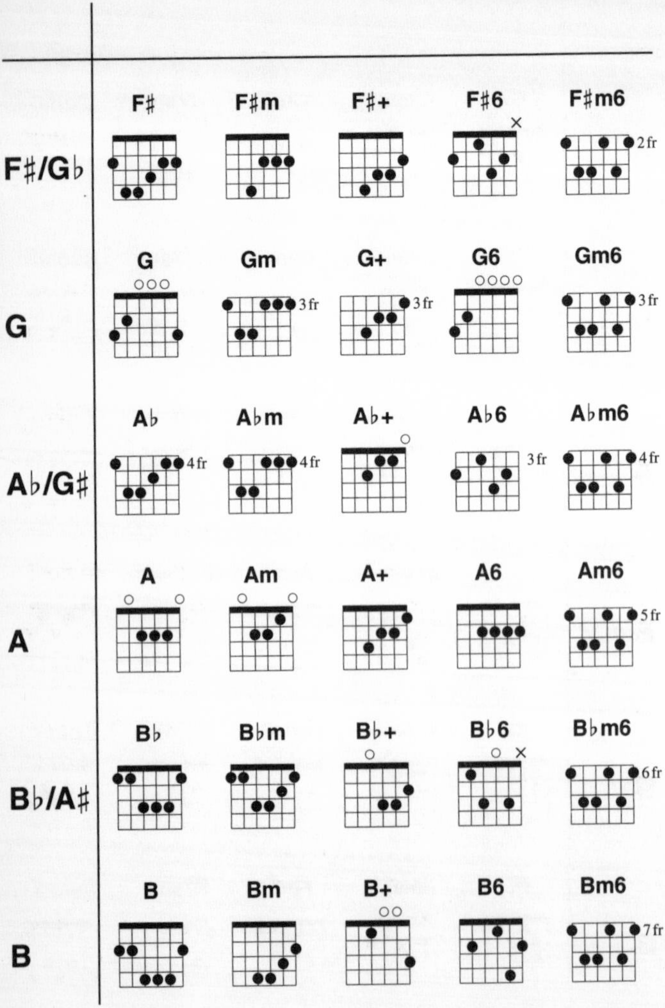
F♯/G♭
F♯
F♯m
F♯+
F♯6
F♯m6
2 fr
G
G
Gm
3 fr
G+
3 fr
G6
Gm6
3 fr
A♭/G♯
A♭
4 fr
A♭m
4 fr
A♭+
A♭6
3 fr
A♭m6
4 fr
A
A
Am
A+
A6
Am6
5 fr
B♭/A♯
B♭
B♭m
B♭+
B♭6
B♭m6
6 fr
B
B
Bm
B+
B6
Bm6
7 fr

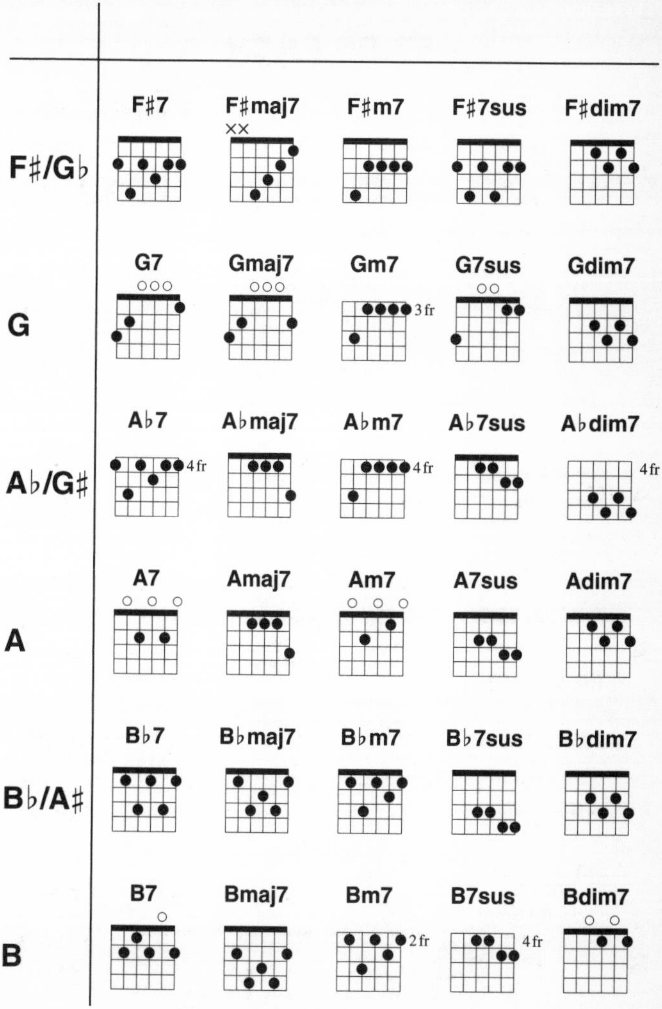
F♯/G♭
F♯7
F♯maj7
F♯m7
F♯7sus
F♯dim7
G
G7
Gmaj7
Gm7
3 fr
G7sus
Gdim7
A♭/G♯
A♭7
4 fr
A♭maj7
A♭m7
4 fr
A♭7sus
A♭dim7
4 fr
A
A7
Amaj7
Am7
A7sus
Adim7
B♭/A♯
B♭7
B♭maj7
B♭m7
B♭7sus
B♭dim7
B
B7
Bmaj7
Bm7
2 fr
B7sus
4 fr
Bdim7